MERRILL F. UNGER

BIBLICAL DEMONOLOGY

A
Study of
Spiritual Forces
at Work
Today

T0321319

KREGEL
PUBLICATIONS

Biblical Demonology: A Study of Spiritual Forces at Work Today
by Merrill F. Unger.

Published by Kregel Publications, a division of Kregel Inc., 2450 Oak Industrial Dr. NE, Grand Rapids, MI 49505.

Library of Congress Cataloging-in-Publication Data
Unger Merrill F. (Merrill Frederick), 1909–1980.
   Biblical Demonology: a study of spiritual forces at work today / Merrill F. Unger.
       p.   cm.
   Previously published: 5th ed. Wheaton, Ill.: Scripture Press, 1963.
   Includes bibliographical references and index.
   1. Demonology—Biblical teaching. I. Title.
BS680.D5U54   1994   235'.4'0901—dc20   94-17882
                                                                                    CIP

ISBN 978-0-8254-4158-5

CONTENTS

iii

*That no advantage may be gained over us by Satan:
we are not ignorant of his devices (II Cor. 2:11).*

To God-fearing parents,
Whose faith and prayers
Have been a source of inspiration
And encouragement
This book is affectionately dedicated.

ACKNOWLEDGMENTS

THE AUTHOR desires to express sincere gratitude to Dallas Theological Seminary for permission to use that portion of the material contained in this volume, which in 1945 was presented as a dissertation in partial requirement for the degree of Doctor of Theology. He also wishes to acknowledge his indebtedness to President Lewis Sperry Chafer and to Professor John Walvoord for invaluable help from a theological standpoint in the original form of the treatise, and to Dr. Wilbur M. Smith of Fuller Theological Seminary for indispensable aid bibliographically in the final elaboration and enlargement of the work for publication.

The author also extends his thanks to his father, who typed the original pages as a labor of love.

FOREWORD

THIS EPOCHAL work on demonology certainly has
been written for such a time as this; for not since the
days of the Church Fathers has there been so much serious interest
in and discussion of the power of demons in world history as in
these days, when the very powers of the heavens seem to be shaken,
so that both Christians and unbelievers have a deep conviction,
often unexpressed, that what is happening on our earth must be
traced to supernatural and evil powers. In the first four centuries
of the Christian Church, those mighty theologians, many of whom
saw deeply into the Word of God, wrote extensively on demon
power. Justin Martyr in his first *Apology* (LIV) continually insisted
that heathen mythology originated in demonic deception, and
added (LVI):

The evil spirits were not satisfied with saying before Christ's appearance that
those who were said to be sons of Jupiter were born of him; but after He had
appeared and had been born among men, and when they learned how He
had been foretold by the prophets and knew He should be believed on and
looked for by every nation, they again put forward other men, the Samaritans,
Simon and Menander, who did many mighty works by magic and deceived
many and still keep them deceived.

A century later, Lactantius devoted considerable space to the
fallen angels in the Second Book of his still worth reading *Divine
Institutes*, in which he asserts that demons were:

The inventors of astrology, and soothsaying, and divination, and those pro-
ductions which are called oracles, and necromancy, and the art of magic,
and whatever evil practices besides these men exercise, either openly or in
secret. . . . These are they who taught men to make images and statues; who,
in order that they might turn away the minds of man from the worship of
the true God, caused the countenances of dead kings to be erected and
consecrated, and assumed to themselves their names.

Augustine, the greatest of all the Church Fathers, writing three centuries after the death of the last of the Apostles, at a time when Christian doctrine had come to rich maturity, frequently insists upon the terrible power of demons both in the times that had preceded and in the days that were yet to come.

For example, in the Second Book of his monumental *City of God*, he even goes so far as to say (Chap. 25) that demons had fought in some of the great battles of human history, and asks the question:

What spirit can that be, which by a hidden inspiration stirs men's corruption, and goads them to adultery, and feeds on the full-fledged iniquity, unless it be the same that finds pleasure in such religious ceremonies, sets in the temples images of devils, and loves to see in play the images of vices; that whispers in secret some righteous sayings to deceive the few who are good, and scatters in public invitations to profligacy, to gain possession of the millions who are wicked? In the Seventh Book (Chap. 33), Augustine rightly argues that Christianity, the only true religion, "has alone been able to manifest that the gods of the nations are most impure demons, who desire to be thought gods, availing themselves of the names of certain defunct souls, or the appearance of mundane creatures, and with proud impurity rejoicing in things most base and infamous, as though in divine honors, and envying human souls their conversion to the true God."

For nearly a millennium and a half, for some strange reason, the true Biblical doctrine of demons was hardly spoken of. Now and then a sermon would be preached on this subject; here and there a book on good and evil angels would inadequately discuss the matter, and though the power of demons was uppermost in those awful years of superstition and false accusations, when both in Great Britain and Colonial America many men and women, condemned as witches, were tortured, drowned, and burned to death; yet the real Biblical teaching on demons was almost never carefully investigated. In the 19th century the whole subject was sneered at by many as a superstitious idea which we had well got rid of, or was quickly passed over in theological treatises.

As an indication of how general was the ignoring of this Biblical truth in the days of the great Puritan divines, one needs only to recall that in the ten thousand pages of the writings of Richard Baxter, not one reference can be found to the activity of demons, outside of the Gospel records of our Lord's life on earth. The same is true in the writings of Thomas Goodwin and in the twenty some volumes of John Owen. Wesley devotes one page to the subject, in his sermon "Of Good Angels," but not as an active force in his own day. We do not find anything in the writings of Jonathan Edwards which really deals with this problem.

With the coming of the two great World Wars, especially the second, and the frightful destruction brought upon Europe by Adolph Hitler, the awful persecution of Christians on the part of Communism in its swift progress around the world, capturing the attention and devotion of hundreds of millions, together with the deep deceptions that are today abroad, and what Brunner calls "a mass atheism which was formerly unknown," men, desiring to ascertain something of the causes of these appalling eruptions of evil, have turned back to the New Testament to search out its teaching on supernatural beings whose constant mission it is to deceive, and degrade, and destroy men. During the last ten years most of the scholarly volumes devoted to Hitler speak of him as a demon-possessed man, and present abundant evidence that when in some paroxysm of anger, or under what he called inspiration, his eyes looked out with an inhuman luster. Many German writers, as Paul Tillich in his *Interpretation of History* and Cullmann in his important *Christ and Time*, speak of the demon forces controlling modern history, even though perhaps they use the term "demonic" as referring to strange forces in modern civilization, not necessarily derived from evil individuals by an evil spirit. Dr. Reinhold Niebuhr, in his now famous Gifford Lectures, *The Nature and Destiny of Man*, devotes considerable attention to this matter of demonized civilization. E. C. Rust, in his remarkable volume, *The Christian Understanding of History*, writes:

The demonic pretensions of human society have increased since the fulness of time has impinged upon secular history. Since Christ has come and the true meaning of historical existence and society has been disclosed among men, the demonization of any aspect of the life of a group has become increasingly a conscious defiance of the claims of Christ Himself and of the truths of the Christian faith. We have seen emerge in Western civilization, permeated as it is with secularized Christian ideas and values, attempts to demonize the state or nation which have consciously avowed their opposition to the Christian faith and made a serious attempt to exterminate it. Since Christ is the revealer of true historical meaning and because the true law of life has been fragmentarily incorporated into the structure of our Western culture, the idolization of the nation in the modern totalitarian state and the atheism of the modern communist state are consciously opposed to the Lord of life and of history and have reached desperate proportions. In Nazism and the Bolshevism of the 1920's we have a true revelation of anti-Christ. All prophetic voices, and therefore the voice of the church, must be stilled if the unconditioned claims of such ephemeral institutions are to go unchallenged and be accepted by the mass of the people; the influence of Christ must be eliminated if anti-Christ is to reign securely; the demonic tends to become satanic, totally destructive, in opposition to all good and all creativity, and so the groups that glorify themselves beyond measure are brought down in total destruction.

In such an hour as this, philosophy will not help us to understand what is really taking place in the mind of unregenerated humanity; and neither can economics, sociology, or psychology tell us what is yet to come. We turn in this hour of deepening darkness to light emanating from God's Word, the only truly inspired volume—whose predictions consistently, irresistibly come to pass as the time of their fulfillment draws near, and whose analysis of the fundamental forces at work in the last days is a part of the very wisdom of God.

The supreme merit of *Biblical Demonology* is that it holds closely to the Word of God, and discusses exhaustively and reverently the many passages which are interspersed in the divine records of both Old and New Testaments.

The author is excellently equipped to do what is here undertaken. Twenty years ago he graduated with honors from Johns Hopkins University, and after spending some years in teaching and in a pastorate, he was graduated from the Dallas Theological Seminary in 1940; this he followed by graduate work leading to a Doctor of Theology degree, which he received *magna cum laude*, in 1945. He also entered the Oriental Institute of the Faculty of Philosophy at Johns Hopkins University in 1944, and was graduated in 1947 with a Doctor of Philosophy degree in Semitics and Biblical Archaeology. After teaching for a year at Gordon College of Theology and Missions, in Boston, he became the Professor of Semitics and Old Testament in Dallas Theological Seminary. His recent book, *Introductory Guide to the Old Testament*, won the first prize in the Christian Textbook Contest.

A great asset possessed by the author of this book, it seems to me, is his eschatology, his concept of world government, and his views concerning a coming reign of Antichrist. This gives him a background for the proper understanding of the New Testament doctrine of demons, which, in my opinion, is impossible without such an eschatology. When demons are discussed in the Pauline Epistles and in the Apocalypse, they appear in a frame of eschatology, and unless that eschatology is understood, the meaning of the New Testament doctrine of demons cannot be rightly comprehended. The careful reading of this scholarly work will illuminate many passages in the Word of God ordinarily passed over or misinterpreted. It will throw a flood of light upon world events as they are now unfolding, and will lead Christian believers into a deeper experience of intercession and surrender, that they may live day by day delivered from these dreadful powers. I have not had in my hands for many months a book dealing with a major Biblical subject that I have felt should be in the hands of every minister of the gospel today quite so much as this thought-provoking work on a subject concerning which Satan would indeed have us ignorant. It will remain for many years to come the standard treatment of Biblical demonology for all who recognize the Holy Scriptures to be inspired of God.

— Wilbur M. Smith

But 'tis strange;
And oftentimes to win us to our harm
The instruments of darkness tell us truths,
Win us with honest trifles, to betray us
In deepest consequence.
— *from* SHAKESPEARE's *Macbeth*

CHAPTER I

THE PROBLEMS OF BIBLICAL DEMONOLOGY

THE IMPORTANCE of the subject of demonology, whether considered intra-Biblically as a branch of revealed theology or dealt with extra-Biblically as a phase of the science of religion, is indeed vast. Both within and without the Bible its ramifications are significant and far-reaching. Biblically considered, it looms large on the sacred page, and especially in the New Testament is it accorded remarkable prominence. It forms, together with angelology and Satanology, an indispensable branch of systematic theology, dealing with the realm of evil supernaturalism. As such, it constitutes the only true basis for understanding and evaluating strange and bewildering phenomena which have perplexed both the ancient and the modern world. Extra-Biblically considered, it forms a large field of research, whether as a branch of comparative religion or as a study of popular superstitions.

Since demonological phenomena have been found to be almost universally prevalent among peoples of various religions and of varying degrees of culture, from the remotest ages of antiquity to the present, it is practically impossible to interpret accurately and to evaluate properly the religious phenomena and practices of various peoples, which frequently are confusingly involved, without a discriminating grasp of this subject. Without such basic knowledge the student of religions, no matter what his qualifications for his task may otherwise be, cannot be expected to make accurate evaluations or reach valid conclusions. His estimate both of Christianity and of non-Christian religions must be expected to be faulty and misleading.

Despite the importance of Biblical demonology in the sphere of Christian theology and in the domain of comparative religion, the problems and perplexities which surround it are undeniably great and provocative of diligent research and investigation for

1

their solution. First, there is the problem of the silence of revelation; second, the problem of the accuracy of interpretation; third, the problem of the prevalence of superstition; and fourth, the problem of the preponderance of doubt.

A. The Problem of the Silence of Revelation

This phase of the problem, although it does exist, is of relatively small importance. In the first place, the subject of evil supernaturalism, including Satan and demons, assumes such a prominent place on the pages of Holy Writ, and there is such a wealth of pertinent passages to be expounded, that, although there is the matter of the silence of revelation on certain circumscribed phases of the theme, nevertheless, this is no barrier to a comprehensive presentation of the subject. In the second place, this phase of the difficulty is manifestly more imaginary than real; for if God is reticent on certain aspects of divine truth, ought men attempt to speak or desire to know beyond that which is written? May that which is unrevealed not lie outside the realm of legitimate knowledge and, for man in his present sinful state, be nothing more than idle curiosity?

However, the limits of human knowledge must be kept in mind; for example, on such a seemingly important phase of this subject as the origin of demons, Ezra Abbot accurately observes, "the Scripture is all but silent."[1] There are other minor points of the topic, too, where the investigator, with excusable zeal for his subject, could wish for a fuller revelation.

B. The Problem of the Accuracy of Interpretation

Nothwithstanding the apparent bounds set to the limits of human knowledge by divine Omniscience, the *real* problem is that of interpretation rather than the silence of revelation. Has all that has been revealed concerning this theme been accurately and fully expounded? In other words, has every aspect of Biblical demonology been thoroughly, systematically, and exhaustively treated? To this question only a negative answer may apparently

[1]*Smith's Dictionary of the Bible*, I, 584. Cf. John L. Nevius, *Demon Possession and Allied Themes*, 5th ed., pp. 269-70.

be given, thus pointing the direction study and research should take.

It must not be supposed, however, that the misconceptions and confusion which hamper this field of inquiry are due chiefly to neglect, although the attention accorded it can by no means be described as commensurate with its import; and its treatment in the average systematic theology is exceedingly sketchy, if it is given any space at all. The misunderstandings may rather be ascribed to mistreatment; for the literature dealing with it as a phenomenon of the science of religion or as an account of popular superstitions is voluminous.

However, the much that has been written has been victimized by extremism. On the one hand, by ultra-emotionalism, giving free reign to romantic credulity and uncontrolled play of the imagination, resulting in extravagant superstition. On the other hand, by ultra-rationalism, in evident reaction, meticulously ruling out the supernatural and adopting unwarranted presuppositions concerning the miraculous, resulting in faulty interpretations and incorrect conclusions. Hence Edersheim's pointed observation concerning Jewish demonology, namely, that "much that is both erroneous and misleading has been written" concerning it,[2] may very properly be extended to describe the whole range of demonology—ethnic, rabbinic, and Biblical.

C. The Problem of the Prevalence of Superstition

It would be difficult to find a subject anywhere replete with more fantastic distortion and unbridled extravagance than popular demonology uncontrolled by the truths of divine revelation. In this realm popular imagination has run riot and recklessly disported itself since the dim ages of antiquity. Uncounted multitudes throughout the centuries have lived and died in the clutches of appalling fear and absurd superstition, under the thraldom of evil supernaturalism. Excesses have not been confined to the gullible masses of the rude and uneducated, but priests and professional men, rabbis, and Talmudists have in many instances been the promulgators of strange vagaries and the protagonists of popular perversions.

---

[2]Alfred Edersheim, *The Life and Times of Jesus the Messiah*, I, 607. See also "Jewish Angelology and Demonology" in II, Appendix XIII, 748-63.

Even Jewish demonology,[3] in spite of the chaste and lofty example of the Old Testament Scriptures, had by the time of our Lord degenerated into a system of almost incredible and fanciful superstition, in sharp contrast to both Old and New Testament teaching. Rabbinic speculation went to absurd lengths. By the traditions of men the teachers of the law, on this subject as on many others, set aside the counsels of God, and taught for doctrines "the commandments of men" (Matt. 15:9).

Christian demonology under the powerful impact and purifying effect of the New Testament revelation remained on a high level for several centuries, and the demonology of the earliest Church Fathers was practically that of the New Testament.[4] Degeneration, however, soon set in; and by the time of the Reformation, extravagance was so rampant that even the great Luther[5] never shook himself entirely free from it, attributing a morbid and exaggerated activity to demons in such daily occurrences as fires, accidents, and other mishaps.

In modern times, even in enlightened lands, people have not been guiltless of such excesses as burning "witches" at the stake. A curious, though less crude vestige of medieval superstition is the prevailing practice in the Roman Church of lighting sacred candles. The precise significance to be attached to this rite, which harks back to ancient modes for keeping evil spirits in check by fire, is that "in whatsoever places these candles are lit or placed, the powers of darkness may depart in trembling and flee in terror."[6]

In lands more or less untouched by the purifying and enlightening effects of the Bible, the darkness and thraldom of error and superstition are truly pitiable. Through fear, people there have all their lifetime been "subject to bondage" (Heb. 2:15). The entire religious environment out of which ancient Israel was divinely chosen to be a witness and a guardian of the truth of the one true God was full of demonism. The genii of ancient Babylonia swarmed everywhere, creeping under doors, filling every nook, lurking menacingly behind walls and hedges, relentlessly demanding incanta-

---

[3]Edersheim, I, 142, 482; and II, Appendix XVI, 770-776.

[4]F. C. Conybeare, "The Demonology of the New Testament," *Jewish Quarterly Review*, VIII, 600.

[5]L. T. Towsend, *Satan and Demons*, p. 45; Lynn Thorndike, *History of Magic and Experimental Science*, VI, 533, 558, 601.

[6]W. M. Alexander, *Demonic Possession in the New Testament*, p. 45.

tions, magical prayers, and religious veneration for their appeasement. The same condition was largely true of ancient Assyria. A wealth of fantastic demonic conceptions, quite equal to those of Babylonia, is also discoverable in Arabic religion,[7] according to which demons swarm everywhere, lying in wait for the unwary. So thickly do the Arabs people the desert with their "Jinn" that they apologize when throwing anything away, lest they should hit some of them. So when entering a bath, or pouring water on the ground, or letting a bucket down into a well, or entering a place of uncleanness, the well-bred son of the desert will say, "Permission, ye blessed!"

The magic rites and incantations of Arabic folk-lore are hardly less numerous than those of Babylonia; and where they exist, demonic superstition is sure to be found. Arabic folk-lore is incredibly elaborate, dealing freely and fantastically with such abstruse questions as the sex, clothing, food, forms of appearance, habitations, and courts of justice of the demons. They are divided into various classifications, such as water and earth sprites, tree or house demons, and others.[8] Following the vagaries of the Koran,[9] demons are viewed as both good and bad. According to its demonology some evil demons (Jinn) were converted to Islam, and became good and faithful spirits, servants of God and protectors of man.

Persian religion, according to the *Zend-Avesta*, represents demons as creations of the independent destroying spirit in a dualistic system, and regards them as responsible for all that is foul and filthy in this world.[10] The ancient Egyptians divided the body into thirty-six regions with a different demon associated with each part. Evil dreams and nightmares are by general consent accounted for by the jungle savage as the work of evil demons.

Grotesque superstitions and bizarre rites connected with demon worship are practically endless in their variety. The Chinese spirits

---

[7]Taufik Canaan, *Daemonenglaube im Lande Der Bibel*, pp. 1-49. R. Campbell Thompson, *Semitic Magic: Its Origin and Development* (London, 1908), Vol. III of Luzac's "Oriental Religion Series."

[8]Canaan, *op. cit.*, pp. 8-9.

[9]Sura 46:28.

[10]Michael Gruenthaner, "The Demonology of the Old Testament," *Catholic Biblical Quarterly*, January, 1944, VI, 19-20.

need the good things of their former existence, and are therefore
supplied with mock houses, mock clothes, mock money, and other
comforts. In parts of India devil-dances and bloody sacrifices are
often employed to pacify offended demons. The *Zend-Avesta* is
freer from superstition and comes nearer to Scripture when it
represents Zoroaster as warding off demons by chanting, "The will
of the Lord is the Law of Holiness," and also by prayer and the
keeping of the Law.[11] In Judaism rabbis do not seem to have
contemplated such arduous methods of driving out evil spirits as
clubbing, stabbing, shooting, or shaking, though these practices
are still honored in many parts of the world.

D.   THE PROBLEM OF THE PREPONDERANCE OF DOUBT

Today, in an age of scientific progress and enlightenment, the
most effective barrier to the adequate understanding of demonology
is not a fanatical gullibility embracing mere superstition, but a
radical skepticism rejecting the supernatural. This obstacle of an
unbelieving rationalism is particularly formidable, moreover, since
it is widespread among men of scholarship and learning, who would
otherwise be eminently fitted to deal with such a field of inquiry.
The seriousness of the skeptical position is apparent when it is
considered that even a simple definition of demonology as "the
systematic investigation of the subject of evil spirits or demons"
at once projects inquiry into the realm of the supernatural.

Since the supernatural realm is above natural laws of the
physical universe and involves a sphere of reality beyond the control of scientific experimentation and strictly scientific inquiry,
the historian of religions, depending upon purely scientific methods
and deductions without the aid of divine revelation, may not find
here a proper sphere for full-orbed investigation. It is true, he
may confine himself to certain phases of the subject, such as the
examination of demons or evil spirits as a branch of the science of
religion, or as a study of popular superstitions, but his presuppositions with regard to the supernatural will inevitably vitiate his interpretations and invalidate his conclusions. Thus handicapped, he
can at best merely catalogue facts without interpretation or induc-
tion. The moment he attempts more, he steps on territory where he

---

[11]W. M. Alexander, *op. cit.*, p. 49.

is totally unqualified to act, since in ruling out the supernatural, he substantially rejects the testimony of Biblical demonology, which is based upon the supernatural and furnishes the only true criteria for understanding and evaluating the diverse and perplexing phenomena encountered in this field.

The complete impotence of the naturalistic historian of religions in dealing with demonological facts is emphasized when the precise nature of those phenomena is analyzed. The sphere is that of evil supernaturalism. The phenomena may accordingly be described first as "supernatural," second as "evil." In this twofold characterization appears the double difficulty of the subject and the twin reason for the naturalistic historian's incompetence to handle the facts of the case. Knowledge of the supernatural can only come through supernatural revelation, since it is above and beyond natural law. Further, it is obvious that revealed truth can be understood only through faith in the revelation and hence in the Revealer. Faith implies humble realization of creaturely limitation, as well as clear apperception of God's infinite wisdom. Rejection of the supernatural is *per se* unbelief, which cuts off contact with God and shuts up the revelation.

The qualification of "evil" further complicates the matter and makes any naturalistic approach doubly hazardous. The powers to be dealt with are not only above the natural realm, and hence wiser and more powerful than man in the natural realm, but they are "evil." They are desirous and able to deceive and lead astray. They resent light, for they are in darkness. They fight against the truth, because they are in error and rebellion against God, and truth glorifies God. Any naturalistic attempt to discover truth in the realm of the divine revelation, however sincere or scientific it may be, is inevitably foredoomed to failure and deception. The natural man, unprotected and unguided by God's Spirit, not only cannot "receive" or "know" matters which pertain to the Spirit of God (I Cor. 2:14), but he is actually subject to limitless error and perversion, as a prey to seducing spirits and doctrines of demons (I Tim. 4:1).

It is doubtless to this incapacity of the natural man to comprehend spiritual truth, coupled with the clearly taught Scriptural principle of demonic deception, that the extremism, which, as observed, notoriously characterizes this theme, is to be attributed.

However, as far as the final result is concerned, it is of small moment whether excess takes the direction of unrestrained popular emotionalism, issuing in fanciful folklore, or follows the path of infidel rationalism, branding all manifestation of supernaturalism as superstition. In either event the result is substantially the same. In the first instance, truth is perverted by being mixed with error. In the second case, it is distorted in attempted separation from error. In either case, the facts are violated and comprehension of the subject is obscured.

Difficulties and questions of no small moment are thus discovered to encumber study in this field of inquiry. Their solution is imperative to any adequate understanding of the theme as a whole. It may be said that the crux of the difficulty centers in the problem of interpretation. The rich store of material contained in the Old and the New Testaments affords a promising field for sound exegesis. Because of the excesses to which interpretation has frequently been exposed—on the one hand to a naive gullibility and on the other to a rationalistic skepticism—discriminating and valid exegesis to ascertain the truth is made more imperative than ever before. The task is, in short, to steer a clear course between the Scylla of a romantic credulity eventuating in a mixing of truth and superstition on the one hand, and the Charybdis of an unbelieving rationalism issuing in a confusing of reality and fancy, on the other.

> "Why then should witless man so much misweene
> That nothing is but that which he hath seene?"[12]

---

[12]Edmund Spenser, *The Faerie Queene*, edited by J. C. Smith, II, stanza 3.

Chapter II

THE ORIGIN OF BIBLICAL DEMONOLOGY

TO THE QUESTION of the rise of demonology the most perplexing and contradictory answers are given, and the whole inquiry, like that of the origin and growth of religion in general, of which it forms an intrinsic and inseparable part, is vexed with a high degree of uncertainty and speculation. This is not surprising, however, in view of the unwarranted presuppositions which many historians of religion make, following the critical trend. For example, Oesterley and Robinson,[1] assuming that "the religion of Israel's ancestors," in the nomadic, pre-Mosaic age, "included a number of deities," are hard-pressed to justify such a violent assumption, and are driven to the confession, that, of the various objects of worship necessary for such polytheism "we hear nothing, unless we are to include the teraphim stolen by Rachel from her father." Realizing the dilemma of their position, they add: "We are thus forced back on *conjecture,* and must rely on such evidence as can be supplied from comparative religion and from philology."[2]

But this is a most dangerous procedure. Philology is undoubtedly useful and indispensable in numberless instances, but it can never legitimately be used as a mere substitute for facts in supporting a theory. As far as comparative religion is concerned, it is one of the most recent of all the sciences, and largely in consequence of this fact, knowledge of what it actually proves is far from definite. The most contradictory conclusions are drawn from it as evidence, and, as in the case of new sciences in the past, not a few have used it as a shelter from which to attack the truths of revelation, and as a last resort to bolster questionable theories. It could only supply adequate evidence if the origin of

---

[1]W. O. E. Oesterley and Theodore H. Robinson, *Hebrew Religion,* 1937, pp. 125-6.

[2]*Ibid.,* p. 126.

Hebrew religion were identical with that of other Semites. This Oesterley and Robinson assume is the case: "The Hebrews were Semites, and their religion, in its origin, did not differ from that of the Semites in general."[3]

The question remains, however, Did Hebraism begin as pure monotheism, with Abram, in divine separation from a universal degeneration, or did it develop gradually into monotheism from primitive animism, and kindred cruder forms via polytheism? The divine revelation is certainly to be preferred before the speculations of men, however subtle and ingenious they may be. According to its testimony, the religion of the Semites began as monotheism with Shem, the son of Noah (Gen. 9:1, 27), and degenerated into polytheism by the time of Abram (Gen.12:1-3), who was called out of polytheism to be a witness, together with his descendants, to the one true God.

The assumption of Oesterley and Robinson that Hebrew religion did not differ in origin from that of the Semites in general is therefore inaccurate, and a flimsy premise upon which to build any elaborate theory of the beginnings and the development of Hebrew religion, as they do. So far from being identical in origin with general Semitic belief, Hebrew religion was a monotheistic purge from the corruption of general Semitic polytheism, which, in turn, represents a continuous and unbroken degeneration from an original common Semitic monotheism.

The vital bearing on the subject of the beginning of Semitic religion in general upon the problem of the origin of demonology appears in a statement of George W. Gilmore: "The entire religious provenience out of which Hebrew religion sprang is full of demonism."[4]

How is this widespread and deeply ingrained belief in demons among the ancient Semites and their neighbors to be explained? Was it a concomitant feature of an original monotheism? Or is it the result of the solvent of monotheism on a contemporary polytheism? Or is it to be explained as an offshoot of polytheism?

---

[3]*Ibid.*, p. 3.

[4]George W. Gilmore, "Demon, Demoniac," *New Schaff-Herzog Encyclopaedia of Religious Knowledge*, III, 399.

Or, perchance, as an evolutionary development from a primitive animism?

A. Various Erroneous Views

On such paramount and significant points as these, conflicting answers are given and various divergent theories, disagreeing with each other, and at variance with divine revelation, are offered. These explanations are but naturalistic attempts to explain phenomena which are above the natural, and hence fall far short of the truth.

1. The Humanistic View

This theory, which is a revival of an ancient Greek concept, would connect the origin of the demons with the rise of the gods. Religion sprang from the fear of ghosts. The gods are but the spirits of departed men, whom men worship mainly because of dread. Originally, when the gods were but supernatural men, the term "demon" (*daimon*) was used interchangeably with "god" (*theos*). Afterwards, when the gods became more exalted, demons were thought of as intermediate beings, the messengers of the gods to men. Later they were thought of as not only good, but also as evil, as men began to differentiate more exactly between good and evil in their thoughts of the supernatural. Doubtless, contact with Eastern pagan religions, which swarmed with multitudinous evil demons, accentuated the differentiation. These evil demons were viewed as including the spirits of wicked men, and were regarded as authors not only of physical, but of moral evil.

It is sufficient to remark that this explanation not only clashes with revealed truth, but with the facts of secular history. Most tribes from the earliest times clearly distinguish between those deities who had once been men, and the gods proper, who had never been men, and consequently had never died. The theory is not valuable as an exposition of the origin of demonology, but as a commentary on the development of the terms *daimon* and *daimonion* for later Septuagint and New Testament usage.

2. The Animistic View

This is the evolutionary hypothesis of W. W. G. Baudissin[5] and

---

[5]W. W. G. Baudissin, *Studien Zur Semitischen Religionsgeschichte*. Heft I, 110-11, 113-115.

others, according to which the development of demonism is to be traced from its original source in primitive animism, upward through polytheism into monotheism. Primitive man with rude and undeveloped religious ideas looked upon nature about him as alive, and pictured natural processes as due to the operation of living wills. Instinctively looking for causes, he fancied that every object in nature had a personality like his own.[6] He thus found himself in a "cosmic society of superhuman agencies some of which ministered to his well-being, others to his injury."[7] He was confronted by fearful and uncontrollable natural forces which wrought terrifying destruction. Hurricane, flood, earthquake, and fire were fancied to be angry personal agencies whose wrath men would strive to avert or appease. Thus arose popular pagan demonism.

Next, man is supposed to have passed from the animistic to the polytheistic state. Vaguely conceived spirits of the earlier stage are now advanced to the position of deities, dignified with names, fixed characteristics, specific functions, organized into a pantheon, and worshipped through images.[8] Perhaps, some continued to be viewed as less definitely personalized natural agencies, reminiscent of the animistic stage, and thus retained the character of demons, while others, more powerful and fearful, are accorded a virile personality, and assigned the full status of deities.

Biblical demonology is accounted for by a higher step in the evolutionary process. Monotheism, reacting upon contemporary polytheism, is strangely pictured as a solvent, making room for heathenism by reducing its deities to the dimensions of demons. According to the necessities of monotheism, demons are denied the dignity and prerogatives of deity, but not all objective reality.[9]

The objections to this plausible and ingenious theory, however, are so serious as to be fatal to its tenability. First, it is at variance with the truth of divine revelation, which represents religious

---

[6]Hermann Siebeck, *Lehre des Religionsphilosophie*, p. 58 ff.

[7]Owen C. Whitehouse, "Demon, Devil," *Hastings' Dictionary of the Bible*, I, 590-94.

[8]Cf. Louis M. Sweet, "Demon, Demoniac, Demonology," *International Standard Bible Encyclopedia*, II, 827-29.

[9]Cf. T. Witton Davies, *Magic, Divination and Demonology among the Hebrews and Their Neighbors*, pp. 8-17.

faith and practice as subject to degradation rather than progressive improvement (Rom. 1:21-23). Second, it clashes with the witness of comparative religion, which also notes a downward rather than an upward tendency in ethnic faiths. This principle is frequently carried to such lengths that, as Lucretius found in Greece and Rome, religion became a curse instead of a blessing. Professor Renouf notes the same phenomenon in ancient Egypt, where the sublimer portions of Egyptian religion are demonstrably ancient, and the "last stage . . . . was by far the grossest and most corrupt."[10] Modern Hinduism represents a deterioration from the higher religious conceptions in the Vedas. In South Africa, Australia, and elsewhere, traditions still persist of a Creator of all things, but his worship has been set aside in favor of lower and evil deities. The same is true of ancient Babylonia and Assyria. Similar declination has more than once manifested itself in ancient Israel, and in the Christian Church, rendering periodic revival and return to the truth imperative.

Third, the genetic connection between animism and polytheism is far from clear. The precise religious nature of the former is indeed highly problematical, and belongs to the category of primitive philosophy rather than religion. Sayce[11] and Rogers[12] have shown that the two religious phenomena have coexisted without actual combination or assimilation for long periods of history, suggesting a different *raison d' etre*, rise, and development. To construct a theory on such a dubious connection is at most a very precarious procedure.

Fourth, to make polytheism the source of Biblical demonology is indeed a bold step, contradicting the lofty spirit of the Old Testament which manifests how slight and unimportant was the bearing of heathenism upon its thought. The interpretation of pagan deities as demons in no wise proves that polytheism is the source of Biblical demonology. It would rather indicate that the category of demons was already well known to Hebrew

---

[10]P. Le Page Renouf, *The Origin and Growth of Religion as Illustrated by the Religion of Ancient Egypt*, in "Hibbert Lectures for 1879," pp. 261-63. Cf. *International Standard Bible Encyclopedia*, 693.

[11]A. H. Sayce, *Babylonia and Assyria*, p. 232.

[12]R. W. Rogers, *The Religion of Babylonia and Assyria*, pp. 75-76.

thought, and that heathen idolatry was interpreted as initiated
and energized by demonic activity and deception.

3. The Astral View

This theory would account for demons under the supposition
that religion began with the worship of the heavenly bodies, to
which the primitive religious mind attached personality. The
most important of these bodies, such as the sun, the moon, and
the planets were assigned the status of full-fledged deities. The
lesser bodies, such as the innumerable fixed stars, were given
the position of lesser deities (demons). It is not known when
planets were first recognized as distinct from fixed stars, but
planetary worship and divination prevailed at a very early period
in the Euphrates Valley.

The astral hypothesis, for instance, thus theorizes on the
subject of light and darkness: Light is the creation of the good
gods; darkness is looked upon less as a creation of the gods than
as an environment for monsters and evil spirits, who are rendered
incapable of perpetrating their wickedness apart from gloom. Of
the evil spirits that love night, seven particular demons, abetted
by certain of the great gods, were thought to be responsible for
the darkening of the moon by eclipse, or storm, and even for the
disappearance of the lunar disc at the end of the month.[13]

To this theory, mainly a product of Professor H. Winckler
of Germany, and enthusiastically espoused by Dr. Alfred Jeremias,
it may be replied that besides being completely at variance with
revealed truth, it lacks historical corroboration. The evidence of
ancient inscriptions do not support it; so its protagonists plant
its roots deep in a purely imaginary age, where evidence pro or
con is *ex hypothesi* lacking. Moreover, it is destitute of scientific
astronomical support. It is simply an elaborate and fine-spun
figment of German rationalism.

B.   The Biblical View

In tracing the origin of evil supernaturalism, divine revelation
is in sharp contrast to naturalistic theories, in that it goes far

---

[13]Cf. William Cruikshank, "Astral Theory," *Hastings' Encyclopedia of Religion
and Ethics*, 1912, VIII, 63.

beyond them to original sources and ultimate realities. It expands horizons. It goes beyond the creation of man, and the introduction of sin into the human race, beyond even the creation of the angelic orders and the entrance of sin into the moral universe to the unfathomable eternity when God alone existed in sole sublime majesty. It alone conducts one to an eminence of altitude ample for furnishing sufficient sweep and perspective to see and comprehend the origin and nature of evil in the world.

Sin itself began in heaven with "Lucifer, son of the morning," the highest and most exalted of heaven's created beings, who became Satan when he led a celestial revolt that spread to myriads of the angelic beings (Isa. 14:12-20). But Satan was not created evil. As Dr. Lewis Sperry Chafer points out,[14] revelation concerning this eminent being begins with his sinless career, embracing the "dateless period" between the perfect creation of the heavens and the earth (Gen.1:1) and the catastrophic judgment upon this planet (Gen. 1:2; Jer. 4:23-26), which is, in all likelihood, to be connected with his fall. One passage, Ezekiel 28:11-19, despite contention to the contrary,[15] obviously transcends reference to the "prince of Tyre," or to Adam in Eden, and embraces a splendid and detailed portrait of Satan's person in his primeval sinless glory. Dr. Twesten's admonition on this point is wise and significant:

> The position that the devil and his angels were not created evil, but became so in consequence of a fall, the possibility of which was given in their free will, is to be held fast, especially in opposition to the dualistic doctrine of a principle in itself evil.[16]

Further revelation concerning Satan presents him as a king with a kingdom (Matt. 12:26), a portion of which dominion consists of the demons (Matt. 12:24). Concerning the precise origin of the demons, though, nothing dogmatic ought to be asserted or insisted upon, inasmuch as this is ˄ne phase of the subject affected by the problem of the silence of revelation. Of the many hypotheses advanced to explain their origin, the simplest and most likely inference from the facts at hand is that they were created sinless

---

[14]Lewis Sperry Chafer, *Satan,* p. 3.
[15]Michael J. Gruenthaner, "The Demonology of the Old Testament" *Catholic Quarterly Review,* January, 1944, p. 21.
[16]A. C. D. Twesten, "The Doctrine Respecting Angels," *Bibliotheca Sacra and Theological Review,* I (November 1844), 787.

as subjects of Satan in the primal glory, and that he drew them after him in his pride and defection from God. That Satan in his apostasy involved a great host of angels, who, like him, "abode not in the truth" (John 8:44) is assumed as a well-known fact of revelation by the New Testament, where some of them are described as those who "kept not their first estate," whom God cast down to Tartarus, and delivered into chains of darkness, to be reserved unto judgment of the great day (II Pet. 2:4; Jude 1:6), and others are, it seems, represented by the demons. Dr. Lewis Sperry Chafer is of the opinion that, of those fallen spirits who were not incarcerated, "another company became demons."[17] John J. Owen concurs in this view that demons are the evil spirits or wicked angels associated with Satan in his rebellion against God.[18] In fact, this, as G. Campbell Morgan says, is "the generally accepted theory."[19] A. A. Hodge,[20] Charles Hodge,[21] as well as A. H. Strong,[22] and others also espouse it. A. C. Gaebelein says ". . . the fallen angels are demons."[23]

However, many other opinions exist, and there is of course little unanimity to be expected on a subject of this sort, on which, as C. I. Scofield aptly says, "nothing is clearly revealed"[24] and great latitude exists for speculation. Since the various theories of the origin of demons will be dealt with elsewhere, it will suffice here to mention that many writers, insisting on a rigid distinction between fallen or evil angels and demons, trace the rise of the latter to inhabitants of the pre-Adamite earth, whose sin, it is said, caused its destruction, and whose bodies were destroyed in the catastrophe that overwhelmed it, leaving them "disembodied spirits" with a keen desire to re-embody themselves on the earth where they once lived.[25] Others,[26] following an ancient pre-Christian

---

[17]Lewis Sperry Chafer, *Satan*, p. 63.

[18]John J. Owen, "Demonology of the New Testament," *Bibliotheca Sacra and Biblical Repository*, XVI, January 1859, 133-35.

[19]G. Campbell Morgan, *The Gospel According to Mark*, p. 114.

[20]A. A. Hodge, *Outlines of Theology*, p. 255.

[21]Charles Hodge, *Systematic Theology*, I, 643.

[22]A. H. Strong, *Systematic Theology*, p. 455.

[23]A. C. Gaebelein, *The Gospel of Matthew*, p. 247.

[24]C. I. Scofield, *Reference Bible*, note on Matthew 7:22, p. 1004.

[25]Cf. Clarence Larkin, *The Spirit World*, p. 39.

[26]F. C. Conybeare, "Christian Demonology," *Jewish Quarterly Review*, IX, 75.

Jewish exegesis,[27] trace the beginning of demons to the monstrous progeny which was the result of angelic cohabitation with antediluvian women(Gen.6:1-6).[28] In any event, demons are evil and members of Satan's kingdom (Matt. 12:26). Scripture says nothing of "good" demons.

C. The Superiority of the Biblical View

But little consideration is necessary to demonstrate how vastly superior *any* of the explanations of the origin of demons based on Scripture are to the mere naturalistic theories of man. Whereas the Bible, in tracing the course of Satan's apostasy and the introduction of sin into the universe, goes back to first causes and ultimate origins, man's speculations cannot get beyond effects rather than causes, and developments rather than origins. Whereas Scripture at once lifts the whole subject into the realm of supernatural reality from which diverse and bewildering demonological phenomena may be accurately appraised and discriminatingly evaluated, man's hypotheses but leave the whole field of inquiry sunk in indiscriminate confusion, wherein reliable criteria are lacking to differentiate reality from fancy and actual existence from pure imagination; and the whole is, as a result, promiscuously pronounced superstition. And, whereas the Scripture account of the origin and reality of evil supernaturalism offers a solid and substantial basis of explanation for the widespread persistence and manifestation of Satanic and demonological phenomena from the most ancient times to the present, naturalistic speculations can but inadequately attribute the facts to man's religiously superstitious mind, or to some similarly unsatisfactory basis.

D. The Ultimate Source of All Demonology

The Book of Genesis, besides being the inspired account of the oldest traditions of the human race, contains all the elements requisite for the development of a demonology analogous to that of the New Testament. There is evidence of a cataclysmic judgment upon a pre-Adamite earth, no doubt to be thought of in connection with a defection and apostasy among the angels

---

[27]*The Book of Enoch*, Chapter XV.
[28]Cf. Larkin, *op. cit.*, p. 39.

(Gen. 1:2). All the characteristics of Satan as an ominous personality, antagonistic to God and to man, are virtually contained in the paradisaic serpent, and the account of the fall. The frequent appearance of deity as the angel of Jehovah, the striking spectacle of the cherubim eastward of Eden as the guardians of the divine holiness, and the free and familiar intercourse of angels with men in patriarchal times, and in all likelihood earlier, indicate the existence of more than an elementary theology and angelology. Indeed, if the much disputed passage of Genesis 6:1-6 really refers to angelic cohabitation with antediluvian women, as an imposing array of scholars hold, there is not lacking added evidence of an elaborate doctrine of evil angels. Be that as it may, the demonology of the Book of Genesis, especially that of earlier chapters, preserving, as it does, the history of earth's earliest ages, is remarkably complete in its essential elements, despite its simplicity and undevelopment. It could well furnish the root from which the many-branched and complex demonologies of the various nations developed, and easily form the essential foundation of demonological facts around which heathen peoples built a superstructure of error and superstition.

The basic similarity between primitive demonological traditions recorded in Genesis, and those preserved in the archaeological records of the earliest nations of the earth, despite the accretions of error and extravagance to the latter, indubitably points to a common source for both and supplies evidence that they are due to a common inheritance of traditions concerning the early history of the race, upon which both have drawn. Thus the demonology of the Book of Genesis and the demonological systems of the earliest nations of antiquity present two forms of the same early traditions, with this important difference, however, that the inspired Mosaic account gives the original pure and unadulterated form of these truths, uncolored by extravagances and as they primitively existed; while the ethnic records offer a version of these primeval traditions of mankind so incrusted with error and the excesses and exuberances of centuries, that even the essential core of reality out of which they were developed is, in many cases, almost wholly obliterated.

A similar phenomenon of historical development may be observed between other primitive traditions of the human race, as preserved in ancient inscriptions and those recorded in Genesis. Most of the great nations of antiquity have preserved traditions of such epic events as the creation of the world, the origin of man, the story of the fall, and the account of the flood.[29] Some of these are only vaguely suggestive of the presentation in Genesis, and may be dismissed without mention; while others are so startlingly similar as to require careful consideration. Of the latter variety are the records in the ancient cuneiform language of Babylonia-Assyria. Stories of the creation, of man's forfeiture of eternal life in the "Myth of Adapa," and of the deluge bear such striking resemblances, as well as notable differences, to the Genesis narratives as to demand explanation.

How, then, is the similarity between the passages in Genesis and the versions contained in the inscriptions to be accounted for? It cannot be that the Genesis account is drawn from the traditions, nor vice versa, that these traditions were drawn from the Genesis narratives, for both of these positions are obviously untenable. Neither can it be because similar traditions just "happened" to arise due to "the natural tendencies of the human mind in its evolution from a savage state."[30] Effects are not produced without causes. The only explanation is that which has already been given to account for the similarity between primitive demonological facts and inferences contained in the earliest chapters of Genesis, and the traditions preserved in the records of the earliest nations of the earth. Their likeness is due to common inheritance possessed by all the civilized nations of antiquity, of drawing from the same original source of primitive tradition, which dates from a time when the human race occupied a common home and held a common faith. The differences are due to the purity and accuracy of the Genesis traditions. Reproduced, as they are in the Scriptures, by divine inspiration, they are given exactly as they existed in their pristine simplicity and unadulteration in the earliest ages of the human race.

Biblical demonology, then, as it exists in its elemental though essential form in the earlier chapters of Genesis, is the ultimate

---

[29]Ira Maurice Price, *The Monuments and The Old Testament*, pp. 98-130; Alexander Heidel, *The Babylonian Genesis*, 2nd ed., pp. 130-39; and *The Gilgamesh Epic and Old Testament Parallels*, pp. 260-67.

[30]Price, *op. cit.*, p. 129.

source and basis of all demonology—ethnic, later Biblical, Jewish, and Christian. Genesis as the book of beginnings catalogues the beginning of the earth and the human race, the beginning of human sin and death and the beginning of human government and language. It also suggests the origin of demons. But inasmuch as demons are certainly to be traced back to the fall of Satan and the angels, which the Book of Genesis assumes as background material in the same way it assumes the existence of God as background material (Gen. 1:1), it cannot validly be charged that there are no demons in the opening book of the Bible. In any event or upon any possible inference based on revealed facts, they are there, whether as fallen angels, or as the disembodied spirits of a pre-Adamite race (Gen. 1:2), or as the result of the cohabitation of angelic beings with antediluvian women (Gen. 6:1-4). In the Book of Genesis the author assumes the existence of demons just as plainly as he assumes the existence of God or the fall of Satan and his angels.

CHAPTER III

BIBLICAL DEMONOLOGY
AS A STANDARD OF EVALUATION

SCRIPTURE IS intensely realistic. Invariably it presents a vividly true-to-life portrait of whatever it may be depicting. This is what would naturally be expected in a revelation inspired and given, as it is, in accordance with the highest standards of divine truth and inerrancy. On its pages there is no room for romanticism, or looking through "rose-colored glasses" in portraying either the character of individuals, or things, or the state of nations. People and conditions are presented as they are. Good as well as evil is drawn in true color. God's closest friends, as well as his avowed and implacable enemies, His own people Israel, as well as the heathen nations surrounding them, are photographed in "candid-camera style" and presented with remarkable life-like reality.

In no sphere is this fidelity to reality and verity more advantageously displayed than in the domain dealing with demonological phenomena, wherein distortion and extravagance are elsewhere so notoriously rampant. Whether it be a matter of the revelation of basic demonological truth, or the appraisal of varied demonological phenomena, or the complex description of a people under the paralyzing power of evil supernaturalism, the Bible's unerring criteria are absolutely trustworthy. The character of Biblical demonology itself, as clear and unerringly recorded truth, qualifies it as a wholly reliable standard of evaluation in appraising the character of demonology in general—rabbinic as well as ethnic.

A. THE CHARACTER OF BIBLICAL DEMONOLOGY

Some of the more general characteristics of Biblical demonology have of necessity been touched upon elsewhere. Here, how-

ever, it is necessary to say something more definite and detailed
concerning its more salient and distinguishing features.

1. BIBLICAL DEMONOLOGY LOFTY IN ITS TONE

Demonology in the Old Testament as well as in the New
moves upon a high plain. Critics, supposing Old Testament
demonology to be an evolutionary development from animism
through polytheism, or some other crude elemental faith, into
monotheism, must certainly be embarrassed by the elevated spirit
of the Old Testament. This is in striking contrast to the crude
and gross tenor of contemporary religious thought, and eloquently
indicates how slight and insignificant was the impression of pagan
thought upon it. Attempts to substantiate the evolutionary hypothesis,[1] in Israelite religion, by laborious efforts to ferret out
so-called "remnants" of animism, totemism, taboo, and ancestor
worship in the Old Testament, as evidences of an imagined development from so-called "earliest stages of belief," are vain and
useless. These attempted evidences are at variance with the
grandeur of Hebrew monotheism and are in disagreement with
the historical growth of Hebrew religion, the basis of which is
separation, not syncretism.

In the call of Abram, and the creation of the nation Israel,
God purified and separated a small stream from the vast polluted
river of humanity. His purpose was to keep this branch pure and
separated, that with it He might eventually cleanse the great river
itself. Its purity consisted in its clear-cut separation to the one true
God in the midst of universal idolatry (Deut. 6:4; Isa. 43:10-12).
Israelite religion began as pure monotheism, in a radical and complete purge from polytheism, and the genius of it lay in its perpetuation as such by rigid and uncompromising isolation. This is
the secret of the loftiness of its demonology, and of its religion
in general. Note also the following statement of George W. Gilmore:
"Yet it is to be observed that not even in its monotheism does the
religion of Israel show a loftier elevation above the faiths of the
surrounding peoples than *in its demonology.*"[2]

---

[1]Cf. W. O. E. Oesterley and T. H. Robinson, *Hebrew Religion*, pp. 3-108.
[2]George W. Gilmore, "Demon, Demonism," *New Schaff-Herzog Encyclopedia
of Religious Knowledge*, p. 399.

2. BIBLICAL DEMONOLOGY FREE FROM EXAGGERATION AND SUPERSTITION

Perhaps no one would be so bold as to deny that the obvious loftiness of the tone of Biblical demonology is manifestly superior to the crudities of contemporary systems. Yet there are those who would deny that it is wholly free from popular exaggeration and superstition. Whitehouse's statement concerning New Testament demonology, that it "is in all its broad characteristics the demonology of the contemporary Judaism stripped of its cruder and exaggerated features"[3] is to be taken as voicing the opinion of many concerning Biblical demonism as a whole. They are reluctant to acknowledge that it is completely uncontaminated with exaggeration and superstition. This tendency is but the recurrence of one of the difficulties which embarrass this field of inquiry: the problem of doubt.

Skepticism seems to center in the apparent great increase of demonic activity in the time of our Lord, and the large number of striking cases of demonic possession. Since this phase of the study will be treated at length later, it is sufficient to remark in passing that so far from there being anything crude or exaggerated in these narratives, savoring of the popular demonism of the day, to jeopardize intelligent faith, there is rather to be noted a chaste influence, curbing curiosity, restraining imagination, severely limiting the sphere of demoniacal operation, laying emphasis upon the connection of demons with moral disorders of the human race, and conspicuously ignoring magical methods.[4] In this, as in every other instance, Biblical demonology remains upon its lofty plain. Its freedom from superstitious excesses and exaggeration offers every possible inducement to devout and enlightened faith.

3. BIBLICAL DEMONOLOGY ACCURATE AND RELIABLE IN ITS SPHERE

This trustworthiness has frequently but groundlessly been called in question regarding many demonological phenomena, but especially with regard to the New Testament cases of demon possession. Such instances, it is maintained, were not what they

---

[3]Owen C. Whitehouse, *Hastings' Dictionary of the Bible*, I, 593.
[4]Cf. Louis M. Sweet, "New Testament Demonology," *International Standard Bible Encyclopedia*, II, 828.

are plainly described to be, supernatural occurrences, but merely attacks of unusual diseases of body and mind, and that our Lord, in ascribing them to demon inhabitation, accommodated himself to the superstitious ignorance of his auditors and the popular beliefs of the time, in order to make himself understood, especially by the sufferers themselves.[5] This position not only violates every principle of sound exegesis of the plain words of the text, but accuses the Lord Jesus, who exposed and denounced superstition in matters of far less moment, of sanctioning particular error which has ever been the bastion of superstition.

The case of the entrance of the demons into the swine at Gadara (Mark 5:11-14), and the violent effect produced upon them, is sufficient, without further arguments to show the falsity of this contention. It is a mere naturalistic rejection of the supernatural, the outcropping of the ever-recurring problem of unbelief. The authenticity and accuracy of these Biblical narratives, however, remain intact.[6] Skepticism may not be able to accept the Scriptural accounts, but its flimsy arguments cannot dispose of them.

4. BIBLICAL DEMONOLOGY VAST IN ITS SWEEP

Evil is not an insignificant passing fad or some trivial temporary aberration affecting only mankind, to be lightly regarded and triflingly dealt with. Far from being inconsequential, the whole subject is invested with the weightiest consequence. Sin is plainly sinful, alienating from God, and dooming eternally. Its blighting and terribly destructive manifestation in the moral universe calls forth the mighty demonstration of God's infinite goodness and grace in Christ, in His redemptive plans and purposes embracing the ages (Eph. 1:4-5). The original majestic and sinless career of Satan (Ezek. 28:12-19), his dramatic revolt (Isa. 14:12-14), his organization in the heavenlies of a stupendous host of evil angels under him (Eph. 6:12), his agency in the fall of man (Gen. 3:1-8), his present relentless and sinister activity (I Pet. 5:8), his future expulsion from the heavenlies (Luke 10:18; Rev. 12:7-9), and his final doom with all who follow him (Matt. 25:41; Rev. 20:10)

---

[5]Cf. Alfred Barry, "Demon, Demoniac," *Smith's Dictionary of the Bible*, I, 584 ff.

[6]Archbishop R. C. Trench, *Notes on the Miracles of Our Lord*, pp. 153-54.

present a scene of awful grandeur and magnitude, and illustrate the extent and importance of Biblical demonology.

5. BIBLICAL DEMONOLOGY PRACTICAL IN ITS PURPOSE

Some would view the whole subject of Biblical demonology as accidental and essentially purposeless, a mere incursion of popular contemporary superstitions into the Biblical accounts.[7] Others would trace the facts to remnants of animistic or polytheistic belief in the evolutionary process from a more primitive and cruder faith.[8] The emptiness of such baseless naturalistic hypotheses, however, is emphasized by the eminent practicality and intrinsic purposefulness of Biblical demonology. So far from satisfying an idle curiosity, or pandering to a morbid imagination, its chaste reticence is indicative of its high aim to enlighten and warn the unwary against the ever-impending peril of evil supernaturalism, and to point the way to deliverance and victory. More knowledge than this is not needed, and hence more than this is not given. This is likely the key to the explanation of the problem of the silence of revelation, so noticeable in many aspects of this study. What we wish to know, may not always be what we ought to know, for edification and practical godliness.

We could wish, perchance, to know more about the precise origin and nature of demons, but what we need to know is how to be able "to stand against the wiles of the devil" (Eph. 6:11), that "our wrestling is not against flesh and blood, but against the principalities, against the powers, against the world rulers of this darkness, against the spiritual hosts of wickedness in the heavenly places" (Eph. 6:12), that our adversary "goeth about as a roaring lion," devouring, (I Pet. 5:8), as an "angel of light," deceiving (II Cor. 11:14), and that if we would not suffer disadvantage from him, we must, like the great Apostle, not be "ignorant of his devices" (II Cor. 2:11).

6. BIBLICAL DEMONOLOGY SOUND IN ITS THEOLOGY

Demonology as portrayed in the Bible is consistent with the doctrine of the sovereignty of God. In this respect it is unique,

---

[7]F. C. Conybeare, "Christian Demonology," *Jewish Quarterly Review*, 1896-97, IX, 602.

[8]Oesterley and Robinson, *Hebrew Religion*, pp. 23-50.

and stands in trenchant contrast to both rabbinic and ethnic conceptions, in which the malignity, the power, and the independence allowed demons are compatible only with a polytheistic creed. Born and bred in rigid monotheism, Biblical demonism was purified at its source, and kept itself unpolluted from those crooked and gross superstitions which impinge upon the majesty of God. The enslaving and fear-inspiring nature of the popular demonism of neighboring contemporary cults was intensely alien to Israel's long experience of Jehovah's uniqueness, goodness, and power. Even frequent apostasy, and the inroads of idolatrous contamination made little or no impression upon crystallized theological thought, and these transient aberrations inevitably met with a virile monotheistic reaction that purged away defilement. Revealed truth remained untouched, and continued to be the impregnable standard to call back straying people from the error of their way.

Israel's monotheism, moreover, kept its demonism singularly uncontaminated from a threatening dualism. Persian religion, for example, divides the world into two distinct empires, good and bad. Each is presided over by an absolutely independent god. The "destroying spirit," ruling over the evil realm, is not responsible to anyone for his actions. He reigns with unimpeded sway over his particular dominion. He will be vanquished by the god of the good realm only at the end of the world. He actually created the demons, who are the authors of sin, and all that is evil and polluting in the world.

In complete contrast to this conception is the sublime undualistic tone of Biblical demonology. Satan as a fallen *creature*, and head of a vast kingdom of evil spirits, though majestic and puissant, is completely under the suzerainty of Jehovah, who alone is the Creator and all-powerful God. Satan can create nothing, nor can he perpetrate any evil, physical or moral, without Jehovah's sanction. His purpose in the divine program is outlined, the span of his perpetration is set, and his inevitable doom is sealed. In spite of this evident antithesis, it is frequently asserted that Persian demonology affected the Biblical conception of Satan.[9] To this contention it is enough to say that all the essential characteristics of Satan were already contained in the Edenic serpent, and

---

[9]Eduard Koenig, *Theologie des Alten Testaments*, 4th ed., p. 231, note 5.

in the Book of Job (which has never yet been proved to be post-exilic); so that Jews needed no imported influence whatever to conceive of his personality.[10]

Biblical demonology is also congruous with the doctrine of man's free moral agency. The almost unrestricted range of activity, and practically uncurbed power of demons over human beings in popular Semitic demonism, left little dignity to man's free will. Human volition was of slight protection against malignant demonic caprice. In the exuberance of popular fancy, man was little more than a helpless victim of teeming hosts of demons, lying in wait for him, and besieging him with every imaginable ill.[11]

In antithesis to this affluence of morbid fancy, Scripture sacredly guards the dignity of human choice. No one choosing light can be invaded by the forces of darkness. It is only as the enlightened will deliberately chooses darkness, or yields to sin, that it exposes itself to demonic power. It was certainly Saul's repeated deliberate disobedience to the divine will (I Sam. 13:13; 15:22, 23) that rendered his weakened will susceptible to demonic influence (I Sam. 16:14). It was when Israel, enlightened by the knowledge of the true God, rejected that light, and served idols, that they "sacrificed their sons and daughters unto demons" (Ps. 106:37). Rejection of truth for a lie lays one open to "wandering spirits and doctrines of demons" (I Tim. 4:1). Even in the case of demoniacs, Edersheim maintains a moral element is involved, entailing the personal responsibility of the demonized, inasmuch as the demoniac state is not permanent. During "the period of temporary liberty" the demonized might "have shaken themselves free" from the evil power, or sought release from it.[12] From the time of the Fathers,[13] many Christian theologians have contended that a moral responsibility is involved in the demoniacs, sin being a precursor to the demonized state.[14] John Lightfoot,[15] Herman Ols-

---

[10]Michael J. Gruenthaner, "The Demonology of the Old Testament," *Catholic Biblical Quarterly*, January 1944, Vol. 6, No. 1, p. 19.

[11]R. W. Rogers, *The Religion of Babylonia and Assyria*, p. 145.

[12]Alfred Edersheim, *Life and Times of Jesus the Messiah*, I, 484.

[13]Cf. *Clementine Recognitions*, 2:72; 4:34.

[14]Origen, *Contra Celsum*, III: III: 2.

[15]John Lightfoot, *Horae Hebraicae*, I: 639; II: 175.

hausen,[16] J. L. Nevius, [17] and J. Weiss, [18] among many others, have
vigorously held this position.

7. BIBLICAL DEMONOLOGY RELIEVED BY EFFECTUAL DELIVERANCE

Scripture indeed gives a vividly realistic picture of the horrible wreck and ruin caused by sin. The effects and ramifications
of the entrance and development of evil into the moral universe
assume stupendous proportions. The whole dark drama, at first
glance, might appear to be a tragedy of unparalleled scope, unmitigated in its woe. But, on the contrary, the cataclysm of diabolical darkness calls forth an effulgence of divine light. The
eruption of hellish hate evokes a flood of divine love. The doleful
spectacle of rebellion and destruction becomes the occasion for
the greatest and grandest event of the ages, the demonstration
of God's unfathomable grace in the revelation of Himself in Christ,
who completely conquers all enemies, and "put away sin by the
sacrifice of Himself" (Heb. 9:26). "For this purpose the Son of
God was manifested, that He might destroy the works of the devil"
(I John 3:8).

Except for His redemptive work—His sinless life, His vicarious
death, His triumphant resurrection, His glorious ascension, His
present intercession, and future coming again—the vast drama
of evil would truly be the blackest tragedy of the ages, unilluminated by any ray of hope. But it is He who brings salvation out
of ruin, and triumph out of disaster. His glorious Person and
finished work constitute the only but all-sufficient ground of deliverance from the baleful power of evil supernaturalism. He is
"the Way," leading out of darkness; "the Truth," protecting from
error; and "the Life," delivering from death (John 14:6). In Him
there is full redemption; apart from Him, unalleviated woe.

Contrast with non-Biblical demonologies is complete. Weighted
down with paralyzing fear, and cruel superstitions, they offer no
emancipation from the dread tyranny of sin. Supposed deliverance
by their false deities is but the chimera of a darkened imagination.
Moreover, there is little improvement over polytheism in the vagaries of a monotheistic system like Mohammedanism. Moslem doc-

---

[16]*Commentary, Matthew* 8:28-34.
[17]*Demon Possession and Allied Themes,* 5th ed., p. 287.
[18]*The Life of Christ,* II, 81 ff; also cf. W. M. Alexander, *op. cit.,* p. 171.

tors grant scant respect to Christ's person, and still less to His unique finished work, when they imagine that His birth occasioned the expulsion of the Jinn (demons) from three of the "seven" heavens, while Mohammed's nativity effected their ejection from the remaining four![19]

Perfection and inerrancy may rightly be expected from anything of divine origin, and from whatever is a product of infinite wisdom. The character of Biblical demonology not only proves that it is what it claims to be, a revelation from God, but also, as such, demonstrates that it is true and thoroughly reliable as a criterion of appraisal. It furnishes the model of truth to test error. It constitutes the pattern of reality to try all imagination and unreality. In its light we see light, as well as darkness, crookedness, and unreality. It alone can furnish an infallible norm to differentiate between truth and falsity, fact and fancy. Measured by its sure and trustworthy standards, demonology, whether ethnic or rabbinic, is seen in its true light.

B. THE CHARACTER OF ETHNIC DEMONOLOGY

Without the chart of revealed truth to guide, it would be an impossible and hopeless task to try to steer a straight course through the intricacies and complexities of heathen thought and practice. With such amazing complication of detail, and often with such refined and subtle intermixture of truth and error, the student of religion proceeding on mere naturalistic hypotheses, without the infallible guide of revelation, is like a vessel without chart, rudder, or compass, tempest-tossed on a reef-strewn sea. Truth and accuracy of interpretation must inevitably suffer shipwreck. Only in the light of the Word of God can truth be differentiated from error, fact recognized from fancy, and reality perceived as actuality. A divine standard alone can supply the valid criterion for estimating pagan systems of thought. Only in divine light may the character of ethnic demonology be confidently evaluated.

1. ETHNIC DEMONOLOGY LOW AND DEGRADING IN ITS TONE

Polytheism, which is the corrupt basis of ethnic demonological

---

[19]Thomas Witton Davies, *Magic, Divination, and Demonology among the Hebrews and Their Neighbors*, p. 93.

systems, spreads the leaven of its pollution to all religious thinking of which it constitutes a part. Monotheism, with one infiinite Creator and Redeemer, who is omnipotent, omniscient, omnipresent, and infinitely good and holy, extends its purity to the whole theological fabric of which it forms the warp and woof. The moment departure is made from one Infinite Being, supremely good and holy, and deities are multiplied, by so much are they degraded, and degrade those who worship them. Degraded deities, circumscribed in power, often of questionable holiness and goodness, offer no check to the independence, malignity, and caprice allowed to demonic conceptions. Indeed, the deities themselves, being non-entities (Jer. 16:20; Ps. 96:5), and mere figments of bedarkened minds (Amos 2:4), are nothing but the visible delusive bait for the worship of the invisible demons themselves. The demonizing of heathen gods, so conspicuous in the Septuagint (Ps. 91:6, LXX 90:6; 96:5, LXX 95:5; and Isa. 63:3, 11) is proof, that already in the third century B.C. demonism was recognized as the dynamic of idolatry, and idol-worship was considered but demon-worship, as Paul also declares (I Cor. 10:20, 21).

2. Ethnic Demonology Full of Extravagance and Superstition

As has already been shown in a preceding chapter,[20] it is enough to add here that in ethnic demonology excess characterizes whatever phase of the subject may be under consideration, and in whatever epoch, whether in ancient times or in the modern scientific era. If the number of demons is under discussion, there is little difference between the superstition of the ancient Babylonian who pictured every nook and corner as swarming with mischievous and evil-working spirits, or the modern Arab who sees demons everywhere in the desert, in trees, springs, and rocks. If their form is thought of, demons according to the ethnic ideal, may be anthropomorphic or thermiomorphic, and capriciously change their shape as need or whim may direct. As to the haunts of the genii, Babylonians believed in the howling of the shedhim in the wilderness, and the modern Hindu and Chinese hear the voices of evil spirits in the weird sounds of the night.[21]

---

[20]See Chap. I, sec. C, "The Problem of the Prevalence of Superstition."
[21]Cf. William Menzies Alexander, *Demonic Possession in the New Testament*, pp. 40-50.

Superstitious peoples so multiply the number of demons that no part of the day or night is void of their visitations. Night is especially the fearful season of their activity. Ambushment and attack are constantly to be dreaded. Countless protective expedients are resorted to, such as charms and magical incantations, to frighten them away. Man's ingenuity is taxed to the limit to outwit imaginary foes and make life at all bearable.

3. ETHNIC DEMONOLOGY NARROW AND ENSLAVING IN ITS CONCEPTIONS

Pagan peoples are held continually in the grip of absurd fear and superstitious dread. Body mutilations, curious amulets, odd articles of dress have always had their advocates for the appeasement and subjection of demons. Modes of managing evil spirits are numberless in their variety. Fire has always been deemed efficacious for this purpose, among the ancient Babylonians, as well as among peoples of Africa, Australia, and India today. Devil-dances and bloody sacrifices are practiced in Southern India. Orgiastic rites are not uncommon under the pall of paganism. The whole dreadful scene is an unanswerable proof of the deception of Satan, and the tyranny of evil supernaturalism.

4. ETHNIC DEMONOLOGY IMPRACTICAL AND PURPOSELESS IN ITS INTENT

The overwrought speculation and the exuberant imagination of ethnic systems display an attempt to satisfy idle curiosity or to stoop to morbid fancy, rather than to provide any practical purpose. The enemy is described, but in such a manner that fear of him is increased, while chance of deliverance from his clutches is decreased. Proffered means of deliverance are but deceitful snares that trap the victim more securely or cruel fetters that bind him more hopelessly to the powers of evil.

5. ETHNIC DEMONOLOGY UNSOUND IN ITS THEOLOGY

Faulty conceptions of deity contaminate every aspect of ethnic theological thought, and especially its demonology. This is the tainted source of all the excesses of ethnic demonism. God is considered otherwise than one, and thus the way is opened for endless distortion in demonic conceptions. God's sovereignty being violated, the door is at the same time opened to a dangerous dualism, and all its kindred ills, as in the Persian religion, where an independent evil deity actually creates the demons.

An unsound theology is bound to produce an unsound anthropology. If God's sovereignty is compromised, man's free will can but be imperilled. The craftiness and strategy with which demons waylay and surprise their victims in ethnic thought, leave scant room for the exercise of man's right of choice or responsibility.

Moreover, the uncurbed activity and the uncircumscribed sphere of demon operation, so characteristic of paganism, clashes with a knowledge of the natural world, and the common laws divinely established to regulate it.

6. Ethnic Demonology Unmitigated by Actual Deliverance

Fantastic rites for controlling and appeasing evil spirits, gross and crude methods of exorcism and multifarious expedients for avoiding their baneful attacks, are but miserable substitutes for the one way of salvation in the cross of Christ. Ethnic demonology is truly a somber picture of tragedy, unrelieved by any true way of emancipation.

C. The Character of Rabbinic Demonology in the Light of Divine Revelation

Little that is accurate and conformable to truth can be expected of ethnic demonology, unmoored and unanchored as it is to the divine revelation. Rabbinic demonology, however, having as it does, the chaste and elevated tone of Old Testament demonology as a background, might naturally be expected to be quite different. That such is not the case, but that rabbinic demonology betrays many of the features of contemporary ethnic thought, is not without considerable significance in evaluating New Testament demonology.

1. Rabbinic Demonology Full of Distortion of Biblical Truths

The fall of Satan and his angels, in rabbinic demonology, is strangely imagined as subsequent to the creation of man, and was occasioned by their jealousy and envy of him.[22] And various gross ideas are entertained as to the origin of demons, ranging from their creation on the eve of the first Sabbath, before their bodies could be finished (this is supposed to account for their being spirits), to generation of multitudes of them as the offspring of Eve and male spirits, and of Adam and female spirits, or with Lilith, queen of the female spirits.[23] Still grosser ideas link them to transformations from vipers, or as springing from the backbone of him who did not bow in worship.[24] Fully sexed, they multiply rapidly, and are innumerable. A thousand at your right hand, ten thousand at your left. No one could survive the shock of seeing their actual number.[25] They are arranged in four classes, according to the divisions of the day—morning, midday, evening, and night spirits. The night spirits are the most dangerous and malignant.[26]

2. Rabbinic Demonology Unmistakably Mixed with Abject Heathen Superstitions

The acme of extravagance is perhaps reached in the rabbinic formula for envisioning demons, which for indelicacy and sheer absurdity perhaps equals anything found anywhere in heathen folklore.[27] But rabbinic demonology is not alone in its claim to direct verification. The glimpsing of spirits is frequently claimed by professional men, among the Zulus, Karens, Australians, Greenlanders, Indians, and many others.

Rabbinic methods of managing demons, such as torchlight by night, ablutions, phylacteries, amulets, and magic formulae, bear the strong impress of ancient ethnic custom. Rabbinic modes of expelling demons, through the conviction that the demon could be reached through the avenues of sense, find numerous pagan parallels. Appeals to the sense of taste, by "hell-broths" and vile mixtures, through the sense of hearing, by curses or withering abuse, through the sense of smell, by fumigations, pleasant or odious, through the sense of sight, by shocking or terrific exhibi-

[22]Pirqé de R. Eliezer, Rabbi (trans. by Gerald Friedlander), chap. 13.
[23]W. M. Alexander, *op. cit.*, pp. 25-26.
[24]A. Edersheim, *Life and Times of Jesus the Messiah*, II, 759-60.
[25]*Ibid.*, p. 760.
[26]Alexander, *op. cit.*, p. 30.
[27]Berakhoth 6a, *Prayers and Blessings.*

tions, through the sense of touch, by the infliction of manifold tortures, prove that between the Jewish and the ethnic doctrine of demons, there is substantial agreement.[28]

3. RABBINIC DEMONOLOGY UNRELIABLE AS A STANDARD OF EVALUATION

One large sector of Jewish demonology must be rejected as unreliable because it clashes with a pure monotheistic faith and morality. Rigid application of the monotheistic principle would have prevented the incorporation of these ridiculous vagaries, and purged out the contamination of gross demonic conceptions, impinging on the majesty and glory of God. Another considerable portion must be set aside as colliding with simple laws of nature. Spirits so fantastically numerous, and so ceaselessly and indefatigably active, would leave little sphere for the operation of natural law in an orderly universe. And another section must be regarded as directly attributable to purely paganistic speculation. There is little in Jewish thought in this realm unvitiated by error and excess.

4. RABBINIC DEMONOLOGY A VIVID CONTRAST TO NEW TESTAMENT DEMONOLOGY

There would be little point in cataloguing such abject superstitions, or little utility in even a cursory consideration of rabbinic demonology except that it has a vital bearing upon the question whether or not New Testament demonology was derived from contemporary Judaism. The contention that such was the case "has been so dogmatically asserted," as Edersheim notes, "as to have passed among a certain class as a settled fact."[29] But a casual unbiased observation of the facts is sufficient to demonstrate that such was emphatically *not* the case. Although there may be "similarity of form, slighter than usually," there is "absolute contrast of substance."[30] Greater antithesis could scarcely be imagined than there is between the elevated tone of New Testament demonology and the crude views and practices mentioned in rabbinic writings.

---

[28]Alexander, *op. cit.*, pp. 125-37.
[29]Edersheim, *op. cit.*, I, 142.
[30]*Ibid.*, I, 142.

CHAPTER IV

THE REALITY AND IDENTITY OF THE DEMONS

THE CHARACTER of Biblical demonology demonstrates its incomparable superiority over all ethnic and rabbinic systems and emphasizes its unique position as a thoroughly reliable standard of evaluation. It also indicates the pivotal place and central significance which the Scriptural testimony must be accorded for any accurate understanding and appraisal of the subject as a whole. Moreover, in the light of the uniqueness and importance of Scriptural demonology, it is not difficult to see that the problem of interpretation of the sacred text will be the task of paramount import. What saith the Scriptures? not only becomes the focal question but also the sign post pointing the direction inquiry must take.

A. THE EXISTENCE OF DEMONS

Little should need to be said as to the reality of demons, inasmuch as Scriptural testimony on this point is so clear and unequivocal. Notwithstanding, unbelief is so widespread and the problem of incredulity so vexing in the whole field of inquiry, that a discussion of it here seems necessary.

It hardly requires pointing out that the Bible doctrine of a personal devil and demons has met with a great storm of skepticism in recent years. Many, in a boasted age of science and enlightenment, dismiss the Biblical claim as a mere remnant of medieval superstition, or treat the whole matter as an amusing joke. Men in the church and out of it, blatantly assert that there is no personal devil, that the devil is only evil personified, and that whatever devil there is, is in man himself, and that there is enough of that variety to answer all theological requirements. It is also confidently declared that no longer can a respectable scholar be found anywhere who believes in a personal devil or demons. Thus this aggressive skepticism and militant attacks demand an apologetic approach to the problem. For it is obvious that if demons be imaginary and non-existent, then the whole subject belongs to the realm of fairy-tale and folklore, and not to the sphere of Christian theology.

1. PROOF FROM SCRIPTURE

The evidence of revelation is put first, not because it is expected more effectively to impress the skeptic (he seems unimpressed by any Scriptural declaration), but because intrinsically it is the most important witness. Demons do exist, first and foremost, for God in His Word says they exist. That the *shedhim* (Deut. 32:17; Ps. 106:36-37) of the Old Testament were real demons, and not mere idols, is proved by the Septuagint translation of the term by *daimonia* (demons); the Jews regarded idols as demons who allowed themselves to be worshipped by men (Bar. 4:7; LXX Ps. 95:5; I Cor. 10:20). It seems certain, moreover, that the *seirim* were also demonic conceptions (Lev. 17:7; II Chron. 11:15; Isa. 13:21; 34:14).

That the New Testament writers believed firmly in the existence of demons is capable of ample proof. They declare their existence (Jas 2:19; Rev. 9:20), describe their nature (Luke 4:33; 6:18), and their activity (I Tim. 4:1; Rev. 16:14), mention their expulsion from human bodies (Luke 9:42), suggest their organization under Satan (Matt. 12:26; Eph. 6:12), indicate their abode (Luke 8:31; Rev. 9:11), and point out their final doom (Matt. 25:41). That Christ Himself shared the identical views of the Biblical writers, though this fact is extensively denied, is subject to the same ample proof. He commanded His disciples to cast out demons (Matt. 10:1), cast them out Himself (Matt. 15:22, 28), rebuked them (Mark 5:8), had complete power over them (Matt. 12:29), and viewed His conquest over them as over Satan (Luke 10:17-18).

In the foregoing references there is not a hint that Jesus or any of the New Testament writers had the slightest doubt as to the real existence of either Satan or demons. They believed in their reality quite as much as in the existence of God, or of the good angels. Only slight investigation is necessary to expose the extreme crudity, destructiveness, and untenability of the rationalistic and mythical view of Satan and demons. It not only jeopardizes the character and truthfulness of the Son of God himself, but challenges the authenticity and reliability of the whole

Bible. For if the teachings of Scripture on the subject of Satan and demons are judged mythical, any other doctrine of Holy Writ may likewise be declared mythical at the caprice of the critic, who is disposed to offset his opinions against those of the prophets, apostles, and the Lord himself.

2. PROOF FROM PHYSICAL NATURE

To any reverent student, the witness of the Scripture to the existence of demons is amply sufficient, and further proof is unnecessary. But for those who are not disposed to accept the testimony of the Bible, other evidence, both scientific and philosophical, is not lacking. Nature, which has often been called God's "oldest Testament,"[1] lifts eloquent voice, as is frequently the case, in authentication and illustration of Scriptural truth. Everywhere in the natural world there are illustrations that suggest such beings as Satan and demons in the spiritual world. In the plant kingdom there are pests, insects, and blight that continually harass the farmer. In the animal kingdom there is not a creature that does not have its deadly enemy, killing and feeding upon it. Even the human family is perpetually besieged by a vast multitude of hostile germs awaiting their chance to storm the citadel of the human body and cause disease and death. However, this is not at all to suggest a causal connection between pests, parasites and disease germs of the natural realm and demons of the spiritual realm.

Since the Creator has an ethical purpose in all His works, and will eventually overrule evil for good, and since in numberless cases natural phenomena elucidate spiritual truths, "the invisible things of Him since the creation of the world" being "clearly seen, being perceived through the things that are made" (Rom. 1:20), it seems obviously deducible from the facts at hand that the tormenters and troublers that afflict every sphere of the natural realm are meant to be *illustrations* of the host of evil, malignant, invisible agencies that exist in the spiritual realm. The witness of nature is such as forever to disencumber the doctrine of demons from the common objections urged against it, that it is neither scientific nor philosophic. It is both. Moreover, no valid argument can be advanced against the constitution and administration of the spiritual world

---

[1] L. T. Townsend, *Satan and Demons*, pp. 34-35.

with its hosts of wicked demons that may not, at the same time, be urged with equal validity against the constitution and administration of the natural world, with its myriads of destructive bacteria and parasites.

3. Proof from Human Nature

For those who may be disinclined to accept either the proof from Scripture or proof from physical nature, added attestation of the existence of demons is to be found in the psychological facts of human nature. As Davies declares, "The belief in evil spirits is universal."[2] Townsend correctly states that such a conviction has been as "persistent and widespread . . . as belief in God, in good angels, or in the soul's immortality."[3]

The question of moment which calls for explanation, is, therefore, How is the practical universality of such a conviction to be accounted for? That the belief has ofttimes been vitiated by extravagant superstitions, though perhaps no more than beliefs in God, or Satan, is beside the question. The problem of a widely prevailing predisposition and of an inveterate tendency on the part of the human race remains a subject for scientific inquiry. What vital truth has not suffered distortion and violence at the hands of fallen mankind? For sensible people to discard the doctrine of Satan and demons, because it has been abused, is folly. Following a similar irrational procedure would result in repudiating every vital doctrine of the Word of God, for every aspect of revelation has suffered endless distortion and misrepresentation. The course appears the more foolhardy, inasmuch as beneath the extravagances of almost every belief there lies hidden some important truth.

But how is the preponderance of human belief in demons, from the most ancient times to the present day, to be explained? Is it a mere chance occurrence, a kind of colossal accident? Or is demonism only an invention perpetuated by superstition? Or is it a phenomenon built upon the facts of an original revelation of truth, preserved by human instinct, and nurtured by the facts of experience and observation?

---

[2]T. Witton Davies, *Magic, Divination, and Demonology among the Hebrews and Their Neighbors*, p. 95.
[3]Townsend, *op. cit.*, p. 43. Cf. Father Delaporte, *The Devil: Does He Exist? And What Does He Do?* pp. 13-16; and Walter Scott, *The Existence of Evil Spirits Proved*, pp. 18-19.

The idea of a "chance occurrence" may be summarily dismissed as unworthy of consideration. A causeless effect is bad logic, and worse theology. The notion of "an invention perpetuated by superstition" is more sinister and menacing, inasmuch as skeptics have frequently contended that belief in Satan and demons is nothing more than a superstition, born in the brain of some insane man, seized upon by other men, and so passed on to succeeding generations. But this contention is false even on philosophical grounds. However, assuming it were true, it leaves totally unexplained how a race of sane men has almost universally seized upon an "insane idea." But if the idea of Satan and demons were an invention, all difficulties are by no means obviated. The "invention" is such a significant phenomenon in the field of psychology and religion as to call forth serious scientific study, rather than skeptical sneers and contempt.

The only valid conclusion, therefore, which can be drawn is that belief in Satan and demons, like other religious convictions which have expressed themselves in multifarious ways in different ages, is not an invention at all, nor the fancy of insane men, but it can be traced to its ultimate source in a primitive divine revelation. The basic facts of this revelation have been perpetuated by a God-implanted and ineradicable human instinct and are supported by experience and observation.

Instinctive beliefs thus furnish an answer to the practically universal belief in demons and supply a proof of their existence. This being the case, and God being the Creator of the human mind with its instinctive propensities, it is clear, since God cannot lie in His Word or works, that the belief in demons rests upon as sound a scientific and philosophic basis as any teaching of Christianity, or as that of any general principle advanced in the philosophies of men.

4. Proof from Human Experience

The constitution of the human mind, as it manifests itself in instinctive beliefs common to mankind, does not exhaust the psychological argument in support of the existence of demons. Another important aspect remains in the testimony and facts of human experience. The career of the drunkard, the criminal, the libertine, the harlot, the dope fiend, the demented, the gambler, and the suicide, in many cases shows ample evidence of a deeper cause than mental or physical disease or injury. The course of license and sin which some men and women are pursuing, and the eagerness with which they rush into vice and licentiousness, knowing full well the awful consequences to body, mind, and soul, are the strongest possible evidence, outside the Bible, that there are wicked and unclean spiritual agencies that tempt, get control, and relentlessly drive their victims on over the brink of destruction.

In instances where the human will is overwhelmed and overborne by an irresistible power, as in the case of the alcoholic, the libertine, or the suicide, who can say that this is not due to demon agency? In any case in which the evil does not lie in the body but in the mind, to say that it is "only disease or insanity" is merely to state the fact of the disorder, and make no attempt to name its cause. Insanity, may, of course, arise from physical injury of derangement of those physical organs through which the mind expresses its powers, but far more often it seems clearly attributable to supernatural agencies, acting directly upon, and disordering the mind itself. Self-destruction seems far better explained, at least in the majority of cases, by demonic influence or possession, than by insanity, which is often urged as an excuse for the act. It bears all the marks of Satan, "the murderer and the liar" (John 8:44). Who but he or his minions could paint the sky with such terrible and deceptive luridness that self-murder appears to be the only step for his victim to take? When Luke writes that "Satan entered into Judas" (Luke 22:3), he most certainly implies that the dynamic of his crime and suicide was Satan or demonic agency. The burden of proof, therefore, rests upon the skeptics that invisible personalities have not a share in almost every crime that men commit.

B.   The Identity of Demons

Despite the fact of the reticence of Scripture concerning the origin of demons, its testimony touching the other phases of their identity is emphatically clear. Whether the demons are fallen angels, or the disembodied spirits of a "pre-Adamite race," or the monstrous progeny of angels and antediluvian women, is, after all, not the important or practical issue from the human side. If it were, we may be sure divine revelation would have made the issue crystal clear. The consideration of practical moment, however, as Scriptural reserve reveals, is not whence the demons came, but

that they actually *are*, that they are evil and harmful spirit personalities, that in their fellowship there is no safety, and that against
them continual warfare must be waged.

1. UNSCRIPTURAL IDENTIFICATION

Pure rationalistic explanations scarcely merit serious attention.
But since they have been widely promulgated, and extensively
accepted, thus beclouding and confusing the right understanding
of the subject, they should be given consideration.

Demons Simply Superstitious Designations for Certain Natural Diseases

Popular superstition attributes certain natural disorders of a
very malignant type to the agency of wicked spirits, but such evil
spirits have no veritable existence. They are mere personifications
of violent and incurable diseases. Thus Davies views cases of
demon possession in the time of our Lord and the demonism of
modern China, as nothing more than "certain diseases superstitiously
regarded as due to demoniacal influence."[4]

But the contention that these cases involved diseases only,
the cure of which is all that is meant by the idea of the expulsion
of demons, is almost too ridiculous to require disproof. What kind
of disease was it that cried out, "What have I to do with thee,
Jesus, thou Son of the most high God?" (Mark 5:7)? Since when
has a monstrous physical distemper appeared which begs permission
to enter into a great herd of swine and destroys them in a few
fleeting moments? The substitution of "spirits" (Luke 10:20) for
"demons" (v. 17) shows beyond all doubt that actual spiritual
entities are meant, and not mere diseases. Owen's observation on
this topic is to the point: "The notion that the demons of the New
Testament were only personifications of violent and incurable
diseases is too preposterous for a moment's belief."[5]

Demons the Spirits of Wicked Men Deceased

This notion, apparently devoid of Scriptural support, seems
to have developed from an ancient Greek rationalizing concept,

---

[4]Davies, *op. cit.*, p. 103.
[5]John J. Owen, "The Demonology of the New Testament," *Bibliotheca Sacra
and Biblical Repository*, Jan. 1859, XVI, 119-139.

which explained the origin of the gods as the result of the fear of ghosts. Homeric gods, being but supernatural men, were but demons or spirits of good and great men deceased. As the intervening centuries lowered the concept of demons until they were thought of as evil, the idea that they were limited to the spirits of wicked men took root. Josephus seems persuaded of this view when he speaks of demons as "the spirits of the wicked that enter into men that are alive."[6] This notion agrees well with his superstitious demonology, which is essentially that of contemporary Judaism, and not that of the Bible.

The origin of demons is seldom accounted for in popular belief, although they are often thought of as coming down as elemental spirits. Their numbers, on the other hand, are regarded as continually augmented as the souls of the departed become regarded as malignant.[7]

2. Identification with Alleged Scriptural Support

There are certain intimations in Scripture which would seem to suggest an origin of the demons different from the commonly accepted view that they took their rise from the ranks of the fallen angels. However, many regard these Scriptural allusions as too vague and indefinite to support a theory. Others make much of them, and advance and advocate their theories with great confidence and assurance.

Demons the Disembodied Spirits of Inhabitants of a Pre-Adamic Earth

A pre-Adamite race is thought of as existing on the original earth (Gen. 1:1), under the governorship of Satan in his unfallen state, as "the anointed cherub that covereth" (Ezek. 28:14). This pristine sphere is, moreover, viewed as the scene of Satan's revolt (Isa. 14:12-14), and the invasion of sin into the moral universe, resulting in an awful cataclysm which reduced it to chaos (Gen. 1:2). The members of the pre-Adamite race, whom Pember describes as being "men in the flesh,"[8] were somehow involved in the

---

[6]Josephus, *Wars of the Jews*, 7:6:3.

[7]George W. Gilmore, "Demon, Demonism," *New Schaff-Herzog Encyclopedia of Religious Knowledge*, pp. 399-400.

[8]G. H. Pember, *Earth's Earliest Ages*, pp. 72-73.

rebellion, and, in the ensuing catastrophe, suffered the loss of their material bodies,[9] becoming "disembodied spirits," or demons.[10] The oft-recorded fact that demons are continually seizing upon the bodies of men to try to use them as their own is taken as confirmatory evidence that demons are disembodied spirits, and that their intense desire for re-embodiment indicates that the intolerable condition of being unclothed, for which they were not created, is so overpowering that they will even enter the bodies of swine (Luke 8:32).[11]

The theory rigidly distinguishes demons, as disembodied spirits, from angels, bad as well as good. Angels, it is maintained, are not mere disembodied spirits, but are clothed with spiritual bodies, since the children of the first resurrection receive spiritual bodies (II Cor. 5:2-3), and are said to be "like or equal to angels" (Luke 20:36; cf. Luke 24:39; Phil. 3:21). The Jews are said to have clearly comprehended this distinction, for the Sadducees confessed neither "angel nor spirit," and the Pharisees, "who confess both," said concerning Paul: "What if a spirit hath spoken to him or an angel?" (Acts 23:8-9).

Further evidence of the differentiation between angels and disembodied spirits (demons), namely, the lack of propensity on the part of Satan and his angels to re-embody themselves in human beings, is cited. It is freely granted, however, that they may do this for the perpetration of mischief, not, though, from an inherent inclination, but only because such a procedure is imperative for the prosecution of some great and special conspiracy of evil (Luke 22:3). The two classes of Satan's subjects, angels and demons, which are thus regarded as differentiated in the New Testament, are similarly traced in the Old Testament. Such angels as Gabriel, and the prince of Persia, and of Grecia are placed in the first order, while the "familiar spirits," the *shedhim, seirim,* and Lilith, are considered as identical with the demons.

The classical meaning of the term "demon," especially as it is used by Hesiod,[12] is taken as its essential New Testament connotation, despite the fact that Hesiod's demons, as the spirits of

---

[9]Cf. Clarence Larkin, *The Spirit World*, p. 39.
[10]Clarence Larkin, *Dispensational Truth*, p. 101.
[11]Pember, *op. cit.*, p. 72.
[12]Hesiod, *Works and Days*, pp. 109-126.

deceased men of the mythical "golden age," are tutelary deities or canonized heroes, and are uniformly good, while the demons of the New Testament are invariably bad. The obvious discrepancy is laid at the door of Satan's deceptions, at whom, we are told we ought not to wonder, if, in a "heathen poem," he commends "his own agents."[13] However, in other aspects of Hesiod's account of the origin of demons, the advocates of this theory see a remarkable corroboration of their contentions, in that it represents a perversion of a primitive pure tradition concerning the sinless pre-Adamite earth and the fall that engulfed it.

The golden-race of men, created by the gods when Cronos ruled in heaven, corresponds to God's creation of the pre-Adamite race of men, when Satan ruled as an unfallen creature. The peace, prosperity, and unmingled joy of the golden race is reminiscent of the joyous state of the unfallen pre-Adamite people. The decree of the mighty Zeus transforming the men of the golden age into demons, together with the simultaneous change in the heavenly dynasty, with the expulsion of Cronos, bringing to an end this age of undisturbed joy, is reminiscent of Satan's revolt, the judgment upon the pre-Adamite earth, and the demonization of its inhabitants.

Larkin[14] sees in the conduct of the demonized, when the evil spirit takes possession of his victim for the purpose of physical sensual gratification, a hint that the sin of sensuality was the "cause of the wreck of the pre-Adamite earth."[15]

Such, in brief, is the theory that identifies the demons with the disembodied spirits of a pre-Adamite earth. The question is, How shall it be evaluated? What credence shall be accorded it? Although it is very ingenious, it of necessity rests upon such a great weight of assumption because of the silence of revelation that care must be taken, at least with our present sources of knowledge, not to accord it a higher status than a mere theory, which, although in some respects is suggestive, is subject to fatal weaknesses.

Unfortunately, the whole notion of a pre-Adamite "human" race, or "men in the flesh," which figures as such a vital premise

---

[13]Pember, *op. cit.*, p. 72.
[14]Clarence Larkin, *Rightly Dividing The Word of Truth*, p. 94.
[15]Larkin, *The Spirit World*, p. 40.

in the argument, is pure conjecture, without the least Scriptural support. The Bible says nothing of any human race before Adam (Gen. 1:26, 27). The only created intelligences revealed to have existed before the creation of man are angels. It would seem, that unless we resort to the argument from silence, which is precarious, the demons, if a pre-Adamite origin is posited for them, must be thought of as derived from the fallen angels. It is on this point, however, that the whole theory breaks down. If no other beings than angels can be proved to have existed before Edenic man, and since angels, as purely spirit-beings, are incapable of disembodiment, then the whole theory that demons are disembodied spirits in clear-cut distinction from angels is invalidated as a support for the hypothesis.

Indeed, it is highly questionable whether such a rigid distinction as this theory calls for, between angel and spirit, can be maintained, even if its basic premise were tenable, in the face of the Scriptural identification of angels as spirits (Ps. 104:4; Heb. 1:14), and the use of the term "angel" for the spirit of man (Matt. 18:10; Acts 12:15). It may be added, that the whole contention for demons as disembodied spirits is rendered unnecessary, inasmuch as the hypothesis itself readily grants that Satan and evil angels not only may, but actually do enter into human beings. If demons cannot be proved to be disembodied spirits, the argument of propensity to enter human bodies loses all force.

Finally, it must be said that drawing parallels from Greek mythology on a point where Biblical revelation is silent, or extremely reticent, is exceedingly perilous. An even more audacious piece of exegesis is the incorporation of a classical Greek meaning of "demons" as the "good spirits of departed men of the golden age," into the New Testament, where demons are without exception wicked and unclean spirits. The word "demon," like other distinctive Biblical Greek words, was divinely moulded through the pre-Christian centuries for its unique New Testament meaning, and not incorporated indiscriminately with its original and strictly pagan concepts.

Demons the Monstrous Offspring of Angels and Antediluvian Women

This very ancient theory, which goes back at least to the

second century before Christ, if not earlier, maintains that "the sons of God" (bene-ha'elohim) of Genesis 6:2 are angels, who, cohabiting with mortal women, produced a monstrous progeny, the demons, born at once of spirits and of flesh. The *locus classicus* in the apocryphal *Book of Enoch* runs thus:

Wicked spirits came out of the body of them (i.e., of the women), for they were generated out of human beings, and from the holy watchers (angels) flows the beginning of their creation and their primal foundation. The spirits of heaven—in the heaven is their dwelling, and the spirits begotten upon earth—in the earth shall be their dwelling. And the spirits of the giants will devour, oppress, destroy, assault, do battle, and cast upon the earth and cause convulsions.[16]

Unfortunately, the basic premise of this hypothesis, namely, that the "sons of God" of Genesis 6:2 are angels, has its difficulties, and has been vigorously denied by a great array of piety and scholarship from the time of the Church Fathers. The opposing view that the "sons of God" are simply godly Sethites, and the "daughters of men" ungodly Cainites who inter-married, has been espoused by Chrysostom, Cyril of Alexandria, Theodoret, almost all the later theologians, and in modern times by Hengstenberg, Keil, Lange, Jamieson, Fausset, Brown, Matthew Henry, C. I. Scofield, and many others.[17]

But the "angel theory" is also supported by an equal, if not a more imposing list of expositors, demonstrating that difficulties of no little moment are encountered by both theories, and both have, at least some Scriptural grounds for support to enlist so many able advocates. The "angel hypothesis" seems to have its origin in the Septuagint. At least the manuscripts vary between "the sons of God" (*huioi tou Theou*) and "the angels of God" (*aggeloi tou Theou*) in the Codex Alexandrinus. Very decidedly it is presented in the Book of Enoch, as noted, and in the so-called "Minor Genesis," also by Philo, Josephus, and most of the rabbinical writers, as well as by the oldest Church Fathers—Justin, Tertullian, Cyprian, Ambrose, and Lactantius. Though Chrysostom, Augustine, and Theodoret contended zealously against it, and in the dark ages it fell into disfavor, it was espoused by Luther, and by a

---

[16]*Book of Enoch*, Chapter XV; cf. *Jewish Quarterly Review*, 1896-97, IX, 75.
[17]Johann Peter Lange, "Genesis," *Commentary on the Holy Scriptures, pp.* 280-84.

galaxy of modern exegetes—Koppen, Twesten, Dreschler, Hofmann, Baumgarten, Delitzsch, W. Kelly, A. C. Gaebelein, and others.[18] By no means do all the writers who defend the "angel theory" connect it with the origin of demons. For example, Pember,[19] and Larkin,[20] and others simply connect the alleged angelic cohabitation with mortal women with "the fallen angels," who are imprisoned in Tartarus (II Pet. 2:4-5; Jude vv. 6-7) because of their abnormal crime in seducing mortal women, while Satan's angels, who were not guilty of this special abnormality, remain with him in the heavenlies, and are not incarcerated. Demons are otherwise accounted for than as the offspring of this unnatural union.

The task of fully presenting and evaluating the arguments in support of these various views is immense, and beyond the scope of this present treatise. All that can be undertaken here is to indicate a few of the difficulties involved in the respective views, with a suggestion as to the possible tenability of each.

The general interpretation that refers "the sons of God" to pious Sethites, and the "daughters of men" to ungodly Cainites, while naive and perfectly orthodox, in that it enunciates a simple spiritual principle and assuredly avoids certain obvious difficulties to which a more virile exposition exposes itself, yet is found to be manifestly weak and unconvincing in satisfying the evident breadth and scope of the passage.

To begin, there is no proof that the "daughters of men" were confined to the descendants of the Cainites. On the contrary, the text evidently indicates that the expression means the natural increase of the whole human family, and not a special class. Moreover, the assumption that the "sons of God" must mean the godly line of Seth seems at variance with the uniform use of that term in the Old Testament where it appears restricted to angels (Job 1:6; 2:1; 38:7). Gaebelein says, "The designation is *never* applied in the Old Testament to believers," whose sonship, he rightly observes, is "distinctly a New Testament revelation."[21]

---

[18]*Ibid.*, pp. 280-281.

[19]Pember, *op. cit.*, p. 205-213.

[20]Larkin, *The Spirit World*, pp. 23-26.

[21]A. C. Gaebelein, *The Annotated Bible* (Pentateuch), p. 29. Says W. F. Albright, "Yahweh was believed to have created astral as well as terrestrial beings, and the former were popularly called 'the host of heaven' or 'the

Isaiah 43:6 is often cited as disproving the contention that the "sons of God" in the Old Testament describes only angels, whether good or bad. But it hardly seems convincing, inasmuch as the expression there implies "sons of Jehovah," an entirely different term, and refers to the future regathering of the godly remnant of Israel. It does seem that the term "sons of Elohim," the mighty Creator, characterizes those who were created directly by the divine hand, and not born of other beings of their own order. Hence Adam's designation as a "son of God" (Luke 3:38); also the designation of those who are born again of the Spirit of God (John 1:12).

Again, if the "sons of God" are simply pious Sethites who mixed with the Cainites, the prominent question is left unexplained as to why their progeny should have been "giants," mighty heroes who were of old, "men of renown." The Revisers' obvious dissatisfaction with the Authorized Version's rendering of *nephilim* by "giants," and the mere transliteration of the term by "nephilim," obviously leaves the difficulty unanswered. The Septuagint translators' rendering of the expression by "giants" (*gigantes*) seems clearly an indication that they thought of the *nephilim* in this passage and its only other occurrence in Numbers 13:33 as the offspring of the sons of God (angels) and the daughters of men (mortal women); for the basic idea of the Greek term is not monstrous size, which is a secondary and developed meaning, but *gegenes*, "earth-born," and employed of the Titans who were partly of celestial and partly of terrestial origin. These monstrous beings of mixed birth rebelled against their father Uranus (Heaven), and after a prolonged contest were defeated by Zeus and thrown into Tartarus.

There is no doubt that the Authorized Version misunderstood the Septuagint in translating *nephilim* by "giants," for the form of the Hebrew word denotes a plural verbal adjective or noun of passive signification, certainly from *naphal*, "to fall," so that the connotation is *nephilim*, "the fallen ones," clearly meaning the

---

sons of God.' In Gen. 6:1 ff., for example, . . . the (astral) gods had intercourse with mortal women, who gave birth to heroes (literally, 'meteors,' *nephilim*), an idea that may often be illustrated from Babylonian and Greek mythology. But the Israelite who heard this section recited unquestionably thought of intercourse between angels and women (like later Jews and Christians)." *From the Stone Age to Christianity*, p. 226.

unnatural offspring which were in the earth in the years before the flood, "and also after that" (Num. 13:33) "when the sons of God came in unto the daughters of men" (Gen. 6:4). There is no doubt, either, that the mention of the great stature of the *nephilim*, the sons of Anak, in the evil report which the ten spies brought of the land of Canaan (Num. 13:33), together with the Septuagint rendering, *gigantes*, suggested the translation "giants." The real and original idea in the mind of the ancient translators, however, may well have been "fallen ones," or monsters of mixed human and angelic birth, who, like the rebellious Titans, were exceedingly wicked and violent, so that "every imagination of the thoughts of his heart was only evil continually" (Gen. 6:5).

Delitzsch, who espouses the "angel theory," speaks of this passage as "the fountain of heathen mythology with its legends."[22] Whether one agrees with him, or with Lange, who regards the whole "angel hypothesis" as itself "an evident myth, implanted in the garden of primitive religious history,"[23] one thing is certain, ancient classic writers obtained their conceptions of the gods and demigods, whose amorous propensities for members of the human race led to births half human and half divine, from some source originally pure and uncorrupted. It is not impossible that this might explain the origin.

Again, if the intercourse between the "sons of God" and the "daughters of men" were merely marriage between the Sethites and the Cainites, it seems impossible to explain adequately certain New Testament passages, and the reason why some fallen angels are imprisoned and others are free to roam the heavenlies. Peter vividly describes the crime of certain of these spiritual beings, which seems to refer to a second and deeper apostasy than their complicity in Satan's primeval insurrection. The sin of these more daring rebels deprived them of freedom and positions under Satan as principalities, powers, rulers of this darkness, and wicked spirits in the heavenlies (Eph. 6:12), and resulted in God's casting them down to Tartarus, delivering them "into pits of darkness to be reserved unto the judgment." And what is noteworthy, the whole divine punishment stands in the closest and most significant con-

---

[22]Franz Delitzsch in Lange's *Commentary on the Holy Scriptures* (Genesis), p. 284.
[23]*Ibid.*

nection with the times of Noah, and the cataclysm of the flood
(II Pet. 2:4-5). Jude even more pregnantly portrays the enormous
wickedness of these fallen angels when he says they "kept not their
own principality, but left their proper habitation," and as a divine
punishment are "kept in everlasting bonds under darkness." And
what is also arresting, their heinous crime would seem to be akin
to the unnatural vice of Sodom and Gomorrah (cf. Gen. 19:5)—
fornication of an abnormal character, going after "strange flesh,"
which might possibly point to cohabitation with beings of a different nature (Jude vv. 6-7).

Since they chose to leave their own realm and to break the
bounds and God-ordained laws of two worlds, to work havoc and
vicious confusion, God wiped out the results of their disorder with
a flood, and dashed them down to the lowest dungeons (Tartarus)
to deprive them forever of the opportunity of causing further derangement. The region of their imprisonment appears to be a
more doleful and terrible place of confinement than Hades, and
is clearly distinguished from Gehenna (Rev. 19:20; 20:10). In
Greek mythology Tartarus was a dismal abode, as far beneath
Hades as earth is below heaven,[24] and significantly considered the
prison-house of the Titans.

While bearing in mind some of the difficulties which beset
the view that the sons of God are pious Sethites, it must not be
supposed that the "angel theory" is not vexed by serious questions.
Whether or not they are grave enough to be fatal to its tenability
ought to be decided very discriminatingly. It must ever be remembered in dealing with Genesis 6:1-4, that, as James Orr says, "It
is not easy to be certain as to the interpretation of this strange
passage."[25]

The most formidable objection to the angelic interpretation
is, perhaps, that angels, as spiritual beings, could not take wives
of the daughters of men. Much of the argument hinges on this
avowed problem. To deny such a possibility, though, at least
among the fallen and impure angels, with a sinful and not a sinless
constitution, and especially among those who left their proper
ethereal habitation, is to assume, it would seem, a degree of
knowledge of fallen angelic nature which man does not possess.

---

[24]Homer, *Iliad,* VIII:16.
[25]James Orr, "Nephilim," *International Standard Bible Encyclopedia,* p. 2133.

Certainly, as Jesus said, the angels of God in heaven neither marry nor are given in marriage (Matt. 22:30; Mark 12:25; Luke 20:35-36); for they are deathless, and have no need to perpetuate their species, nor any possibility of the marriage relationship among their *own kind*, as all angels are spoken of as in the masculine gender. But these spirits mentioned by our Saviour are clearly pure, unfallen creatures in their primeval innocence, to which the redeemed in glory are likened, and not impure and fallen agents of Satan. They doubtless alone serve in the "third heaven" (II Cor. 12:2), or the heaven of heavens where Christ sits at God's right hand "*far above* all rule, and authority, and power, and dominion" (Eph. 1:20-21). That wicked fallen angels, however, could leave their own proper spiritual realms, and invade another, so as to work such abominable confusion that cataclysmic extirpation was necessary to preserve an orderly universe, seems not only possible, but probable, especially in an ancient age of freedom when men were unrestrained by law or government, and in the light of the New Testament hints on the subject.

Another criticism of the angel hypothesis is that it denies the basic conceptions of revelation, and "authenticates a fact" which "destroys all distinction between revelation and mythology," between "divine miracle and magic," between the "Biblical conception of nature as conformity to law, and the wild apocryphal stories."[26]

This stricture is not particularly weighty, inasmuch as the divine account in the Old Testament and the inspired comments in the New Testament unanimously represent the whole episode as being a unique and shocking abnormality, breaking down every God-ordained law for both the physical and the spiritual realms, and producing outrageous confusion in both; so that unmitigated incarceration in the lowest pits of Tartarus is the penalty for the angelic offenders on one hand, and a world-engulfing deluge the punishment for human folly on the other.

If the angel hypothesis could be sustained despite the *reticence* of revelation on the matter, the first premise of the theory that demons sprang from angelic cohabitation with antediluvian women, would of course be established. To establish the second, however, that demons were the results of these unholy alliances, is wholly impossible in the face of the *silence* of revelation. It is pure specu-

---

[26]Lange, *op. cit.*, p. 284.

lation to reason as does the writer of the *Book of Enoch* that
the progeny were born wicked earth-dwelling spirits, or to imagine
that the monstrous offspring became disembodied spirits (demons)
when their corporeal bodies were destroyed in the flood, and
instead of being consigned to Sheol as were other wicked ante-
diluvians, as monstrosities, were left to plague subsequent generations of mankind as demons.

3. The Scriptural Identification: Fallen Angels

Examination of theories which would trace the origin of
demons either to the disembodied spirits of a pre-Adamite race,
or to the offspring of angelic cohabitation with antediluvian women,
has demonstrated their essential defectiveness and invalidity. One
possible hypothesis remains, which, with all the Scriptural evidence
at hand, seems to be the best supported and the most clearly
authenticated explanation.

In Satan's primal rebellion it seems that he drew with him a
great multitude of lesser celestial beings (cf. Matt. 25:41; Rev.
12:4). These fallen angels are divided into two classes: (1) those
that are free, and (2) those that are bound.[27] Those that are
free are abroad in the heavenlies under their prince-leader Satan,
who alone of the fallen spirits "is given particular mention in
Scriptures."[28] He is called "Beelzebub, prince of the demons"
(Matt. 12:24), "Satan and his angels" (Matt. 25:41), and "the
dragon . . . and his angels" (Rev. 12:7). These unconfined
wicked spirits under Satan's kingdom and dominion, who are his
emissaries and subjects (Matt. 12:26) and who are so numerous
as to make his power practically ubiquitous, seem to be identical
with the demons.[29] If Satan's angels and the demons are *not* identical, then no *other* origin of demons is anywhere explicitly revealed
in Scripture.

Satan's methods of activity and his highly organized empire
of roving spirits in the heavenlies are set forth in Ephesians 6:11-12.

---

[27]Cf. Lewis Sperry Chafer, *Major Bible Themes*, p. 116.
[28]*Ibid.*
[29]"The demons are very real beings, but mere creatures. Originally they were
made part of the glorious army of the heavens, that is to say, of the angelic
host, who, in the morning of creation praised God in gladness, and of
whom the army of the stars is the magnificent symbol."—Father Delaporte,
The Devil: Does He Exist? And What Does He Do? p. 18.

His methods are suggested by the expression "wiles of the devil," while his organization is gradated as "principalities," "powers," "world rulers of this darkness," and "spiritual hosts of wickedness in the heavenly places." The serried spirits can be none other than his angels or demons with different stations of rank and responsibility, who are the unseen though real agents behind the visible human actors in the great world drama enacted in his wicked world system.

It is thus in the heavenlies that Satan has his abode and base of operation—not, however, in the third heaven, or heaven of heavens (II Cor. 12:2), where the ascended Christ is seated "far above all rule, and authority, and power, and dominion" (Eph. 1:21). From it Satan and his demons are barred. From that all-glorious sanctum he was cast out, evidently not at the time of his primeval fall, but consequent upon Christ's finished redemptive work and glorious ascension (cf. Job 1:6). With his wicked satellites he is confined to the first and second heavens, and as "prince of the power of the air" (Eph. 2:2), he and his demons will be presently cast down to the earth (Rev. 12:7-12) for their tragic role in the closing days of this age (Rev. 19:20; 20:2-3).

But the fallen angels that are bound must not be confused with the fallen angels that are free. The latter, as noted, are in all likelihood to be connected with demons. The fallen angels that are bound, on the other hand, are those described by Peter and Jude, as ostensibly guilty of such enormous wickedness as no longer allowed them to roam the heavenlies with their leader Satan and the other evil angels, but plunged them down to the strictest and severest confinement in Tartarus, "to pits of darkness, to be reserved unto judgment" (II Pet. 2:4). Jude more fully describes them in the outrage, which brought upon them such a special dispensation of the divine wrath, as not keeping "their own principality," but abandoning "their proper habitation" (Jude v. 6).

That this angelic incarceration cannot be connected with the original rebellion of Satan and the fall of angels is obvious. Satan was not only the sole originator, but the prime offender, in that insurrection. Shall he be still free to roam the heavenlies, while those he deceived be fast shut up in "pits of darkness . . . reserved unto judgment"? Shall the betrayer go unpunished, while the betrayed languish in the most rigorous and stringent imprisonment?

Or shall some of his accomplices go free, and some be castigated inexorably? It seems apparent that both reason and justice are at variance with such an interpretation. But laying aside the moral consideration, and assuming Peter and Jude refer to Satan's primeval apostasy and the fall of angels, another difficulty is encountered. If all the angels who sinned with Satan are those who left their "first estate," and are bound in Tartarus, how shall Satan's angels who are free be accounted for? Their origin can be but an unanswerable enigma.

F. W. Grant stresses the fact that these angels who are bound must be kept distinct from the more "general class of Satan and his angels," who are as yet unconfined.[30] Dr. A. C. Gaebelein expresses the conviction of many scholars[31] when he identifies these angels thus:

They are the beings described in Genesis 6:1-4 as the "sons of God" (a term which in the Old Testament means angels) who came down and mingled with the daughters of men . . . and by their disobedience became the means of corrupting the race in such a manner that the judgment of God had to act in the deluge.[32]

In substantial agreement with this view are J. B. Mayor[33] and Alfred Plummer, the latter thus commenting on Jude 6:

This second instance of the impure angels has nothing to do with the original rebellion of Satan, or fall of angels. The reference is either to Genesis 6:2, or (more probably) to passages in the *Book of Enoch.*[34]

The evil angels that are free and who did not leave "their proper habitation," designated "Satan and his angels" (Matt. 25:41), or "the dragon and his angels" (Rev. 12:7), are the "powers of the air" (Eph. 2:2), the "demons" (Matt. 12:24), over whom Satan is called "prince," and are to be carefully distinguished from the evil angels who did leave "their proper habitation," and who are not spoken of as "his angels" over whom he is "prince," or as the "powers of the air," for they are locked up in deep imprisonment, awaiting judgment, forever beyond Satan's sway and lead-

---

[30]F. W. Grant, *The Numerical Bible,* II Pet. 2:4.

[31]A. C. Gaebelein, *The Annotated Bible,* IV, 82-83.

[32]*Ibid.,* pp. 110-11.

[33]J. B. Mayor, "The General Epistle of Jude," *The Expositor's Greek New Testament.*

[34]A. Plummer, *New Testament Commentary,* III, ed. by C. J. Ellicott, 510.

ership. These are *properly* "the fallen angels," who are bound, in distinction to "the demons," Satan's marshalled hosts, who are free. But the fact must not be overlooked that all demons are not free. In addition to the vast hosts who are at liberty, and serve in Satan's ethereal hegemony, other innumerable multitudes are bound, not indeed in Tartarus with the fallen angels, but in the abyss (Luke 8:31; Rev. 9:1, 2, 10), apparently a temporary prison-house of evil spirits. From this dismal dungeon they shall be let loose to afflict, deceive, and energize wicked earth-dwellers in the last awful scenes of godless rebellion with which this age shall end.

As to the cause or occasion of the imprisonment of these demons, practically nothing is revealed. Were they originally numbered among Satan's free hosts who rove the heavenlies? Was their forfeiture of freedom the divine penalty for their entering into and possessing human beings, to satisfy illicit desires or to perpetuate special heinous wickedness? Did the death of their victims by suicide, or from other destructive effects of their inhabitation, leave them helplessly exposed to the abyss? Or did demon-expulsions automatically result in their consignment to the prison-house of depraved spirits? To all these questions no answer can be given, because no information is revealed.

There is a ray of light shed on the matter, however, in the case of the demons about to be cast out of the Gadarene demoniac, who pleaded with Jesus "that he would not command them to depart into the abyss" (Luke 8:31). It seems reasonable to deduce from this plea, that it was at least habitual for Jesus in His expulsions to reduce the population of the free demons by dismissing them to the abyss. Whether the Apostles and other believers who cast out demons effected the same decrease in the numbers of demons who are at large, and whether any connection is to be traced to the question of the continuance and frequency of demon-possession, of course, cannot be ascertained.

C. Meaning of the Term "Demon"

The derivation of the term "demon" (*daimonion*), in the earlier language *daimon*, is not too certain. Plato indeed derives it from *daemon*, an adjective formed from *dao* and signifying "knowing" or "intelligent."[35] Many modern scholars, per contra, derive it from *daio* (to divide or assign), as though it meant "divider or distributor of destiny." Plato's definition seems preferable; since it points to the superior knowledge of these spirits, who have been credited with superhuman knowledge, and oracles have, accordingly, been sought from them. A survey of the historical development of the term will reveal the divine hand, moulding and preparing the word for its precise Biblical usage.

1. EVOLUTION OF MEANING OF THE TERM "DEMON" IN GREEK

Four principal meanings of the term *daimon* (demon) from the Homeric period to the time of the Septuagint may be traced in the course of the development of the term for its precise use in the Septuagint and in the New Testament. First, in the early history of the language, as in Homer, *daimon* was synonymous with "god" (*theos*). Ludwig Preller notes that the terms gods and *daimones* (demons) are employed for the same beings by Homer and the earlier poets, and contends that the former term expresses more definitely a god's personality, as this is defined by cults and mythology, while the latter expression has reference to his power and activity in manifestation in life and nature.[36] Ramsay also is of the opinion that the *daimon* is the bearer of the divine power operative in nature and human life and that it has not been conceived and defined by mythology and the cultus as a god (*theos*). He also points out that hardly anywhere, except in the *Iliad* (III:420), is a special god called a *daimon,* and that there is a distinct tendency in Homer to attribute a bad influence to the *daimon,* especially in the *Odyssey.*[37]

A second stage in the development of the term *daimon* appears in post-Homeric usage when demons were conceived of as intermediaries between the gods and men. In Hesiod these mediators are the spirits of the good men of the Golden Age, who are appointed attendants and guardians of men by Zeus, and are frequently conceived of as executors of his will.[38] The philosophers

---

[35]*Cratylus* I:398. For the general development and meaning of the term *daimonion* see Liddell and Scott, *Greek-English Lexicon,* rev. ed., I, 365.
[36]Ludwig Preller, *Griechische Mythologie,* I, 112.
[37]W. M. Ramsay, *Hastings' Dictionary of the Bible,* I, 140a, and note.
[38]Ramsay, *op. cit.,* 140a.

give striking expression to belief in these intermediary agents. Plato asserts that "The deity has no intercourse with man; but all the intercourse and conversation between gods and men are carried on by the mediation of demons."[39]

The view also finds expression that every man from his birth is accompanied by a special *daimon*. This *daimon* of the individual is evidently regarded as separable from the man himself, and not identifiable with his soul or spirit, as the *daimonion* of Socrates,[40] who asked questions of it. Attic writers, especially, make reference to *agathos daimon* (a good demon). At this stage, "although the demons are regarded as being inferior to the gods, they do not appear to be conceived of as morally evil, unless, indeed, this may be inferred of some of them by contrast with the good demons . . ."[41]

A third stage of development in the term *daimon* came when the Greeks began to view demons as morally imperfect beings, like man, some good, some evil. This step in the gradual lowering of the concept of the word was the result of an effort to exalt the gods and to make their intermediary "demons" responsible for the passions and scandals attributed to them in the popular mythologies. While Plato endeavored to divest the gods of evils and scandals and to heighten the people's idea of them, his disciple Xenocrates[42] sought to maintain his master's teaching on the subject of the sublime character of the gods by a development of his teacher's notions about demons, making these intermediary agents, whom he conceived as the departed souls of men, the real perpetrators of evil. "He introduced a new idea into philosophic theology in that he was the first to distinguish expressly between good and evil demons, and he emphasized their mediating position. They are

---

[39]Plato, *Symposium*, 202-3.

[40]Concerning the much-disputed saying of Socrates, "I have a divine and supernatural sign that comes to me," Edward Langton well remarks: " . . . it appears to be impossible . . . to affirm that Socrates conceived of his *daimon* as a personal spirit being. The evidence is in favor of the view that the reference was to 'a sudden strongly felt inhibition which Socrates interpreted as given him from without'" (Langton, *op. cit.*, p. 94. Cf. also E. R. Bevan, *Sibyls and Seers*, p. 105; and A. E. Taylor, *Socrates*, p. 43). Nevius interprets Socrates to refer to "conscience, or the voice of God, which was to him so distinct and authoritative that he was almost disposed to attribute to it personality" (*Demon Possession and Allied Themes*, 5th ed.), p. 329.

[41]Edward Langton, *Essentials of Demonology*, p. 87.

[42]R. Heinze, *Xenocrates*, pp. 83-93.

now held to mediate the whole intercourse between gods and men, particularly by means of oracles. They have superhuman power, but even the good demons have not perfect moral purity."[43]

Xenocrates' distinction between good and evil demons was continued by later writers, especially by the Stoics and by Plutarch,[44] who attributes to them degrees of virtue as in men. Posidonius, a Stoic philosopher of the first century before Christ, developed an elaborate theory of demons viewed as spirits of the departed and hence good and evil, the purer inhabitating the higher regions, the impure remaining nearer the earth.[45]

The final stage in this process of development is reached where, as in the Septuagint and the New Testament, all demons are evil, and are members of Satan's kingdom as his active agents (Matt. 12:22-30, *et al.*). Early Christian writings also abound with evidence that all demons are evil. Justin Martyr, for example, obviously following clear Old (Deut. 32:17; Ps. 106:37) and New Testament teaching (I Cor. 10:19-20; I Tim. 4:1; *et al.*) asserts that demons inspired Greek mythology, raised up evil men like Simon Magus, heretics like Marcion, and energized Christian persecutions.[46] Similar emphatic teachings concerning the evil character and ubiquitous activity of the demons appear in practically all the Christian writers of this period—Tertullian, Clement of Alexandria, Origen, Cyprian, and Eusebius, to mention but a few.

2. Meaning of the Term "Demon" in the Septuagint

The expressions *daimon* and *daimonion* are not found very frequently in the Greek rendering of the Old Testament, yet they are employed to translate certain Hebrew words. This fact is not surprising, for the demonology of the Old Testament, as already noted,[47] is of such a chaste and lofty character and in such diametrical contrast to extravagant contemporary demonological thought, that demonic conceptions are relatively scarce. This circumstance does not for one moment militate against the fact of Hebrew popular belief in demons, which is attested by the many

---

[43]Langton, *op. cit.*, p. 88.
[44]*De Defectione Oraculorum* XIII.
[45]Cf. Ehrhard & Kirsch, *Forschungen*, XII, 3, 125-6; also *Encyclopedia Americana* (1951), Vol. 22, p. 421.
[46]*First Apology* 54:53; 56:55; 57:56, *et al.*
[47]See Chapter III of this volume.

Scriptural warnings against sorcery and magic. That the people so constantly needed the admonition of revealed truth speaks more strongly for the abiding belief in demons than the few specific references which are found. The paucity and simplicity of Old Testament demonic conceptions were doubtless intended to be at once a vivid contrast to elaborate and multitudinous ethnic perversions, and at the same time a strong check and rebuke against prevailing superstition and excess.

It is to be noted carefully that Hebrew possesses no precise equivalent for the Hellenistic Greek terms *daimon* or *daimonion*. Indeed, no fewer than five different Hebrew words are translated by it. Of these only the first to be discussed is rendered "demon" by the Revisers.

Shedhim

The word "demon" (*daimon, daimonion*) was introduced in the Biblical sphere through the Septuagint as a translation of *shedhim* and several other words of kindred connotation. *Shedh* (always in the plural, *shedhim*) occurs in Deuteronomy 32:17 and Psalm 106:37, where it is rendered "devils" in the Authorized Version, and correctly "demons" in the Revised Version. The etymology is not too well established, but it is fairly certain that it comes from the root *shudh* "to rule, to be lord," like the Arabic *sala*. The underlying significance is no doubt "idols," properly "lords," since the Hebrews very early regarded idolatrous images as mere visible symbols of invisible demons, who let themselves be worshipped by men (Ps. 96:5; LXX 95:5; Bar. 4:7; I Cor. 10:20). Therefore, in the Song of Moses, the Israelites who lapsed into idolatry are said to have "sacrificed unto demons (*shedhim*), which were not God (or gods), to gods that they knew not" (Deut. 32:17).

It is clear that the *shedhim* are not only identified with idolatrous images, who are denied all reality as gods, but at the same time are separated from them, as being real spiritual existences behind them, energizing their worship. The same double aspect is to be noted in the passage in the Psalms, where, falling again into idolatry, the Israelites are said to have "sacrificed their sons and their daughters unto demons (*daimonia, Shedhim*) . . . unto the idols of Canaan" (Ps. 106:37-38). The "idols of Canaan" are the inanimate idolatrous representations, the visible means of deception.

The "demons" (*shedhim*) are the real spiritual entities inspiring the perverted worship. The name is similar to the Assyrian "shedu," which denotes tutelary deities or genii, evidently looked upon as inferior to the gods, properly so-called, and subordinated to them.

Seirim

The Levitical Law (Lev. 17:1-7) commanded the Hebrews in the wilderness to slay their sacrificial animals at the entrance of the tabernacle, so that they might not go into the desert to "sacrifice their sacrifices unto the he-goats," *seirim*, LXX, *daimonia*, (Lev. 17:7). Unquestionably, these beings are here viewed as objects of worship. Their cult is viewed as an apostasy from Jehovah, and their votaries threatened with extermination (vv. 4, 7). This peculiar variety of demon-worship persisted for centuries among the Israelites, cropping out again under Jeroboam I (929-909), who, rejecting the Levites, "appointed him priests for the high places, and for the he-goats, *seirim*, LXX, *daimonia*, and for the calves which he had made" (II Chron. 11:15). Josiah (638-608), in his sweeping purge of idolatrous contamination, "brake down the high places of the gates," (*shearim*), which is assuredly to be read (so Kittel)[48] *seirim*, "the high places of the he-goats (satyrs)" (II Kings 23:8).

Etymologically the word means "hairy one" or "he-goat," which is evidence that the Israelites considered these demonic conceptions to be goat-like in aspect or attributes. Isaiah, in poetic passages, portrays these demon-satyrs as dancing in the ruins of Babylon, and calling to one another in the desolated city (Isa. 13:21; 34:14). The translation of *seirim* in both of these passages by *daimonia* is conclusive that the Alexandrian Jews considered them to be demons.

Idols

"For all the gods of the peoples are idols (*'elilim*, LXX *daimonia*), but Jehovah made the heavens" (Ps. 96:5; LXX 95:5). This is the classic passage identifying demons with idols, and suggesting demonism as the dynamic of idolatry. Hebrew *'elilim*, the plural of the adjective meaning "of nought, empty, vain," shows plainly

---

[48]Rudolf Kittel, *Biblia Hebraica*, Pars I, p. 546.

the idols are "mere nothings," non-realities. The demons behind them are the real existences.

Gad

"But ye that forsake Jehovah, that forget my holy mountain, that prepare a table for Fortune" (*Gad*), LXX (*to daimonion*) (Isa. 65:11). Again idolatry is connected with demons. The god Fortune (Gad) was worshipped by the Babylonians. He is elsewhere called also Baal, Bel, and was regarded throughout the East as the giver of good fortune. The Septuagint renders him as "the demon," likely because of his conspicuousness and power.

E. DESTRUCTION

"For the pestilence what walketh in darkness, nor for the destruction (*qeter*) that wasteth at noonday"—"the evil spirit (demon) of noonday" (Ps. 91:6; LXX 90:6). This seems to be a trace of a popular demonic conception creeping into the translator's mind. Ethnic extravagances had evil avenging spirits for every moment of the day and night.

Thus in the Septuagint the meaning of the word "demon" is always sinister. In Philo[49] the word appears in the more general sense as equivalent to angels, both good and bad. In Josephus[50] its use is invariably of evil spirits, as in the New Testament. The change, therefore, in the Hellenistic usage is, first, the separation of the good from the bad demons, with the application of the term more and more to the bad ones. Secondly, the extension of the name, in the evil sense, to the heathen deities.

3. MEANING OF THE TERM "DEMON" IN THE NEW TESTAMENT

From Homer down to New Testament times the sense of *daimon* and *daimonion* is seen thus to have increased gradually in its inferiority to *theos*, and to have gathered around it more and more the sense of evil, until it reached its precise and invariable New Testament meaning of an "*evil* spirit" or "messenger and minister of the devil."[51] As spiritual beings, demons are intelligent, vicious, unclean, with power to afflict man with physical hurt, and moral and spiritual contamination.

---

[49]Cf. Alfred Barry, *Smith's Dictionary of the Bible*, ed. by Prof. H. B. Hackett, p. 583; also Langton, *op. cit.*, 102-3.

[50]*Antiquities* 6:8:2, 8:2:5; and *Wars of the Jews* 7:6:3.

[51]Cf. J. H. Thayer, *Greek-English Lexicon of the New Testament*.

CHAPTER V

DESCRIPTION AND DOOM OF THE DEMONS

IN ITS ACCOUNT of the demons, Scripture gives a record that is not calculated to appeal to the ultra-curious or to the highly imaginative. However, the essential facts are presented, but with such simplicity and brevity that the obvious goal of practical instruction and warning is never for a moment lost sight of. In no phase of the subject does this lack of all imaginative particulars and avoidance of all unnecessary details appear more evident than in those passages where evil spirits are described.

A. THE NATURE OF THE DEMONS

The precise character of demons has been widely misunderstood, and has been one of the most prolific sources of superstition, not only in ethnic and rabbinic systems, but in Christian conceptions as well.

1. THEIR SPIRITUAL NATURE

The Gospels prove conclusively that demons are purely spiritual beings, as the following passages show. "And when even was come, they brought unto Him many possessed with demons (*daimonizomenous*), and He cast out the spirits (*ta pneumata*) with a word" (Matt. 8:16). "And the seventy returned with joy, saying, Lord, even the demons (*ta daimonia*) are subject unto us in Thy name" (Luke 10:17). To which the Lord responds: "Nevertheless in this rejoice not, that the spirits (*ta pneumata*) are subject unto you" (v. 20). Likewise in Matthew's report of the lunatic boy it is said "the demon" (*daimonion*) went out of him" (Matt. 17:18). In Mark's Gospel the same demon is called an "unclean spirit" (*to pneumati to akatharto*) (Mark 9:25). Luke recounts the incident of "certain women who had been healed of evil spirits (*pneumaton poneron*) and infirmities," of whom the first recorded is Mary Magdalene, from whom it is said, "seven demons (*daimonia hepta*) had gone out" (Luke 8:2). Demons and evil spirits are therefore one and the same thing.

The spiritual nature of both Satan and his demon hosts is graphically set forth by the Apostle Paul when he emphatically says the believer's intense warfare "is not against flesh and blood," but against the non-material, the incorporeal, which he describes as "powers," "world-rulers of this darkness," "spiritual hosts of wickedness in the heavenly places" (Eph. 6:12). Again, the Apostle seems clearly to designate the "powers of the air," of whom he says Satan is "prince," as "spirits" (Eph. 2:2). Weymouth's translation is well borne out by the original: "the prince of the powers of the air, *the spirits* that are now at work in the hearts of the sons of disobedience." The "powers of the air" are thus the wicked spirits energizing the ungodly, as the Holy Spirit animates God's people.

In like manner the Apostle John bears witness to the incorporeality of the demons when he speaks of the three unclean spirits coming out of the mouth of the dragon, the beast, and the false prophet, as the "spirits of demons" (*pneumata daimonion*) (Rev. 16:14). The expression may be construed either as a common genitive of description denoting the kind of spirits as "demonic," or better, as a genitive of apposition, more particularly defining the general term "spirits," which may be either good or bad, as bad, or "demon-spirits."[1]

Demons, hence, are scripturally presented as purely spiritual beings. In several passages the Bible gives what is practically a definition of "spirit." "God is spirit" (John 4:24). "A spirit hath not flesh and bones" (Luke 24:39). "Demons" are "spirits" (Luke 10:17, 20). "Angels . . . are spirits" (Heb. 1:13-14). The specific attribute of "spirit" is then immateriality, incorporeality. Christ, as the Eternal Word (uncreated Spirit) in the incarnation did not take upon Himself an immaterial, incorporeal body, "the nature of angels" (Heb. 2:16), but actual humanity, in a sphere a "little lower than the angels" (Ps. 8:4-5; Heb. 2:6, 9), that He might lift the believer into His own realm above the angels (Heb. 2:9-10). It is evident, therefore, from these scriptures, that evil, as well as

---

[1]Cf. H. E. Daney and J. R. Mantey, *A Manual Grammar of the Greek New Testament*, pp. 75, 76, 79.

good angels, are in substance spirit, and denizens of the spiritual world, which is above the natural world.

But it must not be supposed that because spirits are immaterial, they are any less personal. Demons, as well as all other created spiritual beings, possess personality, and are everywhere represented as intelligent and voluntary agents (Mark 5:10; Luke 4:34).

If the substance of demons is spirit, what shall be said of their form and visibility? May they assume a definite shape, and be seen by human eyes? Is spirit ever discernible to men in the flesh? These questions are admittedly difficult, and except for a few faint rays of light from the revealed Word, the subject is compassed in darkness. Though no human being in the flesh has ever seen, or could see, the divine essence, God, in His own glorious triune spiritual person (John 1:18; 4:24), yet God, veiled in angelic form, and particularly as incarnate in Jesus Christ, has been seen by mortal eye (Gen. 18:2, 22; Exod. 3:2-4; John 14:9). Though angels, as spirits, are invisible to men (Ps. 104:4), yet power is certainly given them, upon occasion at least, to become visible in the likeness of human form (Gen. 19:1, 5; Luke 1:26; John 20:12; Acts 12:9). Likewise, evil spiritual beings seem evidently to possess a similar power. Satan, the chief evil spirit and leader of the evil spirits (Matt. 12:24), doubtless assumed the semblance of human form in the temptation of Jesus (Matt. 4:9-10), and as he was seen by Zechariah, standing at the right hand of Joshua, the high priest (Zech. 3:1). Under the guise of the Edenic serpent, he first fashioned himself "as an angel of light" (Gen. 3:1; II Cor. 11:14). It would not at all be surprising, therefore, if his satellite demons should so fashion themselves, and assume the semblance of human form, should occasion so require.

Scripture is remarkably reticent on this phase of demonology in complete contrast to ethnic and rabbinic systems, where glimpsing of spirits of the most fantastic shapes and forms is given large prominence. For example, the rabbis divided demons into two classes: one composed of purely spiritual beings, the other of half-spirits ("halbgeister").[2] The latter, as semi-sensuous beings, pos-

---

[2]William M. Alexander, *Demonic Possession in the New Testament,"* pp. 25-26, 50-57. For the multitudinous bizarre forms of demons in ancient Semitic demonology, see Edward Langton, *Essentials of Demonology,* pp. 20-22; and R. Campbell Thompson, *Semitic Magic,* pp. 44, 57, 60, 62, 101.

sessing a psycho-sarcous constitution, involving them in physical needs and functions, could, under certain conditions be seen, and were the source of endless superstition. Scriptural truth, however, at once disposes of the notion of "half-spirits," and with it the greater part of rabbinic and ethnic demonology, where the essential characteristic of spirit is violated.

Presenting demons, then, as purely spiritual beings, Scripture uniformly views them as above the operation of natural law, and not subject to human visibility, or other sensory perception. Hence the Bible's freedom from magical rites and methods, which vitiate and contaminate non-Biblical systems. Notwithstanding this general recognition of the spirituality and non-visibility of demons, it must be carefully noted that the Word of God does recognize the principle of the transcendence of natural law in divine miracle. Under such circumstances, the natural eye may see the spiritual reality, as, for instance, when in answer to Elisha's prayer, Jehovah opened the eyes of the young man, the prophet's servant, to see "the mountain was full of horses and chariots of fire round about Elisha" (II Kings 6:17). Thus it was that Elisha saw the "chariot of fire, and horses of fire," when Elijah was taken up by a whirlwind into heaven (II Kings 2:11). Thus it was that the Patmos seer *saw* the horrible locust demons, in their awful last-day eruption from the abyss (Rev. 9:1-12). And thus he *saw* the three hideous unclean frog-like spirits, which come out of the mouth of the dragon, the beast, and the false prophet (Rev. 16:13-16.)

John glimpsed these denizens of the evil spirit world by supernatural vision. Nevertheless, the demon-locusts and frog-like evil spirits will be invisible to the natural eye, but their presence will be known by the intense suffering they inflict, and the gross deception they cause, which will be unavoidable because of their invisibility and the human inability to provide any material screen against their attack.

Whether or not Satanic power in lands untouched by the truth of the gospel and unliberated from the thraldom of evil supernaturalism, has ever been unchecked to such an extent as to be able to perform diabolic miracles, in transcending natural laws to effect the spread of slavish fear and superstition by the glimpsing of spirits, it is impossible to say. Yet it would be difficult

to deny the possibility of such a fact in the face of the phenomena
of modern spiritism, and the last-day outbreak of miraculous evil
supernaturalism (II Thess. 2:9; Rev. 13:13-15), and in the face
of the claim of both rabbinic and ethnic demonology to direct
verification in the matter of seeing spirits.[3] Denying all possibility
of diabolic miracle as an underlying cause and dynamic, it seems
difficult to account for the perpetuation of such a vast mass of
superstition and fanaticism from the very dawn of historical times
to the present. Where there is a great deal of smoke, there is
likely to be a fire somewhere.

2. THEIR INTELLECTUAL NATURE

That evil spirits are believed to possess superhuman knowledge,
especially foreknowledge, is attested by the widespread practice
of seeking oracles from them. If Plato's etymology of *daimon*
from an adjective signifying "knowing" or "intelligent" is correct,[4]
it hints at intelligence as the basic characteristic in the conception
of demons. Scripture, moreover, uniformly emphasizes their
perspicacity: they know Jesus (Mark 1:24), bow before Him
(Mark 5:6), speak of Him as the "Son of the Most High God"
(Mark 5:7), realize that there can be no fellowship between light
and darkness, between Him and them (Luke 8:28), entreat favors
of Him (Luke 8:31), obey Him (Matt. 8:16), withhold knowledge
of His incarnation and finished sacrifice (I John 4:1-3), prevent
and corrupt sound doctrine (I Tim. 4:1-3), discern between those
sealed by God and those unsealed (Rev. 9:4), and comprehend
the future, and their own inevitable doom (Matt. 8:29).

Although the demons' knowledge is keen and supernatural,
it is not a holy or saving knowledge. Demons "believe and shudder"
(Jas. 2:19), but being confirmed in evil, never seek forgiveness,
never plead for purity. They have a distinct realization that Jesus
is Lord of the spirit-world, but their confession does not involve a
saving trust, or a willing submission. They worship Christ (Mark
3:11), but their worship is not the adoration of love or the joy of

---

[3]Alexander, *op. cit.*, p. 41.

[4]*Cratylus* I, 389. On the intellectual nature of demons, see John L. Nevius,
Demonic Possession and Allied Themes, pp. 33, 83, 150, 296, and E. Langton,
Essentials of Demonology, pp. 153, 179.

holy communion, but the mere bending of a lower to a higher will, in hate and resentment.

As Satan's vast though finite wisdom became corrupted when he sinned (Ezek. 28:12, 17), it is reasonable to conclude that the great wisdom which characterizes angelic beings in general (II Sam. 14:20), was, in the case of the multitude of angelic collaborators who followed him, likewise perverted. This is doubtless the explanation of the pre-eminent but unholy knowledge of the demons, which is used so relentlessly in ceaseless and indefatigable attempts to foil and frustrate God's plans and purposes.

3. Their Moral Nature

The depravity and complete moral turpitude of these unseen agents of evil are everywhere witnessed to in Scripture by the devilish effects they produce in their victims, and by the frequent epithet of "unclean" which is applied to them (Matt. 10:1; Mark 1:27; 3:11; Luke 4:36; Acts 8:7; Rev. 16:13). They use those whom they possess or influence as "instruments of unrighteousness" (Rom. 6:13), to promulgate "doctrines of demons" (I Tim. 4:1) and "destructive heresies" (II Pet. 2:1), leading not only to unmoral, but to immoral conduct. The actions of the demonized seem to indicate that the unclean spirit takes possession in some instances for the purpose of sensual gratification, and uses every type of uncleanness. This may explain the desire of the possessed to live in a state of nudity, to have licentious thoughts (Luke 8:27), and to frequent such impure places as tombs. The vile and vicious nature of demons is further demonstrated by their desire to enter swine (Mark 5:12) and their activity in the proclamation of doctrines of free love (I Tim. 4:3) with the consequent moral breakdown of an orderly society.

Coupled with their superhuman intelligence and moral viciousness is an amazing strength. They have power over the human body to cause dumbness (Matt. 9:32-33), blindness (Matt. 12:22), insanity (Luke 8:26-36), suicidal mania (Mark 9:22), personal injuries (Mark 9:18), and various physical defects and deformities (Luke 13:11-17). They are represented as being of various degrees of wickedness (Matt. 12:45). Their titanic energy is seen in the supernatural strength they can impart to the human body (Luke 8:29). Power and great strength are prominent angelic attributes

(Ps. 103:20; II Pet. 2:11), which, like wisdom, were vitiated and perverted in the rebellious angels (Matt. 12:29).

B. The Activity of the Demons

Satan and evil spirits are untiring and ceaseless in the prosecution of enterprises of deception and wickedness. Satanic diligence and industry are to be noted in such expressions as "going to and fro in the earth, and walking up and down in it" (Job 1:7), "as a roaring lion walketh about, seeking whom he may devour" (I Pet. 5:8). If the prince-leader of the demons (Matt. 12:24) presents such a picture of tireless zeal and unflagging energy, it is not surprising if his host of willing satellites demonstrate something of the same enthusiasm and application.

1. Demon Oppose God and Strive to Defeat His Will

Opposition to God's will is Satan's main objective. The appellation "Satan" means "adversary"—primarily God's adversary (Job 1:6; Matt. 13:39) and secondarily, man's opponent (Zech. 3:1; I Pet. 5:8). The designation "devil" signifies "slanderer"—accusing God before men (Gen. 3:1-5), and men before God (Job 1:9, 11; 2:4-5; Rev. 12:10). It was the intrusion of his will against the divine will in the original apostasy (Isa. 14:13-14), and the concurrence of a vast multitude of angels in the rebellion that forever set the pattern of Satanic and demonic attitude as opposition, and exaltation of self "against all that is called God or that is worshipped" (II Thess. 2:4). From the murder of Abel (Gen. 4:8) to Herod's slaughter of the innocents (Matt. 2:16), Satan's implacable hatred of the Promised Seed, and his antagonism to God's Messiah and the divine purpose in Him, can be unmistakably traced. Since demons serve Satan as king (Matt. 12:26), like him they oppose God.

In the personal appearance of Satan to tempt the Lord Jesus (Matt. 4:1-11), in the tremendous demonic disturbance that everywhere attempted to frustrate His public ministry, in the betrayal of Judas (Luke 22:3) and the denial of Peter (Luke 22:31), and in the terrific blindness and deception of Jewish leaders, may be discerned the venomous resistance of Satan and demons to God's plans and purposes in Christ. The same unmitigated defiance may be perceived throughout the annals of Church history to the last awful demon-energized, anti-God coalition at Armageddon (Rev. 16:13-16).

2. DEMONS OPPRESS MAN AND SEEK TO HINDER HIS WELFARE

Sometimes evil spirits jeopardize man's temporal and eternal well-being by exercising a certain control over natural phenomena. To afflict Job, Satan employed lightning, whirlwind, and disease (Job 1:12, 16, 19; 2:7). The woman who had "a spirit of infirmity" is said to have been bound by Satan for eighteen years (Luke 13:11, 16). The violent Galilean storm, in which the disciples awoke the slumbering Saviour, is traceable to Satanic and demonic agency (Mark 4:39).

More often evil spirits imperil man's well-being by subjecting him to temptation. Many Scriptures specifically ascribe this power to Satan (Gen. 3:1-7; Matt. 4:3; John 13:27; Acts 5:3; I Thess. 3:5), and his solicitations are represented as both negative and positive (Matt. 13:38-39). He not only takes away the good seed, but sows the tares. Assuredly this power of temptation is possessed by Satan's many subordinate evil spirits, through whose instrumentality he accomplishes his nefarious purposes. "The prince of the powers of the air, the spirits that are now at work in the hearts of the sons of disobedience" (Eph. 2:2, Weymouth) may be thought of as conjointly, perpetually, and indefatigably engaged in a vast program of suggestion and solicitation for evil.

It seems evident from Scripture that the activity of demons is so intimately and inseparably bound up with their prince-leader that their work and his is identified rather than differentiated. Thus the earthly ministry of our Lord is described as going about "doing good, and healing all that were oppressed of the *devil*" (Acts 10:38). It is obvious, even from a cursory examination of the facts, that this so-called oppression of the "devil" was largely the work of his emissaries and servants, the *demons*. Doubtless, very crucial cases of temptation (Matt. 4:1; Luke 22:3; 22:31) are the direct task of Satan himself, but since he is neither omnipresent, omnipotent, nor omniscient, the greater part of this colossal activity must be thought of as delegated to demons. Demons also distress mankind by deranging both body and mind in "demon-possession" (Mark 1:23-27; 5:1-20).

3. Nevertheless, Demons Accomplish God's Purposes

Demons are the instruments for executing God's plans for punishing the ungodly (Ps. 78:49). Wicked Ahab was punished for his crimes by a "lying spirit" which Jehovah put in the mouth of all his prophets to lead him to disaster at Ramoth Gilead (I Kings 22:23). Demons lure the God-resisting armies of Armageddon to a similar catastrophe (Rev. 16:13-16).

Satan and his ministers also effect God's plans for chastening the godly. Satan's sifting but accomplishes the Lord's winnowing, as in the case of Peter (Luke 22:31). Job is brought through Satanic testing to a place of spiritual enlargement and refinement (Job 42:5-6). The incestuous believer at Corinth is delivered "unto Satan for the destruction of the flesh, that the spirit may be saved in the day of the Lord Jesus" (I Cor. 5:5). Hymenaeus and Alexander are "delivered unto Satan, that they might be taught not to blaspheme" (I Tim. 1:20).

Satan and demons illustrate, for all time, the nature and fate of moral evil (Matt. 8:29). The consignment of Satan and his angels to the "eternal fire" which is prepared for them and for those who follow them (Matt. 25:41; Rev. 20:10) will not only be a vindication of God's permission of their evil agency, but it will also furnish a demonstration to the entire moral universe of the exceeding sinfulness of sin, and its inevitable penalty and punishment.

C. The Abode of the Demons

Though Satan has great power, he is circumscribed by bounds and limitations, beyond which he may not go. He is now permitted to employ an innumerable host of demons who are free to obey his behests, but he is not permitted to marshall *all* the evil agencies who would fain follow him in his diabolical designs. But, in the last judgments consummating this age, and in augmentation of the punishments of the ungodly, he will be allowed to swell the ranks of his armies with multitudes of evil beings now restrained in the underworld.

1. The Abyss — the Abode of the Imprisoned Demons

Although Scripture mentions the prison of evil spirits, and its multitudinous prisoners, nothing is revealed as to why or when the imprisonment took place. The disimprisonment of its malignant tenants, however, is graphically recounted (Rev. 9:1-11). John saw "a star from heaven fallen unto the earth" to whom was given "the key of the pit of the abyss" (Rev. 9:1). Commentators disagree whether the star represents Satan, or a fallen or an unfallen angel, or an apostate leader, or other being. On the other hand, the unlocking of the pit of the abyss,[5] and the swarms of supernatural, infernal "locusts" which issue from the resulting smoke, it is generally agreed, represent the loosing of myriads of destructive and delusive demons to deceive and torment both Jew and Gentile in the end time.

The pit of the abyss,[6] from whence these teeming demonic agencies emerge, is not Hades, the abode of the spirits of wicked human beings until the second resurrection, nor Tartarus, the prison house of the fallen angels (II Pet. 2:4; Jude v. 6), nor the lake of fire, the final doom of Satan and his angels (Matt. 25:41); but it is the place of the present detention of many fallen spirits, who, for some reason, have been denied the privilege which many of their colleagues enjoy, of ranging at large. To this spiritual gaol some of the demons, who once were loose, have been by divine justice and power remanded (Luke 8:31).

John, the Revelator, gives an account of another vast host of spirit-beings, which like the demon-locusts, are let loose upon the idolatrous and demon-worshipping masses of mankind in the closing years of this age (Rev. 9:13-21). Simultaneously, with the loosing of four angels "that are bound at the great river Euphrates" (v. 14), this invisible infernal cavalry, two hundred million strong, appears as their agent to slay one-third of earth's godless hordes. Whether these strange, bizarre spirit-beings, with their hideous composite constitution, and their death-dealing power, are to be classified as demonic agencies, cannot be clearly ascertained.[7] What is certain is that they belong to the kingdom of evil supernaturalism. "The four angels," whose liberation marks the moment of the

---

[5]For ancient pagan concepts of the abyss, see James Moffatt in *The Expositor's Greek New Testament* (*Revelation*), p. 406.

[6]For a profound discussion on the abyss, see the excursus in Lange's *Commentary on the Holy Scriptures* (Revelation).

[7]That they are demonic agents is extremely likely. Fantastic shapes and forms of demons are among their striking charactertistics in extra-Biblical conceptions; cf. note 2.

commencement of their terrific destruction, seem to be particular magnates in the realm of spiritual evil (Eph. 6:12). The myriads of subordinate agents, whom their loosing automatically calls into action, seem to indicate a distinctive and high rank. Whether the supernatural army (cf. II Kings 2:11; 6:13-17) was all the while free, or like the four angels, bound, and if so, where, is not stated. They simply appear on the scene, and spring into their aggressive and destructive career.

2. Earth and Air — the Abode of the Free Demons

These spirits, as constituting the "powers of the air" (Eph. 2:2), "the powers of darkness" (Col. 1:13), under Satan their prince, are the spiritual foes against whom believers in this age must wrestle (Eph. 6:11-12). They will doubtless retain their freedom to range at large in the heavenlies with Satan until he is cast out of heaven into the earth (Rev. 12:9). With him, they will doubtless be cast into the abyss at the second coming of Christ, to remain there during the millennium (Rev. 20:1-3), and will share his eternal fate in the lake of fire (Matt. 25:41; Rev. 20:10).

D. The Organization of the Demons

Fallen, like unfallen, angelic beings constitute a vast multitude (Dan. 7:10; Rev. 12:4, 7). As the good spirits have various ranks and endowments in an orderly arrangement, it would be strange, indeed, to find Satan's host a mere uncoordinated mob. So far from this being the case, Satan's "kingdom" (Matt. 12:26) is revealed as a highly systematized empire of evil, elaborately organized. Satan's authority, it seems, extends over two distinct orders of beings—the Satanic order of the earth, and the Satanic host of the air.[8]

1. The Satanic Order of the Earth

In this sphere Satan rules over unregenerate mankind. He secured the sceptre of government in the earth from Adam, by right of conquest (Gen. 3:1-6; Matt. 4:8-9; John 12:31), and has organized the present world-system upon his own cosmic principles of pride, ambition, selfishness, force, greed, and pleasure (John

[8]Lewis Sperry Chafer, *Satan*, pp. 63-64.

14:30; 18:36; Eph. 2:2; 6:12; I John 2:15-17). Imposing, outwardly religious, scientific, cultured, elegant, this world-system,
nevertheless, is dominated by Satanic principles, and is beneath
its deceptive veneer a seething cauldron of national and international ambitions, and commercial rivalries. Satan and his elaborately organized hierarchy of evil (Dan. 10:13; Eph. 6:12) are
often the invisible agents, and the real motivating power and
intelligence behind the dictators, kings, presidents, and governors,
who are the visible rulers.[9] Armed force and periodic wars, with
wholesale murder and violence, are its indispensable concomitants.

2. The Satanic Host of the Air

In this category Satan holds sway over the fallen spirits,
who concurred in his primal rebellion. His authority is without
doubt what he has been permitted to retain from his creation.
These spirits, having an irrevocable choice to follow Satan, instead
of remaining loyal to their Creator, have become irretrievably
confirmed in wickedness, and irreparably abandoned to delusion.
Hence, they are in full sympathy with their prince, and render
him willing service in their varied ranks and positions of service
in his highly organized kingdom of evil (Matt. 12:26). Their
initial decision has forever wedded them to his deceptive program
and also to his inevitable doom.

3. The Imprisoned Host in the Abyss

Satan's organization extends not only to his order of the earth
and his host of the air. Even the demon-tenants of the abyss feel
the subtle influence of his efficient systematization. "They have
over them as king, the angel of the abyss: his name in Hebrew
is Abaddon, and in the Greek tongue he hath the name Apollyon"
(Rev. 9:11). This king is not Satan himself. Satan is, to be sure,
prince of all the powers of darkness, but he has potentates and
princelings under him, with their own particular responsibilities
and tasks. It is Satan who opens the door (Rev. 9:1-2) for the
egress of the locust-spirits from the pit in the days of strong
delusion and the "working of error" (II Thess. 2:11), but the

---

[9]See Chapter XI of this text, "Biblical Demonology and World Governments."

immediate king of these malignant demons is one of Satan's angels, "the angel of the abyss."

The king has a descriptive name, given in Hebrew and Greek, demonstrating that the awful demon eruption from the abyss has to do with both Jews and Gentiles in the end time. Christ is called "Jesus," because He is "The Saviour." The king is called "Abaddon," in Hebrew, and "Apollyon," in Greek, because he is a destroyer—the opposite of a Saviour.

E. THE DOOM OF THE DEMONS

Although granted a large sphere of activity, and exercising a powerful and malignant ministry, demons, like their leader Satan, are nevertheless strictly under divine control and have a definite part in the divine plan. The span of their evil machinations is strictly determined, the sphere of their wicked operations is definitely set, and their doom is inexorably sealed. There is no unhealthy dualism in Biblical demonology.

1. THE ABYSS — THEIR INTERMEDIATE DOOM

Evil spirits are by no means ignorant of what lies in store for them and the sure fate that awaits them. That is why they cried out in dismay to Jesus: "What have we to do with thee, Jesus, thou Son of God? Art thou come hither to torment us before the time (before the set time)?" (Matt. 8:29). The demons in the Gadarene demoniac manifested to Jesus a peculiar dread and terror of the abyss, intimating that they viewed it as a place of torment and confinement. "And they intreated (were begging, imploring) him that he would not command them to depart into the abyss" (Luke 8:31).

The abyss appears like Hades, the habitation of the souls of the unrighteous between death and the second resurrection, to be an intermediate place of detention for evil spirits. Hosts of its depraved tenants are set loose from thence during the tribulation to augment Satan's malignant cohorts in their wild work of deception and destruction (Rev. 9:1-11). Into the same dismal dungeon Satan is consigned at Christ's Second Advent to remain shut up there during the Millennial Kingdom (Rev. 20:1-3). Doubtless, his hosts of demon satellites are included, and it is to be understood that they are dispatched thither also, for he is stripped of all power to "deceive the nations" any more, "until the thousand years should be finished" (Rev. 20:3), which could scarcely be the case if the roving bands of his minions were at large to prosecute their mischief.

Again, doubtless his being loosed "for a little time" out of his prison (Rev. 20:3, 7) after the Millennium is to be understood to include loosing them also, at least part of them, and his deceiving of the nations to be aided and abetted by them (20:8-9).

2. Gehenna — Their Eternal Doom

The abyss lodges its wicked tenants only temporarily, and must at length surrender them to the "eternal fire which is prepared for the devil and his angels" (Matt. 25:41). This is unquestionably the terrifying doom the demons had in mind when they cried out to Jesus, "What have we to do with thee, Jesus, thou Nazarene? Art thou come to destroy us?" (Mark 1:24). "Art thou come hither to torment us before *the* time?" (Matt. 8:29).

Satan, after being loosed from the abyss, is again apprehended in the midst of his last awful rebellion against God and hurled to his eternal doom into "the lake of fire and brimstone," to be "tormented day and night for ever and ever" (Rev. 20:10). There can be no question that his demon-accomplices, who have aided him in this his last deception of mankind, at this time will suffer the same fate. Any wicked spirits remaining in the abyss, in all likelihood, are delivered up at the Great White Throne Judgment to be consigned to the eternal flames of Gehenna (Rev. 20:11-15).

Pember[10] sees a possible identification of the abyss, the prison-house of the demons, with "the sea," which is said to give up the dead that are in it (Rev. 20:13). But this idea, which is confessedly ingenious, cannot be proved. The Septuagint does use the term in connection with the chaotic deep in Genesis 1:2, and "the foun-

---

[10]G. H. Pember, *Earth's Earliest Ages and Their Connection with Modern Spiritualism and Theosophy*, pp. 75-76.

tains of the deep" which were broken up to cause the flood (Gen.
6:11), but it is another thing to assume that the abyss may sometimes be used for the sea. If such usage could be established though,
it would explain why "the sea," which is usually explained as
giving up the bodily remains of those buried or drowned in it, is
listed with "Death and Hades" (the unseen world), places not
concerned with the remnants of material forms, but with disembodied spirits.

CHAPTER VI

BIBLICAL DEMONOLOGY
AND DEMON POSSESSION

PROBABLY NO phase of Biblical demonology has called forth more speculation, or excited more doubt and skepticism, than that dealing with the strange phenomenon of demon possession. Unbelief and rationalistic criticism have struggled desperately with this baffling theme, which is at once inexplicable and unmanageable to incredulity. The whole subject is at the same time rendered more acute because of the remarkable prominence accorded demon inhabitation in Scripture, especially during the life and ministry of our Lord.

A. DEMON POSSESSION AND PSYCHISM

Certain remarkable phenomena, which properly belong to the field of experimental psychology, call for special mention in connection with demon possession, because they offer corroborative evidence of the reality of such an occurrence and place it in a light which makes it less of a wonder. While telepathy, or thought transference, and mind-reading are problems of the psychologist, and are fields of investigation, in many respects still in their infancy, and much remains to be discovered concerning them, yet this much is established: the mind of one person cannot only influence that of another, but can mesmerize, or hypnotize, or take control of it to such a degree as to impart to it a knowledge previously unpossessed. Feelings and emotions are also excited that were absent before the person lapsed into the hypnotized state, and in some way or other one mind may read, or become conscious of, what is in the mind of another. The facts are as inexplicable to the initiated as to the uninitiated.

The common Christian belief in good angels, for example, who aid and protect the children of God, finds in the strange psychological phenomena of telepathy a rational support, provided such beings as good angels exist. That they do exist, and have a ministry in behalf of believers, must be conceded by those who believe the testimony of Scripture (Ps. 104:4; Matt. 6:10; Heb. 1:14). Also, the basic Christian tenet that the Holy Spirit can indwell the believer's body and act directly upon the minds of those who submit themselves to God's will, inspiring them with lofty aims and thoughts, guiding them in the ways of righteousness, finds in telepathy a rational basis of corroboration. And, moreover, if there were no Biblical authority or well-authenticated examples of evil supernaturalism to substantiate the claims of modern spiritistic mediums, they could find in telepathy one of their strongest arguments.

The deduction to be made from the foregoing facts is this: if the mind of one person can influence or take control of that of another, if good angels can comfort and otherwise influence the minds of God's people, and if the Holy Spirit can enter, and take possession, and influence for good those who choose the way of salvation, then what valid objection may be offered why Satan and demons, as the Bible teaches, may not also enter into the bodies, and take possession of the minds of those who willingly yield themselves slaves to these evil agencies? This is a question that unbelief must answer, and which no candid philosopher or scientist, who does research in psychology, can reasonably ignore.

B.   THE PREVALENCE OF DEMON POSSESSION

Much skepticism arises from the common erroneous notion, that what is called demon possession was occurrent in only one period of history and characteristic of but one epoch, and is, therefore, to be explained otherwise than what it is actually claimed to be—physical indwelling and bodily control by evil spirits.

1. ITS PREVALENCE IN BIBLICAL TIMES

It can not be denied that the period of Jesus' public ministry was the time of an unusual and startling outbreak of demonism. It seemed as if all the fury of the underworld of evil was concentrated against the Messiah and His public ministry, so that in the Synoptic Gospels cases of demon possession and demon expulsion are extremely common. Not only did the Lord Jesus cast out demons as one of the functions of His ministry of mercy (Mark 1:23-27, 32-34, 39; 3:11-12; 5:1-20; 7:25-30; 9:17-29, 38; 16:9, 17), but He delegated this power to the Twelve (Mark 3:15) to the Seventy (Luke 10:17), and even to believers (Mark 16:17).

But such an eruption of demon power against the ministry of the Saviour ought not to be thought amazing. It was but the critical and inevitable clash of the white light of perfect holiness and truth against the gross darkness of error and deceit. It was the unavoidable collision of the unhindered power of the Holy Spirit, manifested through a sinless life, with the opposing power of Satan. It was impossible for the Son of God to be in the vicinity of evil power, and not expose it, and challenge it. Shadows of twilight and the curtain of night only temporarily hide what the brilliance of the noonday sun reveals.

The Son of God, moreover, was manifested with the specific purpose "that he might destroy the works of the devil" (I John 3:8). It was His avowed intention to engage the enemy in order to defeat him, to challenge his power in order to destroy it, to search out the cancerous sore in order to heal it, to undo, in short, all the woe and wickedness Satan had wrought, and to prove His own deity and Messiahship in the conquest of moral and spiritual evil. Therefore, with head-on impact He collided with Satan's fury and tyranny. It is not to be thought astonishing or unusual that such a phenomenal outburst of demonism should emerge during the Lord's ministry. Indeed, what would be surprising is if such a manifestation had not taken place.

Although the life and times of Jesus were characterized by a great upheaval among Satan and the demons, there were thus definite reasons for it. Let no one suppose, on the other hand, as is often done, that instances of demon possession are confined to that particular period alone. In Biblical times, both *before* and *after* the earthly public ministry of the Messiah, demon possession was by no means uncommon or unheard-of. Exorcisms, with magical words and cures, were the order of the day in contemporary Judaism, and the belief in the possession of men by demons, who were considered the spirits of wicked men deceased, or evil angels, was "thoroughly established among all the Jews, with the exception

of the Sadducees alone."[1] This fact proves that long before the
Advent of the Messiah, demon possession and demon expulsion
were established doctrines in Jewish demonological thought. The
following comment of Johannes Weiss is to the point:

> The historicity of Jesus' successful treatment of demoniacs is admitted in
> principle even by adherents of the critical school. Exorcisms were the order
> of the day, and were expected of a Messianic prophet, and the chief proof
> of their historicity lies in the statements of Jesus, which represent their im-
> portance for Himself and His activity as the Messiah (Matt. 11:5; Luke 7:22).[2]

The presence of demonic phenomena in the Old Testament,
if not actual cases of possession, is strongly suggested by such
instances as the orgiastic rites of the priests of Baal (I Kings
18:28) and Nebuchadnezzar's sudden manifestation of practices
of lower animals (Dan. 4:33). David's feigned dementia (I Sam.
21:13-14) argues for the frequency of such phenomena at that date,
and Saul's persecution mania, which Josephus attributes to actual
demon possession,[3] is clearly a case of demon influence (I Sam.,
chaps. 16, 18-21).

Cases of demon possession and demon expulsion, while not so
frequent, and perhaps not so spectacular as in the ministry of the
Messiah, continued in the early Church, in accordance with the
Apostolic Commission (Mark 16:17; Acts 5:16; 8:7; 19:12). Of
particular interest is Paul's expulsion of the divining demon ("a
spirit, a python") from the soothsaying maid in Philippi (Acts
16:16-18), linking her power of prognostication with the same evil
supernaturalism that inspired the famous heathen oracles at ancient
Delphi. The narrative of Acts 19:13-19 is valuable in showing the
prevalence of itinerating Jewish exorcists, and in illustrating the
contrast between their magical methods for casting out demons
and the simple employment by the Apostles of the mighty name of
Jesus.

The Epistles contain no direct statements concerning demoniacs
or expulsions, but it should not be imagined that Paul did not
believe in these phenomena, when, as a matter of practice, he

---

[1]Alfred Barry, "Demon, Demoniac," *Smith's Dictionary of The Bible,*" ed. by
Prof. H. B. Hackett, pp. 584-585.

[2]Johannes Weiss, "Demoniac," *The New Schaff-Herzog Encyclopedia of
Religious Knowledge,* 1909, III, 402.

[3]Josephus, *Antiquities of the Jews,* 6:8:2; 6:11:2.

cast out demons in his own ministry (Acts 16:18; 19:12). His enumeration of both the gift of "workings of miracles" and "discernings of spirits" among the charismata (I Cor. 12:10), and his connection of demonism with idolatry and false doctrine (I Cor. 10:20; I Tim. 4:1-2), preclude any such false conclusion. The prominent demonology of the Apocalypse strongly implies powerful demonic influence and inhabitation (Rev. 9:1-11, 20-21; 16:13-16).

2. THE PROBLEM OF THE CESSATION OF DEMON POSSESSION

There is a popular and widespread error that labors under the impression that there are now, in an age of science and enlightenment, no longer any demons, nor any cases of demon possession. F. C. Conybeare's faulty criticism is a sample of the pseudo-rationalism of many:

Why no demons any more? I should answer that it is free inquiry, a scientific attitude, modern science, and modern skepticism, which during the last 150 years have rid the civilized world of a burthen which dogmatic theology and Christian rites, and even the New Testament itself, had done nothing to alleviate, and much to aggravate, during seventeen centuries of undisputed sway.[4]

And since there are no demons or cases of demon possession now, it is concluded there never were any. New Testament instances of the so-called "demonized" are viewed as proving that Jesus "was thoroughly immersed in all the popular superstitions of his age concerning evil spirits."[5]

The fallacy of the critical argument becomes apparent, when the fact is realized that it can not be proved that there are neither demons nor cases of demon possession today. Indeed, the whole weight of evidence is to the contrary. Laying aside the Scriptural witness and proof, the facts of physical nature, human nature, and human experience combine to adduce substantial evidence that demons, as well as cases of demon possession, do exist today.

That demon possession by no means ended with New Testament times is irrefutably proved by the witness of early Church history. The "Epistle of Barnabas" (13:19) represents the heart full of idolatry as the abode of demons. "The Shepherd of Hermas" (*circa* 120) contains considerable philosophy of demon possession.

4F. C. Conybeare, "Christian Demonology," *Jewish Quarterly Review*, IX (1896-1897), 600-601.
5*Ibid.*, p. 602.

Justin Martyr views the phenomenon as due to inhabitation by the souls of departed dead, and expulsions were almost as common to the contemporaries of Tertullian and Minucius as to the contemporaries of Jesus.[6] Belief in demons and demon possession have persisted throughout the entire Christian era to the present day, and authenticated cases of expulsion have, from time to time, been adduced.[7]

But what shall be said to the claim that the modern age of scientific inquiry has done away with these beliefs, and no cases of demon possession are now adducible? To such a contention it must be replied that, in spite of the progress of modern thought, and the development of the natural sciences, "the primitive conception of these things as supernatural has by no means been eliminated."[8] The authority of the Scriptural narratives and the general supernatural standpoint from which their exposition is ᵔpproached find strong support in both Roman Catholic and orthodox Protestant Churches.

3. The Prevalence of Demon Possession Today

It is, moreover, a hasty conclusion to infer that there are no cases of demon possession now. The testimony of missionaries to heathen lands is unequivocally to the contrary. Phenomena similar to those described in the Gospels are still met, not only in rude and savage districts, but also in countries of ancient pagan civilization, such as India and China.[9] But it must not be expected that Satanic strategy should be the same in every locality. Demons, notoriously clever and intelligent themselves, have a superlatively wise and cunning leader. It is only reasonable to conclude that they are adapting their stratagems to the enlightenment of the age and the locality. With the crude savage, Satan may best

---

[6]Conybeare, "The Demonology of the New Testament," *Jewish Quarterly Review*, VIII (July 1896), 600.

[7]For a fascinating survey of the history of possession from the most ancient times to the present day in all countries of the inhabited globe, see T. K. Oesterreich, *Possession, Demoniacal and Other, among Primitive Races in Antiquity, the Middle Ages, and Modern Times*, pp. 199-235. See also Edward Langton, *Supernatural: The Doctrine of Spirits, Angels, and Demons from the Middle Ages to the Present Time*.

[8]Weiss, *op. cit.*, p. 403.

[9]G. Buchanan Gray, "Demons and Angels," *Encyclopedia Biblica*, I, 1074.

accomplish his purpose as a "roaring lion," inspiring dread and base fear, but with the cultured and educated, in a so-called Christian society, he can often work more effectively when disguised as "an angel of light."

There can be no doubt, either, that the beneficent effects of centuries of gospel light and Christian faith act as a natural deterrent in restraining the grosser and baser power of Satan manifested in demonic possession (II Thess. 2:7). In heathen societies, with demon power to a great degree unrestrained by the presence and power of the Holy Spirit, demon possession, at least in its cruder forms, is much more in evidence. Then, too, demon possession is undoubtedly often unsuspected because of the prevailing failure to realize demons are capable of inspiring a moral life of self-trust and self-effort, without reliance upon a crucified and risen Redeemer.[10] It is also often present, though unsurmised, in widespread spiritualistic phenomena. As G. Campbell Morgan says, "the moment the word 'medium' is employed, the word 'demonized man' or 'demonized woman' may be substituted."[11]

However, whatever demonic phenomena there may be operative, but unrecognized in lands affected by Christian civilization, it is significant that "manifestations of possession are everywhere in regression amongst primitive people in places where Christian missions have struck deep root."[12] Two reasons are evidently responsible for this fact. The first is the power of Christianity "to inspire the natives with trust in God and to free them from the fear of demons and their attacks on the souls of the living."[13] Another is the effect of civilization, considered largely apart from Christianity, in bringing with it education and, as in the history of modern Europe, an Age of Enlightenment which, in the case of those who do not embrace Christian salvation, frequently gives birth to a naturalistic rationalism that rejects belief in evil supernaturalism. Since "possession begins to disappear amongst civilized races as soon as belief in spirits loses its power,"[14]—as the power of the Holy Spirit decreases among Christians in proportion as they fail

---

[10]Lewis Sperry Chafer, *Satan*, p. 68.
[11]*The Gospel According to Mark*, p. 119.
[12]Oesterreich, *op. cit.*, p. 379.
[13]*Ibid.*
[14]*Ibid.*, p. 378.

to believe the Word of God—culture and education are frequently factors, along with the restraining ministry of God's Spirit through Christians, in diminishing cases of possession and other more overt and direct demonic activities in civilized lands. This does not mean, on the other hand, that Satan does not work in other more subtle ways, hidden from the natural man, and more consonant with the attitude and refinement of sophisticated society, such as deceiving him (Rev. 12:9), blinding his eyes to the power of the gospel (II Cor. 4:4), and holding him in spiritual captivity (Luke 13:16). To be bound by Satan in cruder and more violent ways, as in demon possession, requires, of course, not a rationalistic disbelief in evil supernaturalism, but a greater or less degree of faith in the existence and power of evil spirits, producing a base fear with liable spontaneous or involuntary possession, which may be endured, or a definite yielding of the will to the evil powers, resulting in voluntary possession "systematically provoked."[15]

Cases both of spontaneous or involuntary and voluntary possession are practically universal in extent, there being no quarter of the globe where such phenomena have not been authenticated nor any class of society, primitive or civilized, where they have not occurred, nor any period, ancient, or medieval, or modern, in which cases may not be cited.[16]

A striking feature of demonic possession is the constancy of its nature throughout the centuries. To most people in so-called Christian civilization in Europe and America the book affording the earliest glimpse of the states called "possession" is the New Testament. Despite the strictures of critics, who through ignorance of demonic phenomena in various parts of the world both in primitive and civilized cultures, have accused the New Testament of having "done nothing to alleviate, and much to aggravate" the burden of superstitious beliefs in demons and demon possession,[17] the Bible accounts of the demonized give an accurate picture of these phenomena, which were extremely frequent in the latter days of the ancient world. The authors of the New Testament were evidently quite familiar with cases of demonized persons, "and their accounts, even should they be recognized as of little

---

[15]*Ibid.*
[16]*Ibid.*, pp. 131-380.
[17]Cf. F. C. Conybeare, *op. cit.*, pp. 600-601; Cf. note 4.

or no historical value," says Oesterreich, "bear in themselves the stamp of truth. They are pictures of typical states exactly reproduced."[18]

"Comparing these brief stories with accounts of the phenomena of possession in later times, we find what may be described as the perfect similarity of the facts extremely surprising, while our respect for the historic truth of the Gospels is enhanced to an extraordinary degree. Excluding the story of the herd of swine, the narratives are of an entirely realistic and objective character. In particular, the succinct accounts of Jesus' relation to these events . . . as well as the particulars of his cures, coincide so exactly with what we know of these states from the point of view of present-day psychology, that it is impossible to avoid the impression that we are dealing with a tradition which is veracious."[19]

The constant nature of the phenomena of demonic possession and its persistence throughout the Christian centuries till the present day may be abundantly illustrated from a vast literature. Lynn Thorndike gives a detailed survey of the history of occult literature, beliefs, and practices during the first sixteen centuries of the Christian era, and demon possession and exorcism appear throughout this period.[20] Jules Michelet presents a vivid account of the rampant demonism of the Middle or "Dark" Ages with its reign of Satan, its gross superstitions, unbridled sensuality, and widespread phenomena of possession.[21] "Demons afflict the world throughout the whole period of the Middle Ages."[22] The widespread spiritual retrogression during this period, manifested in an utterly corrupt and paganized church, gave practically free reign to superstition and rampant demonism.

---

[18]*Op. cit.*, p. 3. For an attack on the New Testament accounts of demon possession, see *An Essay on the Demoniacs of the New Testament* by Hugh Farmer. For an exhaustive defense, see John Fell, *Daemoniacs*, pp. 167-400.

[19]Oesterreich, *op. cit.*, pp. 4-5.

[20]*A History of Magic and Experimental Science*, Vols. I-VI, (1923-1941). Cf. I, 18-24, 280,299, 533-4, 722; II, 168, 229, 320; III, 326ff., 466, 533; IV, 286, 306, 587; V, 117-8; VI, 545.

[21]*Satanism and Witchcraft: A Study of Medieval Superstition*, pp. 41-54; 207-220.

[22]*Ibid.*, p. 42.

The Protestant Reformation liberated multitudes from the shackles of Medieval enslavement in gross superstition and demonism. However, giving birth to a church, prefigured by Sardis (Rev. 3:1-6), which had a name to live, but was to a large extent spiritually "dead" (Rev. 3:1), this movement did not possess the vital spiritual power to produce the far-reaching, purifying and emancipating effects so desperately needed. Yet, together with the advent of an age of scientific enlightenment and reason initiated by such men of the seventeenth century as Galileo, Descartes, John Newton and their successors, the crude paganistic demonology of the Middle Ages with its witchcraft, divination, magic, astrology, sorcery, and weird excesses began to be rightly tested in the crucible of human reason and divine revelation.

The progress of scientific enlightenment in the eighteenth century and the far-reaching spiritual revivals and missionary activities of the Philadelphia Church (Rev. 3:7-13) from about 1750 until the twentieth century, have continued to purge out superstition on the one hand, as human reason stressing the working of natural law held sway, and to restrain the outcropping of evil supernaturalism (at least in its lower, less refined forms) by spiritual power and enlightenment on the other hand. This twin effect of Christianity and modern civilization has been to reduce the cruder manifestations of demonism, such as possession, to such an extent that in the present day, critics like Conybeare can say, with some degree of plausibility, "Why no demons any more?"[23]

But there are demons now, the claims of the critics notwithstanding. They are present today working in multitudinous less overt, but none the less real ways. Not only are there demons in so-called Christian civilized lands, but where Christianity and civilization have not penetrated deeply, demon possession and the grosser demonic manifestations are present too. The modern mission field, furnishes abundant evidence of this fact to the honest inquirer after truth. The reason is quite obvious. There the gospel coming into head-on collision with intrenched Satanic opposition and the pagan darkness of centuries, brings the operation and power of evil supernaturalism into sharper focus, and reveals demonic activity amazingly similar to that which occurred in the days of our Lord's earthly ministry.

---

[23]Cf. note 4.

Surveying the results of Christianity in China from 1552-1839 Kenneth Scott Latourette says: "Conversion appears often to have brought relief from the distressing malady known as demon possession."[24] Dr. John L. Nevius, a missionary to China from 1854 to 1892, in the prosecution of his Christian work there was faced with the question, which was constantly forced upon his attention: "Is there such a thing as demon possession in the latter part of the Nineteenth Century?" Dr. Nevius' experiences and careful, unbiased study of strange psychical phenomena in Shantung Province present unequivocal evidence of the widespread existence of demon possession in modern pagan China, the author recording numerous cases, thoroughly authenticated.[25]

What is striking in the accounts given by Dr. Nevius is their close correspondence with the cases of demon possession as recorded in the New Testament. For example, the subject at the time of possession passes into an abnormal state (cf. Mark 9:18). During the transition he is frequently thrown into a violent paroxysm, falling senseless on the ground or foaming at the mouth (cf. Mark 9:18; Luke 9:39, 42). During the attack he evidences another personality, his normal personality for the time being wholly or partially dormant (cf. Mark 5:7). The new personality presents traits of character utterly foreign to those characteristic of the demonized in his normal condition, and this change of character is practically always in the direction of moral impurity (cf. Luke 8:27). Many people while being demon-possessed display a superhuman knowledge. Frequently they appear to know the Lord Jesus Christ as a divine person and show a fear of Him (cf. Luke 8:31). They sometimes converse in foreign languages, of which in their normal condition they are totally ignorant. Prayer in the name of Jesus is the effectual remedy, some victims being delivered very readily, others with difficulty—more earnest intercession with fasting being necessary in some stubborn cases. In no instance, so far as appears, has the distemper returned, if the subject has become a Christian and continues to live a Christian life.[26]

F. F. Ellinwood, in the introduction to Dr. Nevius' book, *Demon Possession and Allied Themes,* thus writes illuminatingly

---

[24]*A History of Christian Missions in China,* p. 194.
[25]*Demon Possession and Allied Themes,* 5th ed., pp. 9-94.
[26]Nevius, *op. cit.,* pp. 143-145.

concerning demon activity in North China: "Antecedent to any
knowledge of the New Testament the people of North China
believed fully in the possession of the minds and bodies of men
by evil spirits. This belief is a part of that *animism*, or spirit
worship, which has existed in China—as in many other countries—
from the very beginning of history or tradition. . . . When therefore Christianity was introduced into China, and the narratives
of demon possession given in the New Testament were read, the
correspondence that was at once recognized by the native Christians
seemed complete. In relation to understanding this particular form
of New Testament miracle there has never been any difficulty on
the part of Chinese Christians."[27]

In an article in the Swedish weekly, *Missions Vannen*, entitled
"Demon Possession in Our Day,"[28] David Almquist, a missionary
to China, makes the following pertinent statement concerning the
New Testament passages that deal with demon expulsion by
our Lord and the early Apostles:

There are many person living in Christian countries who have some question
about these narratives. It seems that we do not meet such occurrences nowadays
and therefore many are inclined to doubt the existence of evil spirits. But
on foreign mission fields these powers of darkness manifest themselves in a
brutally realistic way. One frequently meets cases of demon possession in
those countries, that are counterparts of the instances recorded in the New
Testament. The struggle is intense; the opposition is determined; and one
must abide constantly at the Cross to obtain power for victory over these
forces of darkness.

Almquist appends a striking case of the deliverance of a notorious
Chinese demon-possessed medium by the earnest continuous intercession of Christians.[29]

William H. Chisholm, M.D., F.A.C.S., in the second in a series
of six articles dealing with his experiences as a medical missionary
in Korea, gives the graphic story of the casting out of a deaf
and dumb spirit from a woman for whom the best the hospital
staff could do was of no avail.[30] The case is strikingly similar to
the deliverance of the man's son who had such an unclean spirit

---

[27]*Ibid.*, p. iv.
[28]Translated by Oscar W. Hallin in the *Sunday School Times* for Feb. 28, 1942.
[29]*Ibid.*
[30]"Casting Out a Deaf and Dumb Spirit in Korea," *Sunday School Times*,
Jan. 1, 1938.

and to whom Jesus said, "Thou dumb and deaf spirit, I charge thee come out of him, and enter no more into him." (Matt. 9:25).

C. Gordon Beacham, missionary of the Sudan Interior Mission, thus writes of demonism in the Central Sudan, Africa:

The demons which the people worship are of various orders, each with its own name . . . While the air is supposed to be full of these terrifying spirits, the water is thought to be their special place of abode, reminding one of the Scriptural account of that unclean spirit which 'walketh through dry places, seeking rest, and findeth none.' Many other similarities are to be found between the records concerning demons in the New Testament and those in the life of these backward peoples. I have frequently seen natives who are covered from head to foot with scars of burning, some unseen power having taken possession of them and cast them into the fire. Such occult possession is not to be confused with mere dementia. The native recognizes the difference between insanity and demon possession, and calls each by its appropriate name. Actual conversation is held by normal people with the demons temporarily possessing another individual, and the words which come from the lips of the possessed one are, beyond doubt, the words of some other being.[31]

Robert S. Roseberry, missionary statesman of French West Africa, tells the same story of the paralyzing grip of demonism and superstition which enslaves the natives there. His general description of Africa may also be applied to paganism in South America, Asia, or the islands of the sea.

The powers of darkness hold in bondage countless numbers of the human race. One can easily trace each system back to the great destroyer, Satan himself. Different manifestations, but the same malignant power stands within the shadows, controlling and directing his forces of evil to the destruction of mankind.[32]

The enslavement of paganized peoples and those in Mohammedan lands is appalling. "Many superstitious beliefs hold the people bound all their lives. They become slaves to every practitioner of magic or trickery. This is true of the Mohammedans as well as the pagans."[33] Cases of present-day manifestations of demon possession may be multiplied, too, embracing almost every part

---

[31]*New Frontiers in the Central Sudan*, p. 86. For graphic cases of demon possession recorded, see pp. 86-7. For the difference between demonism and insanity, see *Demonism Verified and Analyzed* by Hugh W. White, pp. 12-20.
[32]*Black Magic*, p. 26. See also his larger volume, *The Niger Vision*.
[33]Roseberry, *Black Magic*, p. 39.

of the globe, but especially in pioneer districts, untouched by Christianity and the enlightenment which civilization brings with it.

C. Various Theories of Demon Possession

The actual expression "demon possession" does not occur in the New Testament, but apparently originated with Josephus,[34] from whom it has passed into ecclesiastical language. The New Testament speaks of those who "have a spirit, or a demon, or demons, or an unclean spirit," but principally of people who are "demonized" (*daimonizomenoi*) as applying to persons suffering from physical disease or mental derangement, under the possession of demons or evil spirits. With regard to the frequent and very prominent mention of demoniacs in Scripture, four principal opinions exist.

1. Unscriptural Views of Demon Possession

The unscriptural views scarcely merit serious attention, but since they are widely subscribed to and staunchly defended, they must accordingly be considered.

The Mythical Theory

The basic idea of this hypothesis, advanced notably by David Friedrich Strauss[35] and the mythical school, is that the whole narrative of Jesus' demon expulsions is merely symbolic, without actual foundation of fact. Demon possession, so-called, is but a vivid symbol of the prevalence of evil in the world, and the casting out of demons by our Lord, a corresponding figure of triumph over evil by His doctrine and life.

Suffice it to reply that in the Gospel accounts, the plain prosaic narration of the incidents as facts, regardless of what might be considered as possible in highly poetical and avowedly figurative passages, would make their statement here, in pure prose, not a figure or a symbol, but a lie. It would be as reasonable to expect myth or figurative fable from Thucydides or Tacitus in their accounts of the facts of contemporary history.

---

[34] Alfred Edersheim, *The Life and Times of Jesus The Messiah*, I, 479.
[35] David Friedrich Strauss, *Das Leben Jesu*, Zweiter Band, Seite 21-52.

The Accommodation Theory

The proponents of the accommodation theory say that our Lord and the Evangelists, in making reference to demon possession, spoke only in accommodation to the prevalent ignorance and superstition of their auditors, without making any assertion as to the actual existence or non-existence of the phenomena described, or the truth or falsity of current belief.[36] It is concluded, that since the symptoms were often those of physical disease (as blindness and dumbness, Matt. 12:22; epilepsy, Mark 9:17-27), or those appearing in common dementia (as in Matt. 8:28; Mark 5:1-5), and since the phrase "to have a demon" was apparently used as equivalent "to be mad" (John 7:20; 8:48; 10:20), and since it is erroneously assumed that cases of demon possession are not now known to occur in our day, therefore, our Lord spoke, and the Evangelists wrote, in adjustment to the common convictions of the time, and with a view to being clearly understood, especially by the patients themselves, but that the "demonized" were merely persons afflicted with uncommon diseases of body and mind.

This ingenious, but false, theory is completely incompatible with the simple and direct attribution of personality to the demons (as much as to men, angels, or God), and, if carried out in principle, must subvert the truth and integrity of the Holy Scripture itself. It is completely overthrown by the single fact of the violent effect caused by the entrance of the demons into the Gadarene swine, which excludes any idea that our Lord or the Evangelists did not assert or imply any objective reality in possession. The theory also employs the popular fallacy, that since demon possession does not occur today—contrary to the testimony of modern missionary history—therefore it never occurred. But even if it were granted that it does not occur today, that would not at all prove that it never existed.

But the essential idea of the accommodation theory is in itself unsound. For our Lord did not speak of demons only to the ignorant and superstitious and uninitiated multitudes, but also in His private instruction to His own disciples (Matt. 17:19-21). Accommodation, however, is practicable, when in things indifferent,

---

[36]Cf. A. A. Hodge, *Outlines of Theology*, p. 257.

language may be employed, which, although etymologically or scientifically inaccurate, yet conveys a true impression (as, "the sun has set"), or, when in things not indifferent, the declaration of truth (I Cor. 3:1-2) is given, which is precise and correct, as far as it goes, but imperfect and partial, because of the arrested or stunted progress of the hearers.

But in the case of demon possession, the matter was far from indifferent. The age was one of scant faith and appalling superstition. Would Jesus sanction, and the evangelists be permitted to record, an idea essentially false, which has continually been the stronghold of superstition? How unthinkable, when superstition, in things of far less moment, was denounced by our Lord (Matt. 23:5, 16-20)!

The Hallucination Theory

Demon possession is explained, under the hypothesis of hallucination, as a mere psychological delusion on the part of the victim, who, diseased and distraught, becomes wrought up to such a high pitch of emotional frenzy or mental excitement that he imagines himself possessed and controlled by another and more powerful being.[37] Under the suppression of human consciousness and the dethronement of reason, he speaks in the character of the fancied demon (Mark 5:7). The cure of this strange illusion is virtually the same as the ejection from him of a real demon.

The theory fails to explain how a person, so bereft of reason, can in the same instant, manifest a knowledge of Jesus' deity and sonship (Mark 5:7) far in advance of the most pious and enlightened people of the whole nation. Nor does it explain the violent effect of the entrance of the demons into the swine (Mark 5:13), which alone is enough to demonstrate the absurdity of supposing the possession to be only an imaginary one.

2. THE SCRIPTURAL VIEW OF DEMON POSSESSION

It is obvious that all attempts to explain cases of demon possession other than as actual occurrences, and in the simple and plain sense in which they are portrayed in the sacred Record,

---

[37]Cf. John J. Owen, "The Demonology of the New Testament," *Bibliotheca Sacra and Biblical Repository*, XVI (January 1859), 124-25. See also Nevius, *op. cit.*, pp. 147-50.

are weak and totally inadquate. It is therefore necessary to present the Scriptural view, which is the natural and literal interpretation of the Biblical narratives, viewing possession as an actual state of inhabitation and control by one or more demons.

As wicked, unclean, and vicious spiritual personalities, willing subjects of their leader Satan, demons were divinely permitted a special activity and manifestation during the days of our Lord and His disciples, to exercise a direct influence over certain persons by residing in them, and thus deranging both mind and body. The influence, exerted by this means, is no doubt to be distinguished from the usual power of temptation and attack wielded by Satan under the permissive will of God. Its relation to it seems to be that of a miracle to God's ordinary providence, or of prophetic inspiration to the regular gifts of the Holy Spirit. Both methods of Satan are actuated by the same general principles and they accomplish the same general results, in attempting to hinder the purpose of God for humanity and in extending the sway of evil supernaturalism; but demon possession seems to be a special and direct manifestation of that which is ordinarily worked out in Satanic temptation by a course of indirect action.

In ordinary temptation and the usual assaults of Satan, the human will yields consciously, and, by yielding, gradually assumes, without forfeiture of its evident freedom of action, the characteristics of the Satanic nature. It is allured, solicited, and persuaded, despite the strivings of divine grace, but *not overborne*. But in demon possession, at least of the spontaneous or involuntary type,[38] the victim seems to undergo a complete or incomplete deprivation of reason or the power of choice, with his personality so eclipsed or overwhelmed as to produce the consciousness of a twofold will in him. Still, however, possession is only a special, and, as it were, miraculous exhibition of the power Satan has over fallen human nature; and there can be no doubt that an examination of its antecedents, probably in the vast majority of cases, would

---

[38]For the distinction between spontaneous (involuntary) possession and voluntary possession, see Oesterreich, *Possession, Demoniacal and Others among Primitive Races in Antiquity, the Middle Ages, and Modern Times,* p. 131.

prove that it was rendered possible, in the first instance, by the repeated consent of the sufferer to temptation and to sin.

Indications are not lacking that sins of sensuality may, in many cases, be the precursors of this awful affliction. The binding power and tyranny of sensual habit and indulgence are matters of common observation. In the case of the libertine, the dope-addict, and the drunkard (especially when struggling in the last throes of delirium tremens), there are many marks of similarity to Scriptural possession. There is, of course, in them also the factor of physical disease, but there is frequently something more.

It is to be noted also that the state of possession, although so frightful in its wretched sense of demoniacal tyranny, might, because of the very fact of that consciousness, be less hopeless and more amenable to instantaneous cure than sins involving deliberate choice and willful hardening of the heart. Some of the actions of the possessed would seem to indicate that the human spirit still retains a keen desire for purity and deliverance (Mark 5:7), although through the flesh and demon power working through the medium of the flesh, it is enslaved. The suddenness and the completeness of demoniacal cures (Matt. 12:22; Mark 5:15), similar to suddenness and thoroughness of conversion, observed in cases of sensualism, compared with the greater difficulty in instances of more refined and spiritual sin, would seem to confirm the thought that sensual transgressions especially were the precursors of the demoniacal state.

It is perhaps not without significance that almost all the cases of demon possession are recorded as occurring among the rude and half-Gentile populations of Galilee. John, dealing mainly with the ministry in Judaea and Jerusalem, where the population seemed to have been more cultured and refined, does not mention an actual case of possession or expulsion, but emphatically recognizes the existence of the phenomenon (John 7:20; 8:48; 10:20). It was, it would seem, natural for the Satanic method to assume the special form in numerous instances of possession in an age of such unprecedented and brutal sensuality as that which preceded the Messiah's Advent, and to continue until the cleansing power of Christianity was felt. This is also why the phenomenon still occurs in rude and Satan-dominated, so-called "heathen," lands.

D. The Nature of Demon Possession

Much apparently remains obscure concerning the precise nature of the demoniacal state, and yet Scripture gives ample detail for the construction of a fairly full and comprehensive picture of the phenomenon.

1. Demon Possession and the Responsibility of the Possessed

Various answers have been given to the question as to what degree the demonized are accountable for their condition. Theories vary from assigning complete responsibility to denying any accountability whatever. Although in the great majority of cases possession is doubtless to be traced to yielding voluntarily to temptation and to sin, initially weakening the human will, so that it is rendered susceptible to complete or partial eclipse and subjugation by the possessing spirit, yet it is scarcely possible to ascribe it in every instance as originating in such moral and responsible conduct; for Mark describes the case of the demonized boy as having been such "from a child" (9:21). In this case, at least, some other reason must be assigned for the child's exposure to demon invasion. If demonization is of the nature of a miracle in the realm of evil, it is futile to attempt to explain it, in every instance, on the basis of natural causation. There may be special divine permission of unusual Satanic operation to accomplish some extraordinary purpose of divine wisdom in accordance with the principles of the divine sovereignty.

Whatever causes may, or may not, be assignable to any given case of possession, one thing is certain, the demonized are incapable of separating their own consciousness and mental processes from the influence of the demon, and their own identity and free volition are merged, and to that extent lost, in that of their invaders.[39] This loss of what may be called "individualism," or the consciousness of a distinct and self-determining individuality, with the power of self-origination in mental and moral actions, which distinguishes the human soul from the animal, accounts for the hideous, inhuman, and often bestial behavior of the demonized. Their conduct is not due to mental disease, where injury to

---

[39] Cf. Nevius, *op. cit.*, pp. 144-5.

the brain or nervous system may cause previously existing mental impressions to be excited without corresponding outward stimuli, as in maniacal disorders, nor is it due to vice, as involving the power of moral self-origination and self-action, but it is attributable to the presence of an inhabiting superior power of evil.

The pivotal question is whether indwelling by the possessing spirit is temporary or permanent. If it is permanent, it is obvious that it involves little or no moral element and consequent responsibility in the possessed; for his personality with its mental and moral actions is completely monopolized by the overpowering demon. In such an event, the only real responsibility to be assigned the victim would be any liability he might have incurred by moral choice in initially laying himself open to the demoniacal state. On the other hand, if the demonized condition is not a permanent condition, the demonized might, in moment of relief, shake himself free from the malignant and overshadowing power, or seek release from it. In that case, the demonized state would involve personal responsibility, although of a diseased and disturbed consciousness. That such a responsibility is involved seems certain, inasmuch as "neither the New Testament, nor even rabbinic literature, conveys the idea of permanent demoniac indwelling,"[40] from which idea the later term "possession" owes its origin. Such New Testament examples as the evangelists record, as that of the scene in the synagogue at Capernaum (Mark 1:21-28), convey the impression of a sudden influence, provoked, it would seem in most cases, by the personal presence and words of the Christ.

It is very difficult, in analyzing the language and conduct of the demonized, to determine whether what is said or done is to be attributed to the demonized or to the residing demon. Indeed, in the presence of a dual consciousness, it must always be remembered that there is a mixture of the human and the demonic. The demonized speaks and acts like a person, under the control of a demon. Edersheim maintains "the demonized would speak and act in accordance with his previous demonological ideas."[41] This seems very reasonable, and would account for indications of popular superstitions in the time of Christ in the conduct and language of the demonized, without attributing to Christ such accom-

---

[40]Edersheim, *op. cit.*, I, 481.
[41]*Ibid.*, I, 609.

modation to the popular notions of the day, as is not only untenable in itself but incompatible with the spirit and language of the narratives.

2. DEMON POSSESSION AND DISEASE

Scripture, while carefully distinguishing between demonic possession and natural disease (Matt. 4:24; 8:16), nevertheless, represents many sicknesses such as dumbness, deafness, and paralysis as due to demon inhabitation (Matt. 9:32-33; 12:22; Mark 5:5; 9:17-18). But as *all* who were dumb, deaf, or paralyzed are not described as demonized, it is evident that all physical or even mental disorders of the same class are *not* ascribed to the same cause. Some may be natural, while others may be demonic.[42] On the other hand, since the demonized state always involves the derangement of body or mind or both, due to demonic and not natural causes, there are, accordingly, always symptoms of disease, more or less violent, in every demonized person; and the severity of these distempers is greatly accentuated in the last fierce paroxysm when the evil spirit quits his habitation. This is an indication that demonic action is primarily upon the nervous system, which forms the nexus between the body and the mind, and the varied physical effects are caused by the different parts of the nervous system acted upon.

Although a particular disease, caused by a demon, may in some cases be permanent, it does not follow that those who are so affected are permanently or constantly under the power of the demon. It seems the disease may remain, even though the person may not, for the time, be in the demoniac state. There is clear indication that the cure of sicknesses caused by demonic power, but not restored while the victim is in the demonized state, as well as diseases due to natural causes, are spoken of more specifically as "healings" (Matt. 10:1; Mark 1:32-34; 6:13; Acts 8:7; 19:12), while actual restoration *in* the demoniac states are more definitely classified as casting out of demons (Mark 1:26, 39; 5:8; 9:28). The more comprehensive term "healing" is, however, sometimes employed to designate both, as obviously the restoration of any derangement of body or mind, whether from natural or demonic cause, whether in the demonized state or out of it, is a healing (Matt. 4:24; 12:22).

---

[42]Cf. A. A. Hodge, *op. cit.*, p. 257; and Nevius, *op. cit.*, pp. 175-206.

Although the demonized state is in some respects similar to maniacal disease, it must not be confused with it. In both there is a loss of individuality, and the consequent power of free and independent choice in moral and spiritual matters. But, whereas in the demoniac, this damage is due to occupancy by an evil spirit, in maniacal disorder it is traceable to physical causes such as disease, or injury to the brain or nervous system.

But after making all allowances for cases of insanity and mental disease which arise from physical injury or derangement of those bodily organs through which the mind expresses its powers, there are yet many more instances where the disorder is certainly to be traced to metaphysical causes, acting upon and deranging the mind itself.

Indeed, in all cases where the malady lies in the mind, and not in the body, to diagnose it as only disease or insanity is merely to state the fact of the disorder and refer it to a class of cases which are known to exist, but to attempt no explanation of its cause. Even in disease, where the mind acts upon the body, as in nervous disorders and epilepsy, the mere disorder of the physical constitution is not the whole reason for the distemper. There is a deeper cause lying in the mind.

It remains to be proved, therefore, that in the many varied and complicated phenomena of so-called physical and mental "disease" in the present day, there is none that may not be attributed to demonic causation. And furthermore, it remains to be demonstrated that there is none in which one gifted with "discernings of spirits" (I Cor. 12:10) may not see clear evidence of genuine demonization.

As W. Menzies Alexander, M.D., says, "The symptoms of the possessed have their parallels among the insane of today, the confession of Jesus as the Messiah *alone* excepted."[43] If this statement from a medical man is true, then demon possession exists today; for certainly the limits of genuine possession cannot, as Dr. Alexander curiously maintains, be confined to what he calls "the classic criterion of genuine demonic possession—the confession of Jesus as Messiah."[44] This was obviously a conspicuous feature of the

---

[43]William Menzies Alexander, M.D., *Demonic Possession in The New Testament*, p. 172.
[44]*Ibid.*, p. 173.

Gospel narratives because of the personal presence of the Messiah in the flesh and, in the very nature of the case, was limited by occasion and circumstances to the earthly ministry of our Lord. It could not possibly occur in demonic phenomena, as there is not the slightest occasion for it. To point to the Messianic confession as the only "superphysical element" in the Biblical accounts of the demonized, and to say the remaining phenomena but demonstrate "the physical element or the presence of mental disease,"[45] is, as noted, to state the fact of the disorder but to give up all explanation of its cause.

The truth is that the Bible, on this phase of the subject as is the case in many other fields of inquiry, without contradicting everyday experience, advances to a realm whither human science cannot follow. As Dr. Alexander himself confesses:

. . . to modern psychological medicine, these (demons and spirits) are un-known as causes of disease. They involve a theory which is alien to the principles of *scientific* pathology.[46]

As generally, Scripture goes back to original causes and refers the introduction of physical and mental suffering into the human race to the Adamic fall, and assigns the power of physical and moral evil to a personal and spiritual source.[47] In addition, it teaches the reality of subservient spirits of evil, who, through the power they are permitted to exercise over the soul and indirectly over the body, are the agents in causing certain physical and mental diseases. This action, however inexplicable it may be to the natural man, as all operation of spirit upon spirit is found to be, cannot *a priori* be declared impossible or improbable, and no one has a right to "eviscerate" the virile expressions of the Scripture "in order to reduce its declarations to a level with our own ignorance."[48]

3. DEMON POSSESSION AND DEMONIC INFLUENCE

It is important in considering the function of evil spirits in Satan's kingdom, as Lewis Sperry Chafer points out, "to distinguish

---

[45]*Ibid.*, p. 171.
[46]*Ibid.*, p. 61.
[47]Cf. Hugh W. White, *Demonism Verified and Analyzed*, pp. 80-93.
[48]Barry, *op. cit.*, p. 585.

between demon possession or control, and demon influence."[49] The New Testament gives ample warrant for making such a differentiation. To demon possession only unbelievers are exposed; to demon influence, both believers and unbelievers. In the one case, the personality is actually invaded, the body inhabited, and a dominating control is gained; while in the other instance, attack is made from without, through pressure, suggestion, and temptation.

The very nature of the believer's salvation, as embracing the regenerating, sealing, indwelling, and filling ministry of the Holy Spirit, placing him "in Christ," eternally and unforfeitably, is sufficient explanation why he is not liable to demon inhabitation. The unbeliever, however, being under "the prince of the powers of the air, the spirits that are now working in the sons of disobedience" (Eph. 2:2, Weymouth), is by the very nature of his plight a prey to all Satanic power and demonic malignity, both from within and from without. And there is no apparent reason why he may not, as in the time of our Lord and His Apostles, suffer demonic invasion of his personality to the partial or total eclipse of his individuality and thus manifest all the symptoms of the possessed, the confession of Jesus as the Messiah, alone excepted.

The believer, we may confidently rest assured, although perpetually faced with the subtle power and cunning of the foe from without, is shielded from the enemy within the gates. But it must not be supposed that disobedience and persistent waywardness in the believer may not eventuate in "a sin unto (physical) death" (I John 5:16), or to the solemn delivering of "such a one unto Satan for the destruction of the flesh, that the spirit may be saved in the day of the Lord Jesus" (I Cor. 5:5). Whatever else this grave procedure may mean, it unquestionably involves severe chastening of the believer who is guilty of immorality, sensualism, or other gross sins, that he "may not be condemned with the world" (I Cor. 11:32). Delivering over to Satan, although seemingly a kind of last-resort method in the divine healing with antinomian abuse of grace, can scarcely mean liability to the demonized condition. But it does mean exposure to demon influence, to physical sickness, perhaps, to mental disease, and certainly, at times, to physical death.

---

[49]Chafer, *Satan*, p. 64.

Demonic influence may assume a great variety of forms. Its sign is always departure from the faith, or the body of revealed truth, and may manifest itself in open apostasy (I Tim. 4:1), or in doctrinal corruption and perversion of the truth, evident in a multiplicity of cults and sects, producing Christian disunity (I John 4:1-2). If an orthodox creed is adhered to, it may show itself in ritualistic formalism, or empty adherence to the letter without the spirit (II Tim. 3:5), or in hypocrisy (I Tim. 4:2-3). Demon influence in doctrine leads to corrupt conduct and practice (I Cor. 10:16-22), resulting in worldliness (II Tim. 3:4) and uncleanness (II Pet. 2:10-12).

Believers who would be spiritual and live victoriously face a tremendous conflict with Satan and demons, who vehemently oppose true spirituality and Christian usefulness (Eph. 6:11-12). The panoply of prayer (Eph. 6:10-20), faith (I John 5:4), and the Word of God (Matt. 4:4, 7, 10), combined with a knowledge of Satanic devices (II Cor. 2:11), are the Christian's resources for triumph.

4. Demon Possession and Exorcism

Strictly speaking there are no exorcisms in the Bible. Use of the word, in its essential etymological meaning, forbids its employment with regard to the expulsion of demons by our Lord or His disciples. The word signifying, as it does, the casting out of evil spirits by conjurations, incantations, or religious or magical ceremonies, is singularly appropriate to describe Jewish and ethnic practice, but is in salient contrast to that of our Lord and His followers, who employed no such methods.

Among ancient and primitive peoples, exorcism depended to a great extent on the efficacy of magical formulas, commonly compounded of the names of deities, and repeated with exorcistic ritual over the bodies of those demon possessed. Power to cast out demons was regarded as existing in the words themselves, and great importance was attached to the correct recital of the right formulas and proper performance of the prescribed ritual.

The prevalent phenomenon of exorcism among the Jews in the time of our Lord (Matt. 12:27) and of the Apostles (Acts 19:13-20) loses its singularity in view of its wide ethnic distribution, manifested, for example, not only in the incantation texts of ancient Babylonia and Assyria,[50] but also in the large numbers of magical papyri, which have been discovered, showing how widespread ancient belief in demonic possession was.[51] And the lengths to which the absurdities and cruelties of superstition have carried men in this direction are amazing.

In the case of Josephus, one is astonished to see how, even in the instance of an educated Jew, the most abject superstition colors his thinking on such subjects. He attributes no little part of Solomon's wisdom to the fact that "God enabled him to learn the skill which expels demons."[52] He also recounts a cure, which he alleges to have seen "in the presence of Vespasian and his sons," performed in accordance with methods of incantation ascribed to Solomon. In the nostrils of the demoniac was placed a magic root, prescribed by Solomon. The demon is fantastically represented as being drawn through the nostrils of the victim, and proof was furnished that exorcism had actually occurred, by placing a vessel of water nearby, which the demon, in compliance with the previous command of the exorcizer, overturned in his hasty exit.[53]

The absurdities and extravagances of this ridiculous incident are more than equalled by the account of an exorcism related in the *Book of Tobit*. The heart and liver of a fish, miraculously caught, are burned upon the ashes of incense, and the resulting smell and smoke disgust and drive away a demon.[54] Rabbinical writers offer little relief from this fanciful vein, but run the gamut of diseased morbidness in their recital of long and repulsive details of various exorcistic methods.[55]

Jesus' method of setting the demonized free is in clear-cut contrast to these Jewish and ethnic exorcisms. His was always the same, and consisted neither in magical means nor in ritualistic rigmaroles, but in His own living word of infinite power. He spoke, and the demons obeyed Him as Lord of the spirit world. In one respect all those who were demonized exhibited the same phe-

[50]Morris Jastrow, *Hebrew and Babylonian Traditions*, p. 202. Also, Robert W. Rogers, *The Religion of Babylonia and Assyria*, 146 ff.

[51]Weiss, *op. cit.*, pp. 402-3. And for a general historical survey of Christian exorcisms, see Oesterreich, *op. cit.*, pp. 100 ff.

[52]Josephus, *op. cit.*, 8:2:5.

[53]*Ibid.*

[54]*Tobit* 6:7; 8: 2-3.

[55]Edersheim, *op. cit.*, II, 775-76.

nomenon. They all recognized Jesus and owned His power (Mark 1:24, 34; 5:7).

The phrase, "in the name of Jesus," (Mark 16:17; Luke 10:17) did not signify that the sacred appellation, formally pronounced, possessed any magical power to accomplish a cure. The "name" was tantamount to the infinite Person behind the name. The expression "in His name" was thus equivalent to "in His power," "in all that He is and does." While it is said that Jesus "cast out the spirits with a word" (Matt. 8:16), the word is obviously not ritualistic, but authoritative. Jesus' own explanation of the method and power used in His expulsions is given when He said, "But if I by the Spirit of God cast out demons, then is the kingdom of God come upon you" (Matt. 12:28). It was, accordingly, by the power of the Holy Spirit, operating in untrammelled fullness in His sinless humanity, that Jesus effectuated His cures, rather than by reliance upon His intrinsic power of deity as the second Person of the Godhead.

The simplicity and effectiveness of the method of Jesus and His disciples in casting out demons, and the loftiness of their demonological conceptions in general, stand in the more arresting antithesis to current thought and usages, when it is realized that the lower range of ideas and practices actually prevailed among the people with whom the Lord and His followers came into constant contact. When the Pharisees attribute the cures wrought by Jesus to demonic agency (Matt. 12:24), they seem to imply that the popular notion of the way to wield control over demons was by obtaining, through magic, power over Beelzebub, the prince of the demons. In reply, Jesus maintains, that since the demons are evil, control over them can come only by opposing them in the power of God.

In His answer to the charge of the Pharisees, Jesus refers to the Jewish exorcists, "who in one way or another, were casting out evil spirits."[56] "If I by Beelzebub cast out demons, by whom do your sons cast them out? Therefore they shall be your judges" (Matt. 12:27). Christ does not defend nor attack these exorcists in this passage. He merely makes reference to them in His argument with their fathers. Plumptre contends Jesus' question requires for its logical validity the admission that the children of the

---

[56]G. Campbell Morgan, *The Gospel According to Matthew*, p. 130.

accusers did really cast out demons, and, that not by Beelzebub.[57] In that case the Pharisees stood self-condemned; for thus were they bringing an accusation against Jesus, to which their own sons were thereby exposed. Plumptre further suggests that one need not assume that the alleged power of Jewish exorcists to cast out demons was always a pretence, or rested only on spells and incantations. He thinks earnest prayer, fasting, and faith may well have been found among the better and truer Pharisees, and resulted in genuine expulsions.[58]

Lange would acknowledge Jewish exorcisms, and holds that they in no way invalidate the authority of the miracles of Jesus. He suggests that the two are fittingly to be compared to the wonders performed by Moses and those wrought by the magicians of Egypt (Exod. 7:8-13, 20-24; 8:6-7, 16-19;9:11), where miracles by evil supernaturalism (magic), in imitation of the divine power, could go so far, and no farther.[59]

Whereas Jesus' reference to Jewish exorcists seems to be to actual expulsions, and that not by evil power, the question is, can ethnic and Jewish exorcistic rites be allowed actual demonic expulsions, under the principle of evil supernaturalism, as Lange suggests? This would seem hard to deny in the face of such widespread and continuous practice of exorcistic ritualism. But at first sight it would seem to be excluded by the Saviour's reference to the inevitable collapse of a divided kingdom or house, or to Satan casting off Satan, or to the despoiling of the strong man's house (Matt. 12:25-29). Upon closer scrutiny, however, it will be discovered that Jesus' reference is solely to the *hostile* invasion of the kingdom of darkness by the actual and effectual power of light, wherein Satan suffers *real* and permanent injury. There is no allusion to Satan's own deceptive, and seemingly self-injurious methods, which are but a feint to extend his power and sway. Jesus is certainly not denying the power of the prince of the demons to allocate his satellites where he sees fit, or to effect their removal from a particular abode, if only temporarily (Matt.

---

[57]E. H. Plumptre, *New Testament Commentary for English Readers,* ed. by C. J. Ellicott, I, 130.

[58]*Ibid.*

[59]Johann Peter Lange, *A Commentary on the Holy Scriptures,* (Matthew), p. 224.

12:43-45), to deceive, to excite fear and dread, and to inspire demon worship. Such expulsions are *not* divisions in the Satanic kingdom, nor Satan casting out himself, but keen Satanic strategy and diabolic miracle to build up and spread out the empire of evil.

As regards Jewish exorcists specifically, it does seem clearly implied by Jesus' allusion to them, that they did, in some cases at least, expel demons, and that not by evil power. Jesus' immediate and emphatic reference, however, to His own expulsions "by the Spirit of God," and in His case the consequent sudden, unexpected coming of the kingdom of God upon His accusers, when they were totally unprepared to receive it (Matt. 12:28), is ostensibly intended as a vivid contrast to *all* exorcistic methods. These methods were ostentatious, elaborate, ritualistic, and superstitious. His method was uniquely simple, instantly and unfailingly efficacious, and thoroughly uncontaminated with showy ritual and ignorant superstition. And yet, despite the character of Jewish exorcisms, there is no dogmatic reason why the rich grace of God might not, in many instances, have overlooked the ignorance and the extravagance of the methods employed, and beneath it all heard the cry of genuine faith and distress and wrought deliverance.

One very important fact, however, must be noted. Although the Shema, "Hear, O Israel, Jehovah our God is one Jehovah" (Deut. 6:4), and similar formulas were employed in Jewish exorcisms, they were never, as Christian expulsions, "in the name of the Lord Jesus" (Act. 19:13). This pregnant phrase necessarily implies personal faith in Jesus as the Christ, and is equivalent to "in His power." The incident, in which the only Biblical reference (Acts 19:13) to the professional exorcist (*exorkistes*) occurs directly by name, is an illustration of this fact. According to the narrative, a group of travelling professional Jewish exorcists, who, of course, were not Christians, witnessing the powerful and instantaneous cures wrought by Paul at Ephesus (Acts 19:12), attempted to do the same by a mere ritualistic use of the name of the Lord Jesus. Their complete and ignominious failure is represented as being due to their lack of faith in the living Christ, by whose power such miracles of healing were wrought, although they were letter-perfect in the use of the formula.

The demons recognized and obeyed Jesus as Lord of the spirit-world. And they knew and heeded Paul as a servant and ambassador of Christ. But an attempted magical and superstitious employment of the name of Jesus, so far from effecting any control over them, instead lay the exorcists open to their punitive fury to impress upon them, and upon all, the error of mixing Christ with magic, and truth with superstition. It is highly significant that the demonstration of God's power in this glaring exposé of superstition resulted in a great revival, in which many who "practiced magical arts" burned their books (Acts 19:19).

Dr. A. C. Gaebelein thinks that those who are mentioned elsewhere (Mark 9:38-39; Luke 9:49-50), who drove out demons by using the name of the Lord Jesus, "but did not follow Him, might have been Jewish exorcists."[60] This, however, is extremely unlikely in view of the incident at Ephesus, and in the light of what the New Testament understanding of the expression, "in My name," implied in the way of faith and obedience. These were, in all probability, men who had received a vision of faith in Jesus as the Messiah, but did not, or could not, attend upon Him constantly, as did the Twelve.

---

[60]A. C. Gaebelein, *The Gospel of Matthew*, p. 248.

CHAPTER VII

BIBLICAL DEMONOLOGY AND MAGIC

EARLY ISRAEL'S virile monotheism was bound to clash violently with surrounding paganism. Its exalted revelation of divine truth could not help exposing the darkness and superstitious ignorance of every form of idolatry. Its own chaste and lofty demonology could not fail to furnish an adequate criterion for appraising the complexities and crudities of pagan practices. Moreover, in the light of Israel's sublime conception of God, refining and purifying every department of its theological thought, especially its demonology, it is not surprising to find the greatest contrast between its belief in demons and the notorious excesses and extravagances of neighboring nations, which, though steeped in gross idolatry, were more or less allied to them.[1] It is also not amazing to discover in the religious literature of ancient Israel, and throughout the entire Bible, the most direct and outspoken hostility toward every type and form of pagan practice and heathen ritual as demoniacally inspired and energized by evil supernaturalism.

Little wonder that Moses, in his parting counsels to Israel, in view of their impending entrance into their covenanted possession of the Promised Land, gives solemn warning and issues stringent prohibitions against every kind of idolatrous custom. Little wonder that he brands anyone who "useth divination," or "practiceth augury," or an "enchanter," or a "charmer," or a "consulter with a familiar spirit," or a "wizard," or a "necromancer," as "an abomination unto Jehovah" (Deut. 18:11-12). Little wonder that he brands these practices as themselves "abominations," and lays the sin of trafficking in them as the actual reason why Jehovah drove these people out of the land before them (Deut.

[1]Franz Delitzsch, *Mehr Licht*, p. 51, and T. K. Oesterreich, *Possession, Demoniacal and Other*, pp. 147-8.

18:12). His clarion call is for the strictest and most uncompromising separation from these defilements and works of darkness, that they might be "perfect with Jehovah" their God, who "hath not suffered" them to do as the heathen (Deut. 18:13-14).

The history of Israel in the land is the recital of a continuous contest with demonic powers of darkness, relentlessly attempting to bind the people of God with cruel fetters, and foist upon them the idolatrous doctrines of demons, against which the great Law-giver of the nation had given such stern warning. At times the battle lagged, as in the latter days of Solomon, when his lapse into demonism and idolatry took its gigantic toll, in the disruption of the kingdom. Henceforth Israel and Judah went their separate ways, both eventually to be drawn themselves into the vortex of demonism, and to be driven from the land, as the heathen nations before them had been.

All Israel's woe may be traced to her defection from Jehovah and her complicity in pagan practices. These heathen customs, so destructive and disastrous to the people of God, assume the shape of various forms of demonology, which are met and condemned in the Word of God. Magic, divination, prognostication, sorcery, witchcraft, necromancy, and ventriloquism are so inextricably connected with idolatry, and so inseparably interwoven with each other, in their character and history, that it is impossible, in every case, to draw definite lines of demarcation between them. Like idolatry itself (Deut. 32:17; Ps. 96:5; 106:36-37; I Cor. 8:4; 10:19-20; Rev. 9:20), of which they are but particular manifestations, demonism is their source and dynamic, and a study of them is the revelation of the depraved heart of paganism.

Notwithstanding the risk of overlapping, it seems advantageous, for the sake of clarity and logical arrangement, to group these seven forms of demonology characteristic of pagan practices, under three principle heads—magic, divination, and necromancy.

A. The Evil Character of Magic

Magic may be defined as the art of bringing about results beyond man's power through the enlistment of supernatural agencies. Its wicked and illegitimate nature at once appears when it is realized that the supernatural agencies used are evil spirits.

The term, in its true scope, thus involves more than what is often classified under this category, such as legerdemain, sleight of hand, or clever jugglery. Sometimes, of course, it is nothing more than shrewd imposture, and cunning manipulation of natural phenomena;[2] but more frequently, as it is encountered in ancient history and in the Bible, it embraces the activity of demons producing "wonders through their knowledge of the powers of nature."[3]

There can be no doubt, if only the authority of divine revelation is allowed a voice, that magic, in the strictest and truest sense, is a departure from religion. Adherence to the testimony of Scripture must ever result in the conclusion that all religions are due to a primitive revelation, the false being corruptions of the true. The connection between magic and religion is very arresting. It is obvious from its character, that it can have no legitimate place in true spiritual religion. And it is also apparent that impersonal magic, which is a species of crude science, viewing natural forces in the world as utilizable under certain conditions, such as incantations, magical acts, and drugs, has little or no connection with religion. But, in personal magic, where living, intelligent, personal agents are appealed to, influenced, and controlled, the connection is real. The magical acts may, in the less corrupt stage, include sacrifice, and the incantations may not be very dissimilar to prayer. Therefore, personal magic, in its higher forms, shades off into religion, and not infrequently do the two exist together.

Although it is a common practice to speak of sacrifice and prayer as constituent elements in ancient and modern religions, it is highly questionable whether such terms, in many cases, are appropriate, as they certainly do not bear the same connotation as they have in Old and New Testament Scriptures. True prayer can be addressed only to God and, since the paternal revelation of Himself in His Son, it is in the name of Jesus Christ. The moment prayer or other religious exercise is directed to any other —deities, angels, demons, or saints, it loses its genuine character, and becomes tinged and contaminated with magic. This magic

---

[2]This is the opinion of R. S. Roseberry concerning the present-day practice of magic by African natives: "While there are undoubtedly true manifestations of demoniacal powers . . . a fair percentage of the magic practiced is trickery, pure and simple." *Black Magic*, p. 39.

[3]Emil Schneweiss, *Angels and Demons According to Lactantius*, p. 129.

may be said to be present in greater or less degree in all non-Christian religions, and also to exist in corruptions of Christianity. It may be said that the more corrupt and degenerate a religious system becomes, the more it is vitiated by the element of magic. The ethical element then wanes, or even disappears. Incantations may be thought of as crude prayers, where the main stress is laid on the mode of utterânce, rather than on the moral condition of the agent. Plants, drugs, and incense, when burned to court the favor of good spirits, or to protect against mischievous and malevolent ones, are but magical perversions of true spiritual sacrifice.

The link between magic and immorality is, therefore, not an imaginary one. The unethical means employed correspond to the unethical nature of the spirit-beings dealt with. In monotheism, where God is infinitely righteous and holy, and demands moral qualifications on the part of those who have dealings with Him, there is no place at all for magic. In proportion as there is deterioration and the element of magic increases, in that proportion does morality sink to a lower level and evil supernaturalism take control.

B. THE BIBLICAL CONDEMNATION OF MAGIC

The attitude of Scripture, inculcating, as it does, the high ethical and spiritual religion of Israel under the Old Covenant, and the sublime and perfect revelation of truth in Christianity under the New, must of necessity be hostile and completely condemnatory of all magic and magical arts. This attitude, especially on the part of the Old Testament, must be strange and inexplicable to those who would trace the source of Israelite religion to anything other than monotheism. But it is perfectly normal, and exactly what would be expected, if Israel's religion began in a divine revelation of truth, despite the fact that the adjoining nations were completely abandoned to superstition, and had elaborate magical rituals.[4] The wide extent of the magical arts may be comprehended from the fact that Scripture alone refers to their being practiced in Babylon (Ezek. 21:21), Assyria (II Kings 17:17), Chaldea (Dan. 5:11), Egypt (Exod. 7:11), Canaan

---

[4]T. Witton Davies, *Magic, Divination, and Demonology among The Hebrews and Their Neighbors,* pp. 64-71.

(Deut. 18:14, 21), Asia (Acts 19:13, 19), and Macedonia (Acts 16:16).

1. Its Old Testament Condemnation

The one great reason which induced the Hebrews to condemn magic was, of course, because it clashed completely with the moral and spiritual religion of Israel, and was intimately and inseparably linked with idolatry. To the Hebrews, deities worshipped by other peoples were evil spirits or demons, with which magicians and diviner's trafficked. To practice magic or divination, or to support them, was to them, at least to the God-fearing and orthodox among them, tantamount to an acknowledgment of idols. This is the reason that Hebrew names for heathen gods (*shedhim, seirim, 'elilim, gad*), which really denoted the demons behind the visible idolatrous representations, have been so translated in the Septuagint.

In II Kings 9:22, magic seems actually to be identified with idolatry, where the "whoredoms" ("idolatries"), and "witchcrafts" (*keshaphim*, "magical incantations") of Jezebel are mentioned. It was a dark day for Judah when Manasseh opened wide the flood gates to demonism, and the practice of every sort of magical art, and, in his idolatrous orgy, "made his son to pass through the fire, and practiced augury, and used enchantments, and dealt with them that had familiar spirits, and with wizards" (II Kings 21:6).

The divine displeasure against this fearful eruption of occultism, which may be taken as characteristic of the divine attitude against all magical arts in general, is graphically set forth in the word of the Lord: "I will bring such evil upon Jerusalem and Judah, that whosoever heareth it both his ears shall tingle. And I will stretch over Jerusalem the line of Samaria, and the plummet of the house of Ahab; and I will wipe Jerusalem as a man wipeth a dish, wiping it, and turning it upside down" (II Kings 21:12-13).

Scripture, on the other hand, just as clearly acknowledges the reality and power of magic as it points out its illegitimacy and heinous wickedness. In the account of the plagues (Exod. 7-11), it is taken for granted that the magicians of Egypt had real power to perform miraculous feats by evil supernaturalism. It is clearly not mere jugglery nor sleight of hand. They are actually represented as throwing their rods down, and they became serpents, and turning the water of the Nile into blood. It is only when they attempt to produce gnats that they fail, showing their power was great, but definitely limited.

It is true the magicians did "in like manner" to Aaron and Moses "with their enchantments" (*belahatehem*, "with their hidden or secret arts"). But this does not signify imposture or fraud. They were not imposing on Pharaoh's credulity, as some suppose,[5] any more than on Aaron's or Moses' perspicacity. These "sacred scribes" (*hartemmim*), skilled in religious writing (hieroglyphics), belonging to a class of Egyptian priests learned in occultism, and conversant with demon-controlled religion, were the instruments of Satan, who manifested his power in them. Similar traffickers in the "black arts" practiced them in Babylon (Dan. 1:20; 2:2, 27; 4:7, 9; 5:11). What they did in the presence of Moses, Aaron, and Pharoah were "lying wonders." The names of two of these agents of darkness, Jannes and Jambres, endued with demonic powers, are given in II Timothy 3:8.

Such mighty demonstrations of demon power seem to occur periodically, like religious revivals, and are found today in spiritism. Occult power will be fully revealed in the tremendous latter-day demonic revival under the Antichrist, which will be attended by phenomenal signs and wonders (II Thess. 2:9-12; Rev. 13:13-18).

Despite the purging effect of Hebrew monotheism and the stern warnings of the law, traces of magic cropped out occasionally, in spite of the uncongenial soil in Israel. The teraphim mentioned in Genesis 31:19, 30, and again, as put away with "familiar spirits, and the wizards . . . and the idols, and all the abominations," during the drastic reforms of Josiah (II Kings 23:24), were household gods in all probability, employed as charms to ward off evil spirits of every kind and to bring good luck.

Rachel's keen desire for the mandrakes, which had been given to Leah by her son, seems to be an example of the popular heathen belief in the magical power of plants, here the "love apple," to stir up sexual passion (Gen. 30:14-24). Instances of the same superstition occur in Arabic literature in connection with what

---

[5]Dwight M. Pratt, "Enchantment," *International Standard Bible Encyclopedia*, p. 942.

is called "Yabruh," which is almost certainly the same plant.[6] Indeed, it would seem the common appearance of magic as a love charm, often exercised by women, is the likely explanation for adultery and magic being frequently named together in the Old Testament (II Kings 9:22; Nah. 3:4; Mal. 3:5).

In the apostasy of Isaiah's day, when occultism had so invaded every phase of life that the "diviner" and the "skilful enchanter" were named among honorable warriors, prophets, and judges (Isa. 3:2), the prophet sternly denounced the wanton women of Jerusalem, not only because of their pride and vanity, as exhibited in their gaudy finery and ostentatious jewelry, but also because many of the fashionable trinkets, such as the "crescents" (*saharonim*, "moonlets" or "moon-shaped amulets") were nothing more than counter charms worn around the neck to protect against evil spirits, and, as such, meant an acknowledgment of heathen religion (Isa. 3:18). Among pagans such protective crescent talismans were even put around camels' necks, as in the case of the Midianite chieftains, whom Gideon slew (Judg. 8:21, 26).

It seems likely that the earrings worn by the Israelites in the desert, out of which the golden calf was made, were amulets (Exod. 32:2 ff.). It is significant that at Bethel Jacob not only put away the idols ("strange gods"), but also the earrings, the latter being as much at variance with Yahwism as the former, because of their heathen origin and import (Gen. 35:1-4).

Israel is urged, under the figure of the wife of the prophet Hosea, to put away her whoredoms from her face" (that is, the nose-ring which was a charm against the "evil eye") and "her adulteries from between her breasts" (that is, the necklaces, also worn as amulets) (Hos. 2:2). These ornaments, when worn, signified sympathy and complicity with heathenism, where they were regarded as defensive against the "evil eye."

Condemnation of the custom of wearing amulets and of trusting in the defence of mere material objects is implied in Proverbs 6:21. A young man is exhorted to "bind" parental admonitions continually upon his "heart," and to "tie" them about his neck. It is significant that the Talmudic word for "an amulet" (*gemia'*) denotes something tied or bound to the person.

---

[6]T. Witton Davies, "Magic, Magician," *International Standard Bible Encyclopedia*, III, 1963-4.

Evidence seems to point to the fact that the phylacteries, worn so ostentatiously by the Pharisees in the time of our Saviour (Matt. 23:5), have a magical connotation. It is certain the practice of using them has no genuine Biblical support, and was introduced by a mere external interpretation of Exodus 13:9, 16, and Deuteronomy 6:4-9; 11:13-21. The Greek name *phulakterion*, whence the English term *phylactery*, in the New Testament period denoted a safeguard, in the form of a counter-charm or defense (*phulasso*, "guard" or "protect") against evil influences. To explain the Greek word as denoting an agency or device to lead the people "to keep" the law is scarcely defensible. This original idea may well have existed in the minds of those who, by a crude literalism first reduced a purely figurative and idealistic Old Testament phrase to a materialistic representation. But this initial corruption only opened the way for further degradation and abuse to fit the mould of the materialistic and superstitious practices of the pagans, so that very soon the most excessive reverence became attached to phylacteries; and, following the general tenor of rabbinic demonology, it was not long before they were regarded as amulets with magical power to avert evils and drive away demons (*Targum on Canticles* 8:3). It is not at all surprising, in view of the essential unscripturalness of the whole custom of wearing phylacteries, that they should have become the prolific source of other abuses besides superstition; and it is but what would naturally be expected, when our Saviour is seen denouncing the empty pride and arrant hypocrisy which this unscriptural custom sheltered and encouraged (Matt. 23:5).

A closely allied case of the perversion of a Biblical concept, under the impact of popular magic, is connected with the literalizing of the same figurative Old Testament passages, whose misconstruction gave rise to phylacteries. The injunction to write the words of Jehovah upon the "door-posts" (*mezuzoth*) of their houses and upon their "gates" (Deut. 11:20) led to the actual inscription of the words from Deuteronomy 6:4-9 and 11:13-21 upon folded parchment, which was encased in a little box, called the "Mezuzah" and exhibited over the doorpost of a Jewish home, to the right of the entrance.[7] Although the word "Mezuzah" occurs over a dozen times in Biblical Hebrew, it is invariably in the sense

[7] Alfred Edersheim, *The Life and Times of Jesus the Messiah*, I, 76, 228.

of "door" or "gate-post," and never in the sense of an amulet put on the door-post, which the Hebrew word came to denote in later Judaism.

2. Its New Testament Condemnation

The New Testament, of course, places the same stern ban against every form of the magical art as does the Old Testament. The sinister and corroding reality of the art of magic is everywhere acknowledged, and the manifestation of its polluting influence is everywhere inexorably denounced.

In Matthew 6:7, Jesus condemns needless repetition in prayer, which savored of the heathenistic modes of magical incantation. "Do not repeat yourself (*me battologesete*) as the heathen." Unless such pagan contamination had been prevalent among the Jews of His day, the Saviour would not have deemed it necessary to give this warning. Repetitions of certain formulas were among the ancients, as among certain modern ascetics of India, considered efficacious in proportion to the number of times they were recited.[8] The same spirit prevails among Moslem dervishes, who multiply their shrieks and whirlings, imagining the more this is done the greater is the power which Allah has over them. According to Herodotus,[9] Battos, a Greek poet, stuttered and employed many repetitions; so the verb *battologeo* ("to prattle, babble, talk excessively") is mimetic, and very expressive.

The Book of Acts contains several striking examples of the clash of Christianity with magic. The first illustration is Simon, the magician of Samaria (Acts 8:9-24).[10] The immediate occasion of the exposé of his demoniacal powers was the potent Samaritan revival under Philip's preaching. This sinister character is described as one "who beforetime in the city used sorcery" (*prouperchen mageuon*, "had been practicing magic") and had "amazed the people of Samaria, giving out that himself was some

---

[8]Davies, *Magic, Divination, and Demonology among the Hebrews and Their Neighbors*, pp. 59, 60.

[9]*Herodotus*, edition by A. D. Godley, I, 55.

[10]For an excellent discussion of Simon the Magician see Sir W. M. Ramsay, *The Bearing of Recent Discovery on the Trustworthiness of the New Testament*, 4th ed., pp. 117-131. On the magicians in the Book of Acts, see Ramsay, *op. cit.*, pp. 106-116.

great one" (Acts 8:9), pretending he was more than human. He appears as a cunning exponent of evil supernaturalism, and as a malign instrument of Satan. He belongs to a class—all too common at the time—that of Jews trading on the mysterious religious prestige of their race and imposing on the credulity of the heathen, boasting, in addition to their sacred books, of supernatural powers, exercised through spells, charms, and incantations which they alleged had come down to them from King Solomon.[11]

The mighty miracles attending Philip's evangelistic campaign (Acts 8:6-7) were performed to show the power of God, to attest the preaching of the truth, and to expose the counterfeit evil works of Simon. He, like the ancient Egyptian magicians, had to own the divine omnipotence (Acts 8:13).

The instance of Bar-Jesus, the magician of Paphos in Cyprus, is parallel to Simon of Samaria, and marks another vivid collision of Christianity with magic. Bar-Jesus is more fully and specifically identified than Simon, but both were of the same class: Jewish sorcerers, especially endued demonic emissaries of Satan. The former is designated as "a certain sorcerer" ("magos" or "magician"), "a false prophet, a Jew" (Acts 13:6), "Elymas, the sorcerer" ("the magos, the magician") (v. 8), "son of the devil" (v. 10), the latter term linking him directly and intimately with the prince of the powers of darkness.

The title "Magos," used of Bar-Jesus, is of pre-eminent interest and import because it is the identical word rendered "Wise Men" (Matt. 2:1, 7, 16), and descriptive of the distinguished visitors who came from afar to worship and present gifts at the feet of the infant Saviour. But in the case of these eminent sages the word is used in a good sense; whereas, in the case of Bar-Jesus, the connotation is distinctly evil. Even in the days of Sophocles the bad signification had already begun to attach to it; he makes Oedipus revile Tiresias under this epithet, as practicing magic.[12] The Magi, even in Herodotus' time, had gained a reputation for magical arts.[13] It is significant that the English word "magic" is

---

[11]On the character of magicians and the diversity of their art in New Testament times, see Ramsay, *op. cit.,* pp. 106-113.

[12]*Oedipus, Rex.* 387.

[13]W. St. Clair Tisdall, "The Magi," *International Standard Bible Encyclopedia,* III, 1962-3.

derived from the name of the Magi, or Zarathustrian (Zoroastrian) priests. Magic is, hence, historically the art practiced in ancient Persia by the recognized priests of that country. The term "Magi" is used in the Septuagint, by Philo, Josephus, and profane writers "alike in an evil and, so to speak, in a good sense."[14] In the former case, the practice of magical arts is implied; in the latter, researches involving the study of the stars and the heavenly bodies,[15] and other deep knowledge; though of course it was not untinged with superstition. To this latter group the Magi portrayed by Matthew must have belonged, and they may be thought of as the scientists of their day, the heirs of the learning of Babylonia and of the lore of ancient Persia.[16]

It is not difficult to perceive how easy it would be, in an ancient age of unparalleled superstition, and in lands unilluminated by divine revelation, for such a noble calling to degenerate, in many cases, into fraud, deception, and every form of occultism; so that, as in the instance of Simon of Samaria and Bar-Jesus of Cyprus, the exponents of the Magi were little more than demon-possessed magicians. There is scarcely any doubt that the Magi of Bethlehem belonged to a class that had come in contact with the purifying revelation of God's truth—perchance, through the children of the captivities, either in Babylonia, Persia, or Assyria; and we may confidently believe that this salutary influence kept them from occultism, and if not, at least from the grosser deceptions and pollutions of evil supernaturalism, evident in Simon and Bar-Jesus.

The Jewish magician has two names. Bar-Jesus is his Jewish patronymic. "Elymas" (*Elumas*) is an appellative name, or title, describing his claims to wisdom and supernatural powers. Luke interprets it as meaning "the magician" (*ho magos*) in Acts 13:8. It is derived either, as is generally thought, from the Arabic *alimun* ("wise, learned"), or, according to the more likely opinion of Delitzsch, from the Aramaic *'alima'* ("powerful").[17]

---

[14]Edersheim, *op. cit.*, I, 203; also Ramsay, *op. cit.*, p. 141.
[15]Cf. Johann Peter Lange, "Matthew" in *Commentary on the Holy Scriptures*, 8th rev. ed., p. 56.
[16]On the Magi at the birth of Jesus, see Ramsay, *op. cit.*, pp. 140-149.
[17]Franz Delitzsch, *Zeitschrift für die Lutheranische Theologie*, p. 7.

The sinister and malign character of Elymas appears when he "withstood" Paul and Barnabas, "seeking to turn aside the proconsul from the faith" (Acts 13:8). Special tools of Satan, such as he, frequently come into view in the Book of Acts—generally, as here, when the gospel was being carried into some new unevangelized region. In Samaria it was Simon; in Macedonia, the demon-possessed damsel; here in Cyprus, Elymas the magician. Paul's scathing denunciation of him may be taken as the Bible's condemnation of all magic and traffickers in occultism in general:

You who are full of every kind of craftiness and unscrupulous cunning—you, son of the Devil, and foe to all that is right, will you never cease to misrepresent the straight paths of the Lord? (Acts 13:10, Weymouth).

The Apostle Paul, warning of the grievous times of the last days when erroneous doctrine and occultism would abound and false teachers would resent and oppose the truth, as Jannes and Jambres, the magicians of Egypt, withstood Moses (II Tim. 3:1-12), declares that "evil men and impostors shall wax worse and worse, deceiving and being deceived" (II Tim. 3:13). "Impostors" (*goetes*, from *goao*, "to wail, sigh, utter low mystical tones") is employed of a class of magicians who chanted magical formulas in a strange guttural voice. Herodotus mentions them as being in Egypt,[18] and elsewhere.[19] They are also referred to by Euripedes, Plato, and subsequent writers.[20] The Hebrew New Testament of Salkinson and Delitzch render *goetes* by *qosemim* ("diviners"). "Sorcerers" would, perhaps, be the nearest English equivalent, and points to the subtle magical occultism to be encountered in the closing days of this age.

---

[18]*Op. cit.*, II, 33.
[19]*Op. cit.*, IV, 105; VII, 101.
[20]J. H. Thayer, *Greek-English Lexicon of the New Testament*, p. 120.

CHAPTER VIII

BIBLICAL DEMONOLOGY AND DIVINATION

A VERY PREVALENT manifestation of superstition and evil supernaturalism, divination plays a conspicuous role in human history, especially in the ancient world. Closely allied with magic and other demonological phenomena, it cannot easily be distinguished, in all cases, from them. It is always, however, characterized by man's inveterate and insatiable desire to know the future, which accounts for its widespread practice, in many lands, from the most ancient times.

A. THE MEANING OF DIVINATION

Divination is the art of obtaining secret or illegitimate knowledge of the future, by methods unsanctioned by and at variance with the holiness of God. Two main species exist. First, artificial divination, or augury, wherein dependence is placed upon the skill of the agent in reading and interpreting certain signs or omens. Second, inspirational divination, in which the medium is under the immediate influence or control of evil spirits or demons, who enable him to discern the future and to utter oracles embodying what he sees.

Ancient Romans were almost exclusively given to artificial divination, but the Greeks used mainly the inspirational type. Cicero, in his famous treatise on "Divination," clearly recognizes the two distinct ways of obtaining knowledge of the future, yet he disavows personal belief in any superhuman communication.[1] Despite the etymology of the Latin word *divinatio* (from *deus*, God, or *divus*, pertaining to God, divine), suggesting prognostication due to inspiration by superhuman beings, the term was confined almost exclusively to obtaining knowledge by outward signs.

---

[1]*De Divinatione*, I: 18; II: 63 ff.

The Greek soothsayer (*mantis*), of a more imaginative and emotional race, claimed to be inspired from without, and to be supernaturally informed, and in this respect bears a close resemblance to the Hebrew prophet. The Greek term for divination (*mantike*) is descriptive of the activity of the "diviner" (*mantis*), and scarcely ever signifies divination of the lower kind—by means of omens.

1. The Fundamental Assumption of Divination

The basic presupposition underlying all methods of divination is that certain superhuman spiritual beings exist, are approachable by man, possess knowledge which man does not have, and are willing, upon certain conditions known to diviners, to communicate this information to man. The word, in its etymological significance, as noted, carries with it the notion that the information is obtained, at least ultimately, from supernatural beings. Even Cicero, who would deny any superhuman communication on the part of the diviner, heartily endorses a definition of divination as "a power in man which foresees and explains those signs which the gods throw in his path."[2] Among the ancients generally (Babylonians, Egyptians, Greeks, Romans, and similar peoples), the conviction prevailed that not only oracles, but also omens of all description, are vouchsafed to men by the gods (demons), and express the mind of these supernatural existences.

Astrology, which is really astronomancy, is but one form of divination, and its fundamental concept is the attribution of personality to the celestial bodies, which are conceived as deities directing the destinies of men, and revealing future events. Even hepatoscopy, or divination by the examination of the liver of animals (Ezek. 21:21), certainly involves the common idea of supernatural beings behind the omen. The common explanation, that the liver was considered to be the seat of life,[3] and that the liver of an animal sacrificed (generally a sheep), took on the character of the deity to whom it was offered, seems probable. The soul of the animal, as seen in the liver, then became the reflector of the soul of the god. Whatever the significance might be, all methods and forms of divination presuppose supernatural person-

---

[2]*Ibid.*, II:63.
[3]Kohler Kaufmann, "Divination," *The Jewish Encyclopedia*, IV, 622-24. See also *Hebrew and Babylonian Traditions*, pp. 139-40.

alities; and the almost universal prevalence of divination, in one form or another in the ancient world, is a powerful argument for the existence of demons.

2. Divination and Magic

In a broader view, divination is but a species of magic. And if magic is defined, in its modern accepted sense, as the art of effecting results beyond human power by superhuman agencies, then divination is merely a specialized form of magic used in an attempt to obtain secret knowledge, especially insight into the future. The relation existing between divination and magic is similar to the relation between prophecy and miracle. Divination and prophecy imply special knowledge; magic and miracle special power. In prophecy and miracle the knowledge and power are divine. In divination and magic they are demonic.

3. Divination and Prophecy

Similarities between inspirational divination and Old Testament prophecy ought never to be allowed to blind one to their radical and essential differences. It is true that both take into account the human instinct for secret knowledge, especially that appertaining to the future, and they agree in the conviction that such knowledge is possessed by certain spiritual beings[4] who are willing, upon certain conditions, to divulge it, and that such secret information is imparted to special classes of men called diviners, seers, and prophets. But the likenesses end here. All the rest is in fundamental contrast.

The Old Testament prophet believed in a personal God, uniquely one, infinitely holy, righteous, and powerful, whose spokesman he claimed himself to be. When he spoke or wrote, it was by direct inspiration from the Spirit of God. "Thus saith Jehovah" was the authoritative formula that stamped his message with the finality and infallibility of divine truth. The Greek and the Roman "soothsayer" (*mantis*), on the other hand, having no sublime ethi-

---

[4]On the ancient belief that demons possessed knowledge of the future, see Emil Schneweiss, *Angels and Demons According to Lactantius*, pp. 128-29. T. K. Oesterreich says: "To primitive people the possessed stand as intermediaries between the world of men and the spirit-world; the spirits speak through their mouths." *Possession, Demoniacal and Other*, p. 236.

cal God, but gods many and lords many, went through various crude contortions, until he worked himself up to the necessary pitch of ecstasy, by music, drugs, sacrificial smoke, and similar helps. When, finally, in his insane excitement, he did speak, it was not truth by divine power, but error and deception by demoniacal cunning. In some instances he deemed it efficacious to swallow the vital part of the bird or beast of omen. The heart of a crow, mole, or hawk, thus imparted to him, he thought, the presaging soul of the creature.[5]

The *mantis* plied his art as a lucrative business, charging expensive fees, and refusing his services, when the emolument was not sufficiently remunerative. The oracular shrines were operated for selfish personal and political ends.[6] The Old Testament prophet, in complete antithesis, spoke as he was bidden by God. Personal ambition and selfish aims had no claim whatever upon him. Conviction and truth were all-important, no matter how these might clash with the desires of kings, dignitaries of the state, or the common people, and no matter what suffering, poverty, imprisonment, or even death, loyalty to God's Word might entail. Isaiah's fearless denunciation of Ahaz's sin in summoning the aid of Assyria (Isa. 7 ff.), as well as Jeremiah's scathing censure of the iniquitous actions of the leaders of the nation of his day (Jer. 2:36 ff.) are examples of godly intrepidity, beautiful to behold. Both of these valiant men of God suffered severely for their courage, especially Jeremiah, who stands out as one of the finest recorded examples of what, in the face of the most formidable opposition, a servant of God ought to be. Had Micaiah, the son of Imlah, lied to please the unscrupulous Ahab, he might have been clothed in purple and lodged in a palace. As it was, the unprincipled monarch could only fume, "I hate him, for he doth not prophesy good concerning me, but evil" (I Kings 22:1-25), and vent his offended rage by casting the prophet of God into a dungeon.

In view of the similar and yet antithetical nature of prophecy and divination, the early Church Fathers were correct in viewing

---

[5]T. Witton Davies, "Divination," *International Standard Bible Encyclopedia,* II, 863; also J. G. Frazer, *The Golden Bough: The Magic Art,* II, 355.

[6]The complete lack of the ethical element in divination is brought out by Bouché-Leclerq in the preface to his monumental work, *Histoire de la Divination dans l'Antiquité.*

the divination of heathenism as demoniacally inspired, and the aping work of Satan as discrediting the truth by producing phenomena among pagan races very similar to the operation of the Holy Spirit. Heathen divination is, then, not so much a corruption of prophecy, as a Satanic imitation of it. It is needless to say that the view of such anthropologists as Frazer,[7] and Tylor,[8] and such Old Testament scholars as Wellhausen and W. Robertson Smith, that prophecy is but a development from a higher form of divination, is totally at variance with the spirit and testimony of Scripture.

B. THE BIBLICAL DENUNCIATION OF DIVINATION

Pure Yahwism, in its basic principle, is and must ever have been inimical to divination of every type, despite the fact that the inspirational variety bears certain resemblances, and even affinities, to prophetism. The underlying thought of all forms of this forbidden art is that by resorting to certain means, at variance with an infinitely wise and holy God, men may obtain desired knowledge otherwise beyond their grasp. But since the religion of Israel made Jehovah the sole legitimate source of that information, and the prophet the constituted medium through which it came to men, all recourse to illegitimate methods, or appeal to spiritual beings other than God, or search for forbidden or illicit knowledge which could not pass the divine scrutiny, is taboo. This means, in short, that all divination of every form and description, is excluded from the religion of Israel.

Little wonder, then, that "one that useth divination," or "one that practiceth augury," is placed in the same category with the sorcerer, the medium, the wizard, and the necromancer, as "an abomination unto Jehovah," and is unequivocally condemned (Deut. 18:10-14); while the prophet of Jehovah is contrasted with diviners of all kinds, as the only authentic and duly authorized agent of supernatural revelation. Meanwhile, the antithesis furnishes the occasion for the sublime and far-reaching prediction of the coming of the supreme and perfect Prophet, the Revealer par excellence, of the heart of God to man, Jesus Christ, the Prophet of the prophets (Deut. 18:15-19).

---

[7] *Op. cit.*, I, 346; II, 355; III, 342.
[8] E. B. Tylor, *Primitive Culture*, I, 78-81, 117-133; II, 155.

The Deuteronomic passage also gives truth, as spoken by Jehovah through the prophet, as the basic criterion for evaluating the genuineness of an alleged spokesman of the divine revelation. If, like the heathen diviners, he speaks "in the name of other gods," or presumptuously, in Jehovah's name, what has not been divinely commanded him to speak, so that "the thing follow not, nor come to pass," he is to be accounted a false prophet of the stamp of pagan diviners, and to be put to death (Deut. 18:20-22). This regulation for the conduct of the people of God may seem harsh and unnecessarily severe. But not so. It was divinely framed to be obeyed strictly and uncompromisingly, so as to act as an efficient check against the formidable and ever-present peril of contamination from the almost universally prevalent heathen practice of divination. Its inexorable tone alone was consonant with pure Yahwism. The deliberate and persistent violation of its sound and health-ministering precepts is the only adequate and valid explanation of the presence of various forms of divination in the Old Testament.

It is emphatically not a case of the Bible's appearing, as Davies imagines, "to speak with two voices, generally prohibiting, but at times countenancing various forms of divination."[9] The Scriptural attitude toward divination is *always* that of prohibition and condemnation, never that of favor or abetment. As the revelation of the divine will, the Bible enjoins things as they ought to be. As divine truth it portrays them as they are. And though things as they are may be far from what they ought to be, and may, in the divine patience and forbearance, be temporarily allowed, they are, nevertheless, still under the same divine sentence of censure and disapprobation, whether such is openly expressed at the time or not.

1. CASES OF ALLEGED BIBLICAL SANCTION OF DIVINATION

The case of Balaam (Num. 22-24) is often cited as an instance in point where divination is tacitly or expressly sanctioned in the Bible. Careful analysis of Balaam's character, however, will demonstrate that this is a hasty and inaccurate conclusion. That he was a heathen diviner, whose words of blessing or cursing were

---

[9]Davies, *op. cit.*, p. 861.

believed, at least among the heathen, to have magical efficacy, cannot be denied (Num. 22:6). He is explicitly called "Balaam . . . the soothsayer" (*haqqosem*, "the diviner") (Josh. 13:22); and the elders of Moab and Midian, who went to fetch him for Balak, king of Moab, to curse Israel, took with them the alluring bribe or fee for such service, called *qesamim*, "the rewards of divination" (Num. 22:7). As a heathen diviner, he also resorted to "enchantments" (*nehashim*, from *nahash*, referring to the hissing, serpentlike utterances of divinatory formulas) (Num. 24:1).

The question is, Was Balaam, the soothsayer, the diviner, also a prophet of Jehovah? Nowhere is he called a prophet, though plainly he does the work of a prophet, and it is scarcely possible to conceive of anything more magnificent in all prophetic literature than the parables he delivered, which bear, in every detail, the superlative seal of divine inspiration.[10] It is certain, too, that he had communion of some sort with God (Num. 22:9, 20, 22-35; 23:4, 16). He is plainly a heathen magician under the divine dealing, who, very probably, like Jethro (Exod. 18) and Rahab (Josh. 2), was conducted to acknowledge Jehovah by the overpowering influence of God's prowess manifested in Egypt and in the wilderness, which had made an indelible impression upon the neighboring nations (Exod. 15:14; Josh. 2:9-10; 5:1). He resolved to serve Jehovah, probably with the ulterior motive that serving such a powerful God would be more lucrative. He, therefore, decided to perform his enchantments henceforth in Jehovah's name.

Balaam's case is indeed a strange anomaly. He knew the Lord, Jehovah of the Israelites, but his knowledge was dimmed and distorted by heathenistic corruptions, and vitiated by covetousness. Such a combination of paganistic magic and personal greed with the service of Jehovah could not be permanent or static. It was compatible only with a transitional state in his experience of the divine dealing. He must soon abandon his heathenism and his inordinate love of gain, or give up Jehovah. The period of decision

---

[10]R. A. Watson speaks of elements in these oracles "that have the ring of inspiration" (*The Expositor's Bible*, I, 457). For an exhaustive study of this subject, see *The Soothsayer, Balaam* by Serafim, Bishop of Ostrog., published in England in 1900. Cf. also, L. E. Binns in *Westminster Commentaries* (1927), and J. H. Greenstone, *Numbers with Commentary*.

was fast approaching when the message of the king of Moab reached him.

Balaam took his first step backward in his ascent out of paganism, when, in secret hope of base gain, he refused the directive for the permissive will of God (Num. 22:12, 20). His second act of retrogression occurred, when, with liberal sacrifices, and the employment of elaborate enchantments (24:1), he persistently, but vainly, tried to cajole Jehovah into allowing him to curse Israel (Num. 23:4), so that he might reap the rich reward of the wages of unrighteousness. It was not until he saw that Jehovah was inflexibly set to bless Israel, that he forsook his vain enchantments, and his mercenary ambition, and yielded himself to the ennobling influences of "the Spirit of God"—which then "came upon him" (24:2). Thus, for a time, he became a genuine prophet of Jehovah. Here was the final opportunity for his better nature, in the rich grace of God, to assert itself permanently over the dark forces of paganism. But he rejected his chance, and chose base gain. He taught Balak how to corrupt the people, whom he could not curse (Num. 25:1-3; 31:8, 16). His wicked example of covetousness, and of easy world-conformity, as the typical hireling religious teacher, serves as a repeated warning throughout Scripture (Mic. 6:5; II Pet. 2:15; Jude v. 11; Rev. 2:14).

In the light of these essential facts concerning Balaam, what shall be said to the claim that his case constitutes a Biblical sanction of divination? "So far," we are told, "is his vocation from being censured, it is actually called into the service of Yahweh."[11]

To this charge, it may be replied, that Balaam's case is ostensibly altogether unique and special. To begin, he is a heathen, a Gentile, and an enemy of Israel. Yet in the sovereign will and wisdom of God, he is raised up to be a prophet (a phenomenal and un-heard-of thing for a non-Israelite), and in spite of himself, is inspired and constrained to prophesy blessing upon Israel. The fact that he was also a pagan diviner, and was lifted up to the dignity of an inspired prophet, is only one of the many exceptional, and altogether singular, features of the whole extraordinary incident. To take this feature as an example of the Biblical sanction of divination, is, however, totally unwarranted, in view of Balaam's previous knowledge and intercourse with Jehovah, as a heathen

[11]Davies, *op. cit.*, p. 861.

soothsayer coming out of paganism, and inasmuch as the whole episode represents him as being under the divine preparation and discipline for the demonstrably special task of being the instrument by whom God would testify on behalf of His people rather than, as usual, to them.[12]

Jehovah's sovereign and special use of Balaam as his mouthpiece, despite the fact that his knowledge of truth was clouded and corrupted by heathen conceptions, appears in the manner in which he is enabled to deliver his prophetic parables. While he sought enchantments (Num. 23:15; 24:1), in his pagan ignorance and superstition, in vain attempts to wheedle Jehovah into permitting him to curse Israel to further his secret hankering for material gain, nothing is said of his being inspired by the Holy Spirit. It is, apparently, simply a mechanical procedure, seemingly independent of his moral state, and in no sense is it to be construed as a sanction of his vocation as a diviner, nor of his personal avarice. "And Jehovah put a word in Balaam's mouth" (Num. 23:5, 16). It was not until Balaam saw the futility of his enchantments to affect Jehovah, whom he discovered altogether righteous and holy, and not until he turned away from his pagan ritualism, as well as from his own sordid plan to change Jehovah's will for personal advantage (24:1) that "the Spirit of God came upon him" (24:2). He thus attained the status of a *bona-fide* prophet of Jehovah— but only after renouncing his heathenism. Surely, in this there is no sanction of heathen divination, tacit or expressed. Rather the implication is unequivocal condemnation.

Balaam's own testimony concerning Israel, which is really Jehovah's "word in his mouth" (23:16), is most pertinent and conclusive: "Surely there is no enchantment with Jacob" (*nahash*, "divinatory method of any kind in Jacob"), "neither is there any divination with Israel" (*qesem*, "divination of any sort in Israel") (Num. 23:23). His subsequent lapse, after his special task was finished, is beside the point, and in no way affects the incident as a revelation of the Biblical attitude toward divination.

Another instance, often cited, of the alleged Biblical sanction of certain forms of divination, is the case of dreams. And there is

---

[12]For a suggestive study on this subject, see William Foxwell Albright, "The Oracles of Balaam," *Journal of Biblical Literature*, 63 (September 1944), pp. 207-33.

no doubt that Scripture assigns to them, at least to those of a certain variety, an important place as a legitimate means of revealing future events. In fact, in dispensations of God's dealings with man, unconnected with regularly constituted prophets, and with limited or no written revelation, as in the days of the patriarchs (Gen. 31:10-14; 37:5-9), and judges (Judg. 7:9-14), or in periods before the giving of the Holy Spirit (John 7:39) or the completion of the Scriptural canon, as in the case of all Old Testament saints, there is no reason why the divine method of revelation may not have made use of the medium of involuntary dreams, or such as come unsought, for guidance in human affairs. Neither is there any reason, as far as moral considerations are concerned, why God may not make use of involuntary dreams in any dispensation, particularly as a special means of leading in human affairs (Matt. 1:20; 2:13; Acts 2:17). It is true, in this age of the indwelling Holy Spirit, with a full written revelation to guide, that we walk by faith, and have no need of such special methods of guidance (II Cor. 5:7). Yet even now, should God see fit to lead in this extraordinary manner, there would be nothing in it incompatible or inconsistent with His holiness, neither would it savor of divinatory means, since it would involve no search for secret or illegitimate knowledge through methods at variance with the divine character, for by its very nature it is God-given, and involuntary on the part of the human instrument.

On the other hand, the case is quite different with dreams that are voluntary, and sought for, and which are thus definitely divinatory in character. These are unqualifiedly condemned in the Word of God. To this variety belong such dreams as are induced by what is termed "incubation," or sleeping in some shrine where the patron god of the place is believed to reveal his secrets to the sleeper. Herodotus makes mention of this practice among an Egyptian tribe by the name of the Nasamonians, who used to practice divination by sleeping in the graves of their ancestors. The dreams which came to them there were stoutly believed to be revelations from the deified progenitors.[13] There is reference to this heathen superstition in the Bible, where it is catologued among other heathen abominations, and sternly denounced as a pagan corruption to which God's people yielded. They are

---

[13]*Herodotus,* edition by A. D. Godley, IV, 172.

described as those who "sit among the graves, and lodge in the secret places (vaults)" (Isa. 65:4). Solomon's dream (I Kings 3:1-15) came to him at the high place of Gibeon; but it was manifestly God-given, involuntary on the king's part, and not a case of incubation.

Besides the foregoing examples of inspirational divination, certain types of the artificial, or augural variety, have been adduced as countenanced by Scripture. Among the latter, sortilege, or the casting of lots, is the most conspicuous. With regard, however, to the Biblical practice, it is very questionable whether the custom can be classified as divinatory at all, at least not under any ordinary definition of the term. In cases where it is used legitimately, and by God's people, it is not in any sense an "art," but a simple process like drawing straws, or flipping a coin. No abstruse or forbidden knowledge of the future is sought, but some simple matter of very practical import, as, for example, which of the two goats was to be sacrificed to Jehovah, and which was to be driven alive into the desert (Lev. 16:8-10), or, which of two men very similar in qualifications and abilities was to be chosen to take Judas' place (Acts 1:26). No methods were employed, either, which were unsanctioned by, or at variance with, the divine holiness. The lot was simply a pebble, or a potsherd, or a bit of wood. If people were to be selected, their names were inscribed on their respective lots, which were thrown together into an urn, shaken together, and he whose lot first fell out upon the ground was chosen.[14] Hence, the expression, "the lot falls upon" someone (cf. Acts 1:26).

Jehovah himself gave direction for the apportionment of the land of Canaan "by lot" (Num. 26:55). He specified the choice of the two goats on the Day of Atonement, one for Himself and one for Azazel, by lot (Lev. 16:8). The divine direction for the apprehension of Achan was by lot (Josh. 7:14). Always, when properly used by God's people, it was associated most intimately with Jehovah's leading. The invariable attitude among the pious was: "The lot is cast into the lap, but the whole disposing thereof is of Jehovah" (Prov. 16:33). Very likely the same principle of the lot was operative in the *Urim* and *Thummim* of the high priest. These two words, though etymologically obscure, stand for two objects,

---

[14]Homer, *Iliad*, III, 316, 325.

perhaps, stones, one denoting "yes," or its equivalent, and the other "no." Whichever the high priest took from his ephod was believed to be the answer to the question asked.

Nothwithstanding the divine permission of the employment of the lot, a practice in itself harmless enough, yet it is a question whether or not its prevalent use in Old Testament times was not a divine accommodation to the undeveloped spirituality of "children under the rudiments of the world" (Gal. 4:1-3). Certainly, now when God has "sent forth the Spirit of His Son into our hearts" to guide us (Gal. 4:6-7), we have no need of such "elements." It is highly significant that the last Scripturally recorded use of the lot by God's people was just *before* the Holy Spirit came (Acts 1:26) to "guide into all the truth" (John 16:13).

A peculiar species of divination by water, called hydromancy, is sometimes alleged to be recorded by the Bible without disapproval. Joseph, in Egypt (Gen. 44:5), is said to have practiced this form of augury without censure on the part of the narrator. But Joseph purposely represents himself to his brothers as making use of the silver cup which was hidden in Benjamin's sack for divinatory purposes, merely to enhance the value of the cup. It is plain from the circumstances of the story that he did not actually so use it. However, many forms of hydromancy were practiced among ancient nations, as among modern Arabs and others. Generally, a precious stone, or a piece of gold, or silver was thrown into a vessel containing water. The resulting movements of the water and the images formed were construed according to certain fixed signs.[15]

Gideon's fleece is frequently referred to as another instance of augury implicitly approved of in Scripture (Judg. 6:36-40). But the sign is clearly a divine accommodation to Gideon's faltering faith and persistent plea for such an omen (Judg. 6:17, 36, 39), and, not at all, an implied approval of his method of ascertaining the divine will. The Angel of Jehovah (deity) had appeared to him, and given him repeated and remarkable assurances of his success against the Amalekites (Judg. 6:12, 14, 16), which should have been fully sufficient for all normal requirements of faith, without his asking for further corroboration.

---

[15]*The Geography of Strabo,* XVI: 11:39.

Thus, even these foregoing cases, which some deem doubtful, demonstrate how consistently and steadfastly the religion of Israel set itself against augury. This fact is all the more remarkable when one recollects how rife this augural type of divination was among all the environing peoples. It is the more inexplicable, too, to those who would deny the evidence of special divine guidance in every phase of Israelitish history.

The divine condemnation of the "one who practiceth augury (*me'onen*) (Deut. 18:10) is unequivocal. But the precise etymology of the Hebrew term is uncertain. Some would derive it from the root '*anan* ("to cover"), "one who practices hidden or occult arts." This explanation, though, has no real support from usage. Others would connect the word with '*anan* ("cloud"), "one who observes the clouds with a view to obtaining an oracle." Still others would make it a denominative from '*ayin* ("eye"), "one who smites with the evil eye." But nothing in the context would suggest any of these views. The most likely explanation is that the expression is from the Semitic root meaning "to emit a hoarse nasal sound" (Arabic, *ranna*), such a sound as was customary in reciting magical formulas (Lev. 19:26; II Kings 21:6). "The oak of Meonenim" (*'elon me'onenim*, "the augurs' terebinth") is interesting as an ancient tree, near Shechem, famous for divination, which the Canaanites consulted, very likely, in some augural way (Judg. 9:37).

2. Cases of Unequivocal Biblical Condemnation of Divination

All divination savors of idolatry, and, as such, is anathema to God. Some forms are so crude and gross as to call forth special divine denunciation. Of such a mode is hepatoscopy, or "looking in the liver" (Ezek. 21:21). This method was very prevalent in the ancient world among the Babylonians, and other Semites, and among the Greeks and the Romans. Although one of the most ancient and venerable forms of prognostication, it is still in vogue in Burmah, Borneo, and Uganda. No evidence is available that it was ever practiced among the Israelites. In the passage from Ezekiel's prophecy, the king of Babylon is said to have "looked in the liver." This verse is classic for the description of the three kinds of divination common among the Semitic nations (arrows, entrails, and teraphim).

As a specific variety of the general term for "divination," *qesem*, the primary idea of which is probably that of "cutting" or "dividing," like the Arabic *qasama* ("to divide out"), the significance to be attached to hepatoscopy seems clearly to be "division." Each of the various parts of the liver, the lobes, the ducts, and so forth, had a special importance assigned to it. The theory, apparently, is that the god to whom the animal was sacrificed revealed his will by the manner in which he fashioned the organ, which was considered to be the seat of the victim's life.

Belomancy, or divination by arrows, is represented by Ezekiel as being practiced in Babylon, along with hepatoscopy and consulting the teraphim: "For the king of Babylon stood at the parting of the way, at the head of the two ways, to use divination (*qesem*); he shook the arrows to and fro, he consulted the teraphim, he looked in the liver" (Ezek 21:21). The arrows were either marked in such a way as to indicate certain courses of action, and one was drawn or shaken out, or else they were thrown promiscuously into the air, and the augury was deduced by the way in which they fell to the earth.

Rhabdomancy, or divination by the use of the divining rod, is referred to by Hosea, as practiced by the Israelites in their defection and apostasy. The prophet condemns it. "My people ask counsel at their stock" (*'tz*, "tree" or "piece of wood"), "and their staff" (*maqlo*, "divining rod") "declareth unto them (their oracles)" (Hos. 4:12).

"Consulting the teraphim" (I Sam. 15:23; Ezek. 21:21; Zech. 10:2) is a form of divination which may have been effected by consulting the dead. This seems very likely, if, as is probable, the teraphim were ancestral images, superstitiously raised to the rank of household gods. The method of consultation is not known. It is not impossible that the modern medium's frequent use of a portrait of a deceased relative, for the alleged purpose of entering into communication with the departed spirit, may furnish a hint.

An extreme mode of obtaining an oracle is the one almost certainly referred to in the cruel and inhuman heathen practice of sacrificing children by burning. This is corroborated by its inclusion in the context of Deuteronomy 18:10, where the words "maketh his son or his daughter to pass through the fire" assuredly indicates human sacrifice, and the sense is "that burns his son or his daughter in the fire." Commenting on this passage, Keil and Delitzsch aptly remark:

> Moses groups together all the words which the language contained for the different modes of exploring the future and discovering the will of God, for the purpose of forbidding every description of soothsaying, and places the prohibition of Moloch-worship at the head, to show the inward connection between soothsaying and idolatry, possibly because februation, or passing children through the fire in the worship of Moloch, was more intimately connected with soothsaying and magic than any other description of idolatry.[16]

Astrology, or astromancy, is another form of divination condemned in Scripture. Although no explicit mention is made of it in the Deuteronomic list (Deut. 18:9-15), it is certainly to be closely associated with Moloch-worship. Two very difficult passages (Amos 5:25-26 and Acts 7:41-43) seem plainly to link the cult of Moloch with the worship of the planet Saturn. Although some scholars deny this, there appears ample support, both in the Hebrew, and in the Septuagint of the passage from Amos, that the prophet is alluding to the worship of Saturn, and planetary divination in general—and, as connected with Moloch-worship and Israel's apostasy of the golden calf. "Did ye bring unto me sacrifices and offerings in the wilderness forty years, O House of Israel? Yea, ye have borne the tabernacle of your king (*siccuth malkecem*, LXX, *skenen tou Moloch*), and the shrine (*kiyyun*) of your images, the star of your God, which ye made to yourselves" (Amos 5:25-26).

Stephen, quoting this very passage, connects it with the idolatry of the golden calf (Acts 7:41), and the worship of "the host of heaven" (v. 42), and, following the Septuagint, with the cult "of Moloch and the star of the god Rephan" (v. 43). The consonants of the Hebrew text of Amos will permit the vocalization, "Molech (*molek*), for example with the vowels of the common Hebrew word for "shame" (*bosheth*). This is congruous with a common Hebrew custom of pointing names of heathen gods with the vowels of some word, like "shame" (*bosheth*), to show their consummate contempt for the foreign deities. Undoubtedly, then, "Molech" (*molek*) is the true pointing in view of the Holy Spirit's application of the passage through Stephen, rather than "king" (*melek*) as the Masoretes vocalized it.

---

[16]Carl F. Keil and F. Delitzsch, *Commentary on The Pentateuch*, III, 393.

The word "Chiun," in the same passage, offers a similar parallel. As the name of a heathen deity, its vowels represent an assimilation to some such word as *shiqqutz,* "a detestable thing." The Syriac version has preserved the correct vocalization; apparently the Septuagint does also, albeit the consonants have suffered corruption, especially in the Greek manuscripts of Acts 7:43, where "Chiun" strangely appears as "Rephan." There can be no doubt that the vocalization should be as Rudolph Kittel[17] gives it and the correct transliteration, "Kaivan," which was the name of the planet Saturn among the ancient Arabs and the Syrians, while "Kaimanu," "constant" or "regular," was its name with the Assyrians. The seeming discrepancy between "Chiun" and "Rephan" is due, either to the latter being a local Egyptian or Coptic name for the planet Saturn and therefore employed by the Septuagint as its equivalent, or to an error in the particular text from which the Seventy were translating, the initial "k" being taken as an "r." The readings of "*Siccuth,* your king" (E.R.V.), or "tabernacle of your king" (R.V.), and "shrine of your images" (R.V.) (Amos 5:26) lack the authority of the Septuagint, corroborated by the New Testament quotation and application, and miss the parallelism of the text, and its general line of thought, which support the reading given by some of the ancient versions, and followed by the Authorized Version.

Not only do Amos and Stephen link the worship of Moloch with that of the planet Saturn, but what is even more difficult, both also appear to represent the adoration of the golden calf in the wilderness (Acts 7:41) as identical with the same cult. But this problem disappears if the explicit statement of Stephen is accepted, that God gave Israel up (cf. Ps. 81:12) "to serve the host of heaven" (Acts 7:42). The worship of the golden calf was plainly star worship. The representation was that of the solar bull, the constellation Taurus, as marking the position of the sun at the time of the spring equinox.

Moloch the king, the idol of the Ammonites and of the Phoenicians, was inseparably connected ·with both the solar bull and the planet Saturn. The rabbis describe his statue as of brass, with human body and bovine head. Diodorus Siculus gives a vivid description of the Carthaginian worship of Moloch or Saturn:

---

[17]Rudolph Kittel, *Biblia Hebraica.*

Among the Carthaginians there was a brazen statue of Saturn putting forth the palms of his hands, bending in such a manner toward the earth, as that the boy who was laid upon them, in order to be sacrificed, should slip off, and so fall down headlong into a deep burning furnace . . . The ancient fable likewise that is common among all the Grecians, that Saturn devoured his own children, seems to be confirmed by this law among the Carthaginians.[18]

The Israelites, professing to be carrying the tabernacle of Jehovah, upon which the Shekinah glory rested, in giving themselves over to the worship of Moloch, were, in spirit, carrying the tabernacle of the cruelest and most abominable of all heathen deities, and were rejoicing in the light of the planet assigned to that deity.

The god Moloch, then, was the sun as king, especially as he entered upon what was viewed as his special domain, the zodiac from "Taurus" to "Serpens" and "Scorpio," the period when the sun is highest and hottest. Despite the fact that such a connection of the sun with Saturn may seem forced, evidence is not lacking from ancient monuments, that the Babylonians believed in such a relation, as Thompson's quotation from the following inscription will show:

When the sun stands in the place of the moon, the king of the land will be secure on his throne. When the sun stands above or below the moon, the foundation of the throne will be secure.[19]

It is obvious that the "sun," in this inscription, cannot be the actual sun, and it is defined on the reverse side of the monument as being "the star of the sun," the planet Saturn:

Last night Saturn drew near to the moon. Saturn is the star of the sun. This is the interpretation: It is lucky for the king. The sun is the king's star.[20]

The connection between the sun and the planet Saturn likely arose because both were in a peculiar sense symbols of time. The sun returns to the beginning of the zodiac to mark the consummation of a year. Saturn, the slowest moving of all the celestial bodies, revolves through the signs of the zodiac once in about

---

[18]*Bibliotheca Historica*, Book XX, chap. 1.
[19]R. C. Thompson, *Reports of The Magicians and Astrologers of Nineveh and Babylon*, obverse of No. 176.
[20]*Ibid.*, reverse side.

thirty years, a full generation of men. Saturn was thus, in a particular sense, the symbol of time, and because of time, of destiny.

The earliest astrological tablets, as would be expected, are related principally to omens dependent upon the two great lights, the sun and the moon. When the planets were first recognized as distinct from fixed stars is not known. It could not have been very long after the recognition of the constellations. One planet, Chiun, or Saturn, is mentioned in the Bible, as noted. Safe inference may be made that others were known, since this particular body is the least spectacular both in luminousness and motion, and was likely discovered after some of the others. Be that as it may, planetary worship, and its concomitant, planetary divination, prevailed in the Mesopotamian world at a very early period.

The close interrelation between the worship of the calves, of the heavenly host, and of Moloch, and divination and enchantments, appears in the terrible divine arraignment against apostate Israel. The acme of all the abominations of the backslidden ten tribes, which brought upon them the Assyrian Captivity, is represented as their making "molten images, even the two calves" and an "Asherah," their worshipping "all the host of heaven," their serving Baal, their causing their "sons and their daughters to pass through the fire," and, in closest connection with the enormities, their employment of "divination and enchantments" (II Kings 17:16-17).

The defection of recreant Judah was very similar to that of faithless Israel, and precisely the same demonological elements accompanied it. In his sweeping reformation, Josiah "put down the idolatrous priests" who "burned incense unto Baal, to the sun, and to the moon, and to the planets (*mazzaloth*), and to all the host of heaven" (II Kings 23:5). He also "defiled Topheth . . . that no man might make his son or his daughter to pass through the fire to Molech" (v. 10). "Moreover, them that had familiar spirits, and the wizards, and the teraphim . . . did Josiah put away" (v. 24).

It is evident that the idolatries to which the Israelites of both kingdoms were most addicted were related to the adoration of the heavenly bodies. Inseparably bound with these pagan cults, was the passion to employ celestial omens as indicators of future events, thus producing every kind of divination and witchcraft.

The word rendered "planets" in II Kings 23:5 is *mazzaloth,* translated "twelve signs" in the Revised Version margin. Concerning this expression, Thompson says:

The places where the gods stood in the zodiac were called "manzalti," a word which means literally "stations," and we are probably right in assuming that it is the equivalent of the *mazzaloth* mentioned in II Kings 23:5.[21]

In late Hebrew, *mazzal,* though literally one of the twelve constellations of the zodiac, is applied promiscuously to any and every star; for example, in "Bereshith Rabba": "One *mazzal* completeth its circuit in thirty days, another completeth it in thirty years."[22]

The reference is ostensibly to the moon, with its lunation of about thirty days, and to Saturn, with its revolution of about thirty years. These being the two planets with the shortest and the longest periods respectively. By a natural metonymy, *mazzaloth,* the complete circuit of the zodiac, came also to signify the bodies that performed this circuit.

A passage in Isaiah is remarkable for its clear-cut classification and subtle scorn of Babylonian diviners, who used stellar omens. "Let now the astrologers, the star-gazers, the monthly prognosticators, stand up, and save thee" (Isa. 47:13).

The astrologers are the "dividers of the heavens" (*hovre shamayim*), who cut up the sky for augury, or to take a horoscope. The significance of any stellar conjunction was made dependent upon the particular quarter of the firmament in which it happened to occur. The earliest of such divisions seems to have been into the four quarters, north, south, east, and west; and astrological tablets, illustrating this fact, have been uncovered in considerable numbers. Thus one tablet[23] lists the solar eclipses for the first half of the month Tammuz, with the signification of each eclipse depending upon the quarter in which it was visible. On the first day the eclipse is associated with the south; on the second, with the north; on the third, with the east; and on the fourth, with the west.[24]

---

[21] *Ibid.,* Introduction, p. xxvii.
[22] E. W. Maunder, "Astrology," *The International Standard Bible Encyclopedia,* I, 299.
[23] W. A. I. III, 56,1.
[24] Maunder, *op. cit.,* p. 299.

Very meagre astronomical knowledge is indicated by these tablets, and the evidence is that the omens, either based on the sun, moon, or the constellations of the zodiac, were not derived, as has frequently been supposed, from some spectacular event occurring at or near the time of the observed eclipse, but must have been drawn up on an entirely arbitrary plan. Hence, they must have been extremely unreliable. Isaiah's clever sarcasm is better understood in the light of these facts. "Stand now with thine enchantments, and with the multitude of thy sorceries, wherein thou hast labored from thy youth. . . . Thou art wearied in the multitude of thy counsels. Let now the astrologers, the star-gazers, the monthly prognosticators stand up and save thee. . . . Behold, they shall be as stubble, and fire shall devour them" (Isa. 47:12-14).

"The "star-gazers" (*hahozim bakokavim*) are literally "those looking up, or contemplating, the heavenly bodies," for the purpose of revelations and oracles. The verb "contemplate" (*hazah*) has a sacred connotation, and is the common word for seeing God (Exod. 24:11; Job 19:26), and for what is divinely presented to the mind of Jehovah's true prophets by inspiration (Isa. 1:1; Hab. 1:1; Amos 1:1). In its use as a description of planetary diviners is couched a tacit rebuke to all "seers of the stars." One of Thompson's "Reports" may be cited as an illustration of this class of astral prognosticators: "Saturn has appeared in Leo. When Leo is obscured, for three years lions and jackals . . . kill men."[25] As the planet Saturn requires three years to pass through the constellation "Leo," the ravages of lions are predicted to last that long.

The "monthly prognosticators" were diviners who were acquainted with the omens of the new moon, and who, at each new appearance of the slender crescent, professed thereby to tell what was to happen. Their designation was very expressive of their art. They were "those who make known (omens) at the time of the new moons" (*modhi 'im lehadhashim*). Signs were drawn from the various positions, and even from the directional pointing of the horns of the lunar disk, when first seen. The right horn was assigned to the king, and the left to his enemies: "When, at the moon's appearance, its right horn is high (literally, "long")

---

[25]*Opus cit.*, No. 216.

and its left horn is low (literally, "short,") the king's hand will conquer land other than this."[26]

The "monthly prognosticators" either were ignorant of the fact that the right-hand horn is always the higher, and that the degree of its elevation depends on the season of the year—or, for some reason, they kept the knowledge to themselves.

In a number of passages in the book of Daniel (1:20; 2:2, 10, 27; 4:7; 5:7, 11, 15) several classes of diviners are listed. In the Babylonian world there were several types of prognosticators who stood at the service of the king to obtain for him stellar and other types of oracles and to interpret dreams and omens.[27] The lists in Daniel include those skilled in interpreting astrological omens, but they are not described as "dividers of the heavens." The expression rendered "magicians" (*hartummim*) represents Egyptian magic (the word is used in the Egyptian stories in Genesis 41:8; Exodus 8:7; and others). The "enchanters" (*ashshapim*) represent Babylonian magic, where, as Montgomery notes, "a correct Babylonian term is used, *ashipu.*"[28] In Daniel 2:2 two other classes are added to the "magicians and enchanters" of 1:20, namely, "the sorcerers" (*mekashshephim*) and the Chaldeans (*Kasdim*).

The sorcerers describe the occultists who by magical petitions and songs gain the assistance or control of evil spirits for divining (Exod. 7:11; Deut. 18:10). Their profession "is condemned through the Old Testament as representing black magic," e.g., Exodus 22:17, or in the figurative scenes of immoral seduction, as in Isaiah 47:9.[29] The "Chaldeans" were the dominant race under the Neo-Babylonian Empire, who so exclusively filled ecclesiastical positions that at the capital "Their name became synonymous with the priests of Bel Marduk."[30] So highly were they esteemed as possessors of wisdom that "the several classes of wise men were

---

[26]*Ibid.*, No. 25.

[27]Morris Jastrow, *Die Religion Babyloniens und Assyriens* (1905), chapter 19, "Das Orakelwesen." See also *Keilinschriften und das Alte Testament* by Zimmern and Winckler, pp. 604 ff.

[28]James A. Montgomery, *The Book of Daniel: International Critical Commentary*, p. 137.

[29]Montgomery, *op. cit.*, p. 143.

[30]*The Westminster Dictionary of the Bible*, rev. by Henry S. Gehman, p. 97.

summed up in the comprehensive term 'Chaldeans.' "[31] Both "magicians" (4:6) and "wise men" (*hakkimin*) (2:48) are employed in a similar comprehensive sense in Daniel.

One other significant term in Daniel remains in the expression rendered "soothsayers" (*garzin*) in the Revised Version (2:27), apparently coming from the common root *gzr*, "to cut" (Dan. 2:34), then "decree" (Job 22:28; Esther 2:1), the infinitive being used of a divine "decree," and *gezirta*, meaning "fate" in Rabbinic and Syriac. "Hence the generally accepted meaning is (fate) determiners, i.e., astrologers. Thus it is rendered by the "Jewish Version"[32] in opposition to the Authorized and Revised Versions' rendering "soothsayers," and specifies the type of divination in which these prognosticators specialized as dealing with celestial omens. However, the etymology may embrace the idea of the cognate Arabic verb "to slaughter" (cf. *jazzar*, a slaughterer). If so, the meaning would then be such as slay animals for the purpose of examining the liver and entrails as omens, with perhaps the concomitant idea of sacrifices as an appeal to deity.

The New Testament episode of the maid at Philippi who had "a spirit of divination" (Acts 16:16, R.V.), that is, "a spirit, a python" (*pneuma Puthona*, "a Pythian spirit," where, with the conjunction of two substantives, the second has the force of an adjective), is very valuable in demonstrating the close connection between divination and demonism. In Greek mythology, "Python" (*Puthon*) was the name of the mythical dragon, that dwelt in the vicinity of Pytho, at the foot of Mount Parnassus, in Phocis. It was said to have been the guardian of the most famous of all Greek oracles at Delphi, and to have been slain by Apollo. Pytho is thus the oldest name of Delphi, or the region roundabout, in which the famous ancient oracle was situated. Consequently, "the Pythian spirit," as Hesychius correctly defines it, was tantamount to a "divining demon" (*daimonion mantikon*),[33] and, in the course of time, came to be the generic title of the supposed source of the inspiration of diviners in general, including the slave girl, whom Satan used at Philippi to oppose the truth of the gospel.

---

[31]Montgomery, *op. cit.*, p. 144.
[32]The Holy Scriptures according to the Massoretic text (Philadelphia, 1917).
[33]Hesychius of Alexandria, The Lexicographer, as quoted by J. A. Thayer, *Greek English Lexicon of the New Testament*, p. 557.

It is significant in the light of the demon-possessed maid at Philippi that "the vehicles of manifestation resembling possession in the ancient world are almost exclusively women. . . . Among the possessed prophetesses of historic times the most eminent is the Pythoness."[34] The seeress of Delphi, originally a maiden from the surrounding countryside, "prophesied under the intoxicating excitement of the vapors issuing from a cleft in the rocks above which she sat on a tripod; she was filled with the god (Apollo) himself and his spirit. The god, as was believed, entered into the earthly body, or else the priestess' soul, 'loosed' from her body, apprehended the divine revelations with the spiritual mind. What she then 'with frenzied mouth' foretold was spoken through her by the god."[35]

Christians by no means held the Delphic oracles to be priestly trickery or morbid psychic excitation. Like the pagans, they believed them to be inspired, but differed from the heathen in believing the inspiration to be not divine, but demonic. Minucius Felix,[36] Tatian,[37] Origen,[38] and Augustine,[39] as well as later writers,[40] shared the same general views.

In the light of the general facts pertaining to the ancient Delphic Oracle it need not be for one moment doubted that the demon-possessed girl at Philippi had actual powers of oracular utterance by virtue of evil supernaturalism.[41] It is demonstrably weak and unsatisfactory exegesis, betraying ignorance of essential facts of demonological phenomena, as well as disregard for the explicit statements of the narrative, to represent her as a mere "hysterical type," or "none too strong mentality," whose "confused utterances were taken as coming from some supernatural power."[42]

[34]T. K. Oesterreich, *Possession, Demoniacal and Other* (p. 311). Oesterreich gives a good general account of the Delphic Oracle, *op. cit.*, pp. 311-331.
[35]E. Rohde, *Psyche*, II, 2nd ed., 60-61.
[36]*Octavius*, chap. 27. C.S.P.C.K. Translations of Christian Literature, Series II.
[37]*Oratio ad Graecos*, 18.
[38]*Contra Celsum*, Book 7, chaps. 3 and 4 (Ante-Nicene Christian Library, *Writings of Origen* translated by Crombie, Vol. II).
[39]*De Civitate Dei*, XIX, 23. *Works of Augustine* (Edinburgh, 1588), p. 334.
[40]Oesterreich, *op cit.*, p. 33.
[41]Edward Langton, *Essentials of Demonology*, p. 177.
[42]Burton Scott Easton, "Python," *International Standard Bible Encyclopedia*, IV, 2511.

In reality, it was a head-on clash of light with darkness, of the power of the gospel with the power of Satan.

Meyer maintains that this young woman was a "ventriloquist-soothsayer," and correctly following Plutarch's use of the expression *Puthon,* as referring not only to a "divining-demon," but also appellatively to "soothsayers, who spoke from the belly" (*eggastrimuthoi*), makes it what it certainly is, identical with the Hebrew *'ob.*[43]

There can be no doubt that this girl was a spiritistic medium,[44] and the divining demon spoke from within her innermost being, as in the case of one who possessed a familiar spirit (*'ob*). In this sense she may be called a "ventriloquist," ("ventum," belly, and "loqui," speak). But the modern idea that popularly attaches to the word, that is, the idea of chicanery and trickery, in deceptively throwing the voice so that it appears to come from some place other than its real source, in this instance must be excluded.

---

[43]Heinrich A. W. Meyer, *Critical and Exegetical Handbook to the Acts of the Apostles,* p. 313. See also Edward Langton, *Good and Evil Spirits: A Study of the Jewish and Christian Doctrine, Its Origin and Development.*
[44]James M. Gray, *Spiritism and the Fallen Angels,* p. 97.

CHAPTER IX

BIBLICAL DEMONOLOGY AND NECROMANCY

NECROMANCY IS not a demonological phenomenon distinct in itself, but merely a particular aspect and mode of divination. However, its widespread practice among heathen nations of antiquity, its persistence throughout the centuries, and its present-day appearance in the modern spiritualistic revival, entitle it to an important place of special consideration by itself.

Divination embraces all attempts to obtain clandestine information from the denizens of the spiritual world, so that necromancy is to be classified under it, and as a phase of it. Its distinguishing mark is that the knowledge desired is sought from the spirits of deceased persons. The word itself is very expressive of the sphere it embraces, and denotes literally divination (*manteia*) by consulting the dead (*nekros*).

A. BIBLICAL INSTANCES OF NECROMANCY

Examples of consultation with the spirits of the departed dead are not numerous in the Bible, for Scripture invariably condemns this practice as completely at variance with the true spiritual worship of God. But among various nations of antiquity it was not only allowed, but abetted, and widely practised. Among many ancient people, like the Babylonians, Egyptians, Greeks, and Romans, the diviner stood in the service of the states and was consulted before important decisions were made, or wars waged.[1]

That certain classes of pagan prognosticators were categorized as illegitimate, and prohibited from exercising their calling, was

---

[1]Before any important undertaking, the Assyrian kings, for example, "tell us that through the *baru*-priests, as the diviners were called, a favorable day for the enterprise was selected." Morris Jastrow, *Hebrew and Babylonian Traditions*, p. 150. Cf. M. S. and J. L. Miller, *Encyclopedia of Bible Life*, p. 338.

not because their occultism clashed with heathenism, but rather because they were supposed to be in league with the gods of other and hostile nations. Since, in the beliefs of the time, the gods of a particular nation were the protectors of its people, and the deities of rival nations were its enemies, any one suspected of alliance or intercourse with these hostile gods was under rigid governmental prohibition.

1. The Old Testament Ban Against Necromancy

But in a theocracy like Israel, there was no such distinction as legitimate and illegitimate occultism. It was all under inflexible interdict, and traffic in it was, in all cases, viewed as flagrant apostasy from Jehovah and as a crime punishable by the severest penalties. Hence the Mosaic injunctions: "Turn ye not unto them that have familiar spirits, nor unto the wizards; seek them not out, to be defiled by them: I am Jehovah your God" (Lev. 19:31). "And the soul that turneth unto them that have familiar spirits, and unto the wizards, to play the harlot after them, I will even set my face against that soul, and will cut him off from among his people" (Lev. 20:6). "There shall not be found with thee . . . a charmer, or a consulter with a familiar spirit, or a wizard, or a necromancer" (Deut. 18:10-11).

The "familiar spirit" (*'ob*) is the divining demon present in the body of the conjurer. "A man also or a woman that hath a familiar spirit (literally, 'in whom there is a divining demon'), or a wizard, shall surely be put to death: they shall stone them with stones; their blood shall be upon them" (Lev. 20:27). The term "familiar" is applied to the foreboding demon,[2] it would appear, because it was regarded by the English translators as a servant ("famulus"), belonging to the family ("familiaris"), who was on intimate terms with, and might readily be summoned by, the one possessing it. The significance of the Hebrew term is disputed. It is not impossible that it might be related to the Arabic root *awaba* ("to return"), with reference to the spirit who periodically comes back. The commonest view, on the other hand, associates the fundamental etymological significance with the idea of "something

---

[2]For proof that the spirit agents who work through the medium are evil and not good spirits, see John L. Nevius, *Demon Possession and Allied Themes,* pp. 320-332.

hollow," as a "leathern bottle," or "wine skin" (Job 32:19). Assuming the fundamental notion of "hollowness" to be in the word, various explanations are current as accounting for it, such as calling the spirit *'ob* because of the hollow tone of its voice, which indicates a sound that might be expected to issue from any hollow place, or because the divining spirit was regarded as speaking out of a cave or opening in the ground. Among the Greeks and the Romans, oracles depending on necromancy were situated among the deep caverns, which were thought to communicate with the spirit-world.[3] Davies quotes W. R. Smith as of the opinion that divination by the *'ob* was connected with this ancient superstition. Just as *'ob*, meaning "a divining spirit," came to denote the person in whom the spirit resided, so by a similar metonymy—the contained for the container and vice versa—the hollow cavern came to be used for the spirit that spoke out of it.[4] Gesenius suggests that the connection between "bottle" and "necromancer" probably arose "from regarding the conjurer, while possessed by the demon, as a bottle, i.e., vessel or case, in which the demon was contained."[5]

The "wizard" (*yidʿoni*) is properly the "knowing or wise one," as the English word connotes, as well as the Septuagint *gnostes*. Like "the familar spirit" (*'ob*), it means, in the first instance, the alleged spirit of a deceased person (really the divining demon). Then it came to mean him or her who divines by such a spirit. Thus both terms mean, first, the divining spirit, second, the medium through whom the spirit divines. The two concepts, the divining spirit and the divining medium, are frequently so closely identified as to be thought of as one, as in Leviticus 19:31 and 20:6, where the original "unto them that have familiar spirits" is simply "unto the familiar spirits" (*el haʾovoth*). The same is true of the term "wizard." Implicit in its meaning is the thought of the wise and knowing demon, and the clever and cunning medium, who is adept in occult science because

---

[3]This was notably true of Apollo's famous oracle at Delphi. See T. K. Oesterreich, *Possession, Demoniacal and Other*, pp. 312 ff.; E. Langton, *Essentials of Demonology*, pp. 96-98.

[4]T. Witton Davies, *Magic, Divination, and Demonology among the Hebrews and Their Neighbors*, p. 87.

[5]William Gesenius, *A Hebrew and English Lexicon of the Old Testament*, translated by Robinson. This undoubtedly correct explanation was followed by Tregelles in his edition of *Gesenius' Lexicon*.

the intelligent spirit is in him. It is the superhuman knowledge of the spirit inhabitant of his body that makes him a "wizard."

Attempts have been made to distinguish trenchantly between the terms *'ob* and *yid 'oni* in their reference to the divining spirit, but it is doubtful whether any rigid differentiation can be successfully maintained, in view of the paucity of data available.[6] If the two expressions actually refer to different spirits, the "wizard spirit" (*yid 'oni*) certainly points to spirits characterized by superior knowledge. The "familiar spirit" (*'ob*) would then seem to be any ghost that is called up from the spirit-world to answer questions put to it (I Sam. 28:7-8). The "wizard spirit" seems always to speak through a medium, while the "familiar spirit" (*'ob*) may evidently speak directly out of the spirit-realm (I Sam. 28:15). Some passages, at first sight, might seem to suggest that the *'ob* was the "divining demon" in distinction to the *yid 'oni,* the medium possessed by this spirit. But this distinction does not hold, for Saul is said to have put away "those that had familiar spirits (*ha'ovoth*) and the wizards out of the land" (I Sam. 28:3, 9); this could scarcely have been the case, if the former were merely spirit agents.

May not the two distinct terms describe two different aspects of the same spirit? So regarded, the *'ob* would convey the idea that the spirit has come back from the other world, while *yid 'oni* would suggest that the demon so returned possesses superphysical knowledge, and, therefore, would be capable of giving occult information. Indicative of this view is the fact that in all the eleven cases in which *yid 'oni* occurs, it consistently follows *'ob,* strongly suggesting that it is interpretive of it. The *'ob,* in contrast, frequently occurs alone (I Sam. 28:7-8; I Chron. 10:13).

Very likely the two characters are essentially one, and the conjunction joining the two, as in Deuteronomy 8:11, is of the nature of a hendiadys: "he who seeks a departed spirit that is knowing" (*shoel 'ob weyid 'oni*). The remaining expression, "necromancer" (*doresh el hammethim,* "a seeker among [unto] the dead") is obviously a general and comprehensive necromantic term, and includes *'ob* and *yid 'oni.* The whole expression, then may be rendered as follows: "He who inquires of the departed

---

[6]For a discussion of these terms, see S. R. Driver, "Deuteronomy" in the *International Critical Commentary,* pp. 225-26.

spirit that is knowing, even he who seeks unto the dead." This rendering is in harmony, too, with the usages of Hebrew parallelism.

The illegality and wickedness of all necromantic art in Israel appears, besides in the stern and inflexible Mosaic injunctions directed against it, in such passages as describe how "Saul had put away them that had familiar spirits and wizards out of the land" (I Sam. 28:3,9), how later he died for his persistent disobedience, "and also for that he asked counsel of one that had a familiar spirit to enquire thereby" (I Chron. 10:13), and how Josiah, in his thorough and far-reaching purge of paganism, cleansed away the pollution of spiritistic mediums, and occultists of every description (II Kings 23:24). A considerable portion of Manasseh's guilt, in his abominable idolatrous orgy, is traceable to his traffic with familiar spirits and wizards. "He had intercourse with divining demons and wizards" (*asah 'ob we yid 'onim*), that is trafficked in divining mediums and wizards (II Kings 21:6; II Chron. 33:6).

That outcroppings of the practice of necromancy were frequent in Judah up to the time of the captivity and were an unfailing index of the low spiritual ebb of the apostate nation and a contributory cause of their exile, there can be no doubt. Isaiah sternly upbraids the occultists of his day for seeking unto mediums and wizards "that chirp and mutter." Reprovingly he denounces all necromantic divination as wholly opposed to Jehovah and his worship: "Should not a people seek unto their God? on behalf of the living should they seek unto the dead?" (Isa. 8:19).

The common Septuagintal rendering of "familiar spirit" (*'ob*) is "ventriloquist" (*eggastrimuthos*), one who so speaks out of his inmost being that people are made to believe that a ghost spoke through him, as a result of his throwing his voice into the ground, where the spirit was supposed to be (I Sam. 24:8; Isa. 8:19; 29:4). This is precisely the rationalistic explanation of necromantic phenomena promulgated by Lenormant, Renan, and others. But despite the fact that ventriloquial jugglery and imposition were often resorted to by the ancients for the purpose of magic and clever charlatanry, as is also the case with many modern spiritistic tricksters, nevertheless, genuine traffic in occultism was practiced then, as now, and Scripture presents this species of divination, not as mere quackery, but what it was really claimed to be—an actual display of demonism and the operation of real powers of evil supernaturalism.[7]

But mediumship and spiritism are closely connected with the ventriloquial whispers and mutterings, which the seducing demons employ in their human agents in subtle imitation of the utterances of the dead, in order thoroughly to deceive and win over their ready dupes. Isaiah, warning Judah and Jerusalem of impending suffering, says they shall "be brought down" . . . and their voice shall be "as of one that hath a familiar spirit" (*ke'ob*, literally, "like a shade out of the ground") and their "speech shall whisper out of the dust" (Isa. 29:4). The prophet's reference is clearly to the "ghost" (demon) evoked, who, aping the deceased, evidently speaks directly out of the ground, and "chirps and mutters" (cf. Isa. 8:19) out of the dust." The ancients actually thought the souls of the departed returned, and could be communicated with. They little comprehended demonic deception, and did not realize that the supposed "shade," or spirit of the deceased, was not some loved one, or friend returned from the other world, but merely an impersonating demon.[8] Multitudes in modern times are likewise deluded in the clutches of spiritistic error.

2. The Case of Saul and the Medium of Endor

The episode of Saul's visit to the spiritistic medium at Endor (I Sam. 28:1-25) is not only the most prominent and detailed case of necromancy in Scripture, but it stands unique and unparalleled,[9] as not only a glaring exposé of the fraudulency of spiritism, but also as God's unequivocal condemnation of all traffic in occultism, and His sure punishment of all who break His divinely ordained laws in having recourse to it. It is evident that such an account of a wicked occult practice so sternly forbidden any Israelite, and yet so in vogue in heathenism in general, and among the Canaanitish nations in particular, would never have been accorded so much

---

[7]Cf. Langton, *op. cit.*, p. 178; also James M. Gray, *Spiritism and the Fallen Angels*, pp. 17-18.

[8]Gray, *op. cit.* Also, William C. Irvine thus concludes: "With a host of enlightened Christians we believe that what messages are received from the spirit-world are not received from the souls of those who have passed through the veil but from demons who impersonate them." *Heresies Exposed*, 11th ed., p. 175.

[9]Gray is correct when he says, "Samuel's case is unique." (*Op. cit.*, p. 81).

space, nor given such a place of prominence on the pages of divine truth, unless it had a momentous ministry to fulfill and a stern duty to perform, in once for all revealing the complete duplicity of spiritism, and in solemnly warning against the dire destructiveness of all intercourse with evil spirits.

That the woman of Endor was identical with the modern medium appears in Saul's command to his servants to seek him out "a woman that hath a familiar spirit," (*'esheth ba'alath 'ob* literally "a woman controlling, or mistress of, a divining demon") (I Sam. 28:7), that he might inquire of her, and also in his initial request to the medium herself, "divine unto me . . . by the familiar spirit" (*ba'ob* "by means of the divining demon") "and bring me up whomsoever I shall name unto thee" (v. 8).

Saul asked that Samuel be brought up, because he knew there was none like the venerable prophet and judge who knew so well God's mind and future events. The woman doubtless began to make her customary preparations, expecting, as usual, to lapse into a trance-like state, and be used by her "control" or "divining demon," who would then proceed to impersonate the individual called for. The startling thing, however, was that the usual occult procedure was abruptly cut short by the sudden and totally unexpected appearance of the spirit of Samuel. The medium was consequently transfixed with terror, and screamed out with shock and fright, when she perceived that God had stepped in, and by His power and special permission, Samuel's actual spirit was presented to pronounce final doom upon Saul.[10] The sight of Samuel was the proof of divine intervention, and was indubitable evidence that the man in disguise was Saul. The medium's terrified conduct, and her complete loss of poise at the appearance of a real spirit of a deceased person, constitutes a complete and irrefutable Scriptural disclosure of the fraudulency of all spiritistic mediumship.

The woman, to be sure, had the power to communicate with wicked spirits, as do modern mediums of spiritism and psychical research. These deceiving demons represent themselves to their

---

[10]Pember pointedly observes: "For since Saul would seek unto the dead, God had in anger sent up the real Samuel as the bearer of a fearful message of doom." *Earth's Earliest Ages*, p. 274; cf. Gray, *op. cit.*, pp. 83 ff. Ecclesiasticus (46:20) agrees in Samuel's actual appearance: "After death he (Samuel) prophesied and showed the king his latter end."

mediums, and through them to their clients, as the spirits of the departed dead, but actually their messages do not emanate from the deceased at all, but from themselves as lying spirits, who cleverly impersonate the dead.[11]

The return of Samuel from the spirit-world, though actual, is unique and exceptional, under any consideration. To begin, it is not the case of a medium bringing back the spirit of a deceased person. The woman's "divining demon" had nothing whatever to do with Samuel's sudden appearance. She and her spirit accomplice were completely sidetracked at the presence of Samuel, and had nothing more to do with the proceedings. Evil spirits may impersonate the dead, but they cannot produce them. Only God can do that, as He did in this case. Moreover, the incident is the only example in all Scripture where God permitted a deceased person to come back, as a spirit, to hold communication with the living. Others have come back from the dead, albeit not as spirits, but as raised persons, such as Jairus' daughter, the widow of Nain's son, and Lazarus of Bethany. They did not receive resurrection bodies, nor did they, we may confidently believe, retain any consciousness of the spirit-world, and they afterward died again. But Samuel's spirit was not re-embodied, and, therefore, he was not disqualified from relating information from the other world. The case of our Lord, and those who came "out of the tombs after His resurrection" and "appeared unto many" in Jerusalem (Matt. 27: 52-53), were resurrected persons, not spirits (Luke 24:49), nor in any sense examples of spiritism. The same is true of the appearance of Moses and Elijah on the Mount of Transfiguration. They, too, were present not as "spirits," but in their glorified bodies.

Samuel's return in spirit form from the realms of the dead is, then, altogether unparalleled and unprecedented, both in manner and purpose; in manner, because it was by special divine power and permission; in purpose, because it was for the unique intent of divine rebuke and warning to all who resort to occultism, and particularly, to pronounce immediate sentence on Saul for this, his final plunge into ruin (I Chron. 10:13).

After the medium is exposed, and her craft is laid bare as a fraud and a deception by her unseemly fright at the appearance of Samuel, whom she was professing to call up, the whole proceeding

[11]Pember, *op cit.*, p. 273.

quickly passes over to a colloquy between Samuel and Saul. It is manifest that at first, at least, Samuel's spirit was visible only to the woman, whom she described as "a god (*elohim*) coming up out of the earth" (I Sam. 28:13). The expression is difficult and unusual, in that it is the same word for "God" or "gods." But that the particular reference in this passage is neither to Jehovah, nor to heathen deities, or demons, is evident from Saul's immediate query, "What form is *he* of?" (v. 14). Hence, the term "god," as used in this specific instance, refers, in accordance with a well-established Hebrew usage, to a "judge" or "prophet," as those "unto whom the word of God came" (John 10:35; Ps. 82:6), and whom God consequently dignified with authority to bear His own name (Exod. 21:6; 22:8). The designation was pre-eminently apropos of Samuel, the last and greatest of the judges, and the first of the prophets.

After the woman's further description of Samuel, as "an old man" coming up, "covered with a robe" (I Sam. 15: 27), Saul seems to have glimpsed the spirit of Samuel also, for "he bowed with his face to the ground, and did obeisance" (v. 14), and the conversation proceeded directly, without any further employment of the woman. Samuel's pointed and stinging rebuke to Saul is added evidence that his spirit actually appeared, and that it was not an impersonating demon. Most purported communications from the dead are vague and cryptic, couched in abstruse language calculated to deceive, and withal, to leave a favorable impression. This was far from the case with Samuel. In severest terms, he announced that the Lord had wrested the kingdom from Saul, and that tomorrow Saul and his sons would die (vv. 16-19).

Samuel's manner of speech in describing Saul's death has occasioned much confusion. When he said, "Tomorrow shalt thou and thy sons be with me" (*'immi*) (v. 19), it is not necessary to suppose that this, the rendering of the Massoretic text, is perhaps, not the correct reading, but that the translation of the Septuagint (*Codex Alexandrinus* and *Codex Vaticanus*)is to be preferred, "Tomorrow shalt thou and thy sons with thee be fallen" (*'immeka nophelim*). This, although solving an imagined difficulty that bothers some, is obviously a weakened version. There is no reason why Saul and his sons should not have gone at death to be where Samuel was, in the Paradise section of Hades, where all the spirits

of the righteous dead were in Old Testament times (Luke 16:19-31)
It must never be forgotten that Saul is not a type of unbeliever,
but of a child of God, albeit disobedient and under the divine
discipline. His last act of lawlessness, in resorting to necromancy,
resulted in his untimely end on the battlefield of Mount Gilboa,
which is typical of the believer's "sin unto death" (I John 5:16),
and his being delivered "unto Satan for the destruction of the
flesh that the spirit may be saved in the day of the Lord Jesus"
(I Cor. 5:5).

That Samuel was in Paradise, which was before the resurrection of Christ, in the underworld, and not, as now, in the third
heaven (II Cor. 12:2-3), explains the reason why his spirit is
represented as coming "up out of the earth" (I Sam. 28:13-14), and
not as coming down from heaven. Samuel disclosed nothing as to
the state of those in the unseen world, except a hint as to the
condition of the righteous dead, which, he clearly implied is that
of rest and quietness, and that Saul had disturbed his tranquility
by calling for him. In this statement is contained a revelation of
the state of the righteous dead in Paradise between death and the
resurrection of the body.

If it is forbidden in the Scripture for a child of God to resort
to a "familiar spirit," then it is equally wrong for the departed dead,
either godly or wicked, to communicate with the living. By so
doing, both infringe upon the law of God. If the persuasive plead-
ing of the rich man in Hades could not effect the sending back of
the spirit of Lazarus to the earth to warn his brothers, how can a
medium, through the agency of demonic power, prevail upon spirits
of the dead to return? And what need is there for our communication with the dead? We have Moses and the Prophets, yes, and
Christ and the Apostles, with a full revelation concerning the
circumstances of both the saved and the unsaved dead. If the
episode of Saul's recourse to occultism has any lesson at all, it
shows the folly and duplicity of traffic with necromancers.

B.   Necromancy and Witchcraft

The terms "witch" and "witchcraft" have in reality no
proper place in our English Bible, inasmuch as the superstitious
ideas popularly associated with these expressions, are not found

in Scripture. As a result of the extravagant and fanciful demonology of the Middle Ages, the word "witch," which seems to denote etymologically "one who knows," came more and more to denote a woman who had formed a compact with the devil, or with wicked spirits, and, as a result of this league with evil, and complete abandonment to the powers of darkness, became able to cast many kinds of spells, and cause untold mischief of every description to both people and things. "Witchcraft" in modern English denotes the arts and practices of such women.

1. THE BIBLE AND SORCERY

The term "witch" occurs twice in the Authorized Version, and in both cases has been correctly rendered by "sorcerer" or "sorceress" by the Revisers of 1884. "Thou shalt not suffer a witch (R.V. "sorceress, *mekashshepah*) to live (Exod. 22:18). "There shall not be found with thee . . . a witch (R.V. "sorcerer," *mekashshepah* (Deut. 18:10). The Hebrew participles, in each case, denote one who practices magic by using occult formulas, incantations, and mystic mutterings. The feminine ending of the participle in Exodus 22:18 may merely denote one of a class, or even a collection of units, rather than the strictly feminine connotation of "sorceress."[12]

The term "sorcerer" is therefore, a better translation of the Hebrew words because it avoids the superstition time has attached to the designation "witch," and is manifestly sufficiently elastic in scope to comprehend the broader range of demonological phenomena categorized under it. Although the etymology of the expression "sorcerer" (from the Latin, "*sors*," a "lot," "one who throws or declares a lot"), would assign it initially the more circumscribed sphere of augural prognostication, it is evidently commonly employed to include the whole field of divinatory occultism. As such, it embraces and includes the necromancer, who may, accordingly, be classified as a certain type of sorcerer. The appellation "witch" has persistently clung to that which is more accurately a sorceress, sometimes, a necromancer. For example, the phrase "the witch of Endor" occurs widely in literature, and particularly in common parlance, but it is not found in the Bible. The epithet has come from the misleading heading and summary of the Authorized

---

[12]E. Kautzsch, *Gesenius Hebrew Grammar*, ed. by A. E. Cowley, section 122, *s, t.*

Version. This character is defined in I Samuel 28:7 as "a woman who is mistress of a divining spirit." She was, therefore, a sorceress, more precisely a spiritistic medium or necromancer, not a "witch."

The Revisers partially recognized the inappropriateness of the terms "witch" and "witchcraft" in the English Bible, and remedied the situation by eliminating the term "witch" entirely. However, for some incomprehensible reason, they strangely clung to the expression "witchcrafts" (*keshaphim*) in II Kings 9:22; Micah 5:12; and Nahum 3:4, but in all these instances, a proper rendering would be "sorceries" or "magical arts," and not "witchcrafts," which term is inaccurate and misleading. The translation "sin of witchcraft" in I Samuel 15:23 is correctly "the sin of divination" (*qesem*). The phrase "used witchcraft," employed of Manasseh, is correctly translated by the Revisers "practiced sorcery" (II Chron. 33:16), as the word denotes "to practice magic," and is the same verb from which the participles translated "sorceress, sorcerer" in Exodus 22:18 and Deuteronomy 18:10 are derived.

The expression translated "witchcraft" by the Authorized Version in Galatians 5:20 (*pharmakeia*) is the common Greek word for "sorcery," and is so recognized by the Revisers, though it more literally denotes the act of administering drugs, and then of giving magical potions. It naturally came to designate the magician's art, as in the present passage, and in Isaiah 49:7, where the Septuagint renders *keshaphim* by *pharmakeia* ("sorceries"). The verb "bewitch" (*baskaino*), in Galatians 3:1, contains the idea of bringing mischief upon anyone by the blinding effect of the evil eye, and hence has, perhaps, an occult reference. But it has nothing whatever to do with the fantastic notions attached to "witch" or "witchcraft."

Sir Walter Scott deftly exposes the error of the deluded believers in witchcraft and the witch-baiters of medieval and modern times who professed to draw their base superstitions and inhuman cruelties from the Bible.[13] Although ambiguously employing the term "witch" when referring to the medium of Endor and other female spiritistic traffickers in necromancy in the Old Testament, Scott is nevertheless careful to point out that this class of diviners was entirely different from the European "witch" of the Middle Ages. The so-called "witch of the Hebrews" did not rate higher than a fortune teller or a divining woman. Notwithstanding,

---

[13]*Letters on Demonology and Witchcraft*, 2nd ed., pp. 47-58.

hers was a crime deserving of death (Exod. 22:17). Not, however, because she was a hideous creature, the distorted product of Medieval imagination firmly believed in by multitudes, who could transform herself and others into animals, raise and allay tempests, frequent the revelry of evil spirits, cast spells, destroy lives, blight harvests, upset Nature, and cause multitudinous other daily calamities, but because her occultism involved a rejection of Jehovah's supremacy, in that it was a bold intrusion upon the task of the genuine prophet of God, through whom God's Spirit at that time regularly spoke to make known the divine will.[14]

Sir Walter Scott's summary of the Biblical teaching respecting witchcraft expresses the truth succinctly:

> Whatever may be thought of other occasional expressions in the Old Testament, it cannot be said that, in any part of the sacred volume, a text occurs indicating the existence of a system of witchcraft, under the Jewish dispensation, in any respect similar to that against which the law-books of so many European nations have, till very lately, denounced punishment; far less under the Christian dispensation—a system under which the emancipation of the human race from the Levitical law was happily and miraculously perfected.[15]

2. A Historical Sketch of Witchcraft

It is accordingly quite evident that the terms "witch" and "witchcraft" have no proper place in our English Bible, inasmuch as the superstitious ideas popularly associated with these expressions are not found in Scripture and are furthermore completely at variance with the lofty demonology of both the Old and the New Testament. These superstitious ideas, however, are found from ancient times in heathen thought. The priests (or priestesses) of the ancient oracles, whether of Apollo at legend-haunted Delphi, or of horned Hammon amid the sandy wastes of Libya, or phallic Baal upon the lonely heights of Peor in Moab, were all sorcerers. According to Montague Summers:

> They delivered oracles; they chanted incantations . . . they directed, they expounded, they advised, they healed, they dispensed noxious draughts, they pretended to lord it over nature by their arts, they tamed wild beasts, and

---

[14]*Ibid.* Totally abandoned to the Evil One, witches "were supposed to be capable of doing anything the devil could do."—W. M'Donald, *Spiritualism Identical with Ancient Sorcery, New Testament Demonology, and Modern Witchcraft,* p. 98.

[15]*Op. cit.,* p. 57.

they charmed serpents . . . they controlled the winds just as the witches of Lapland and Norway were wont to do, they could avert the hailstorm, or on the other hand they could cover a smiling sky with the menace of dark clouds and torrential rain. . . . These priest-sorcerers had, moreover, the power to turn human beings into brute animals.[16]

In addition, ancient sorcerers were often necromancers. One of the earliest and most significant scenes of necromancy in Greek literature occurs in *The Odyssey* (Book XI), wherein Odysseus is advised by the evil Circe, to take counsel of the shade of Tiresias in the underworld. The Greek goddess of necromancy and all witchcraft was the mysterious Hecate. Both Greek and Roman sorcery abound with necromancy and every possible variety of demonological phenomena.

However, it remained for priest and peasant of the Middle Ages, in the period of woeful apostasy and spiritual declension, so thoroughly to mix pagan superstition with Christian demonological concepts that imps and hobgoblins, and witches who were the very epitome of all the evil powers of ancient sorcerers, and more, were the result. The poor victim accused of witchcraft was considered to have made a pact with the devil, to practice infernal arts and to obey his every command. The pact was believed to have been signed with the victim's own blood, her name enrolled in the devil's "black book," and the agreement solemnly ratified at a general meeting presided over by the devil himself.[17] The witch was bound to be obedient to the devil in everything, while the other party to the pact delivered the witch an imp, or familiar spirit, to be ready at call to do whatever was directed. The most terrifying evil powers, to cast spells, to hurt, and to kill were delivered to the witch, who became a creature utterly dangerous and unfit to live.[18]

Since the thirteenth century the word "witch," which seems to denote etymologically "one who knows," has come to refer to such

---

[16]*The Geography of Witchcraft*, p. 2. For a general survey of witchcraft, see *The History of Witchcraft and Demonology* by the same author. Cf. also, William Perkins, *A Discourse of the Damned Art of Witchcraft*, Vol. III. For the theme of witchcraft in Elizabethan drama, see Robert Hunter West, *The Invisible World*, pp. 136-161.

[17]See A. E. Waite, *The Book of Black Magic and of Pacts, Including the Rites and Mysteries of Goetic Theurgy, Sorcery, and Infernal Necromancy.*

[18]Margaret A. Murray, *The Witch Cult in Western Europe;* and West, *op. cit.,* pp. 253-4.

imaginary grossly wicked creatures. From that time until well into the eighteenth century, church and state joined hands to torture and burn witches. Persecution of witchcraft was not abolished in England and Scotland until 1736, in 'the reign of George II. All the American Colonies had laws against witchcraft similar to those in England[19] and from the first there were occasional witch trials and executions. The Salem outbreak near the end of the seventeenth century did not run its course until fifty-five persons had suffered torture and twenty had been put to death.[20]

The fantastic lengths to which extravagance ran is shown by the widespread idea of general assemblies of witches called "Witches' Sabbaths." To these annual gatherings the witches were believed to come riding on broomsticks, pokers, goats or hogs, the devil himself in the form of a goat taking the chair. Here they did homage to their master, offered sacrifices of young children, and practiced all sorts of license until dawn. Here neophytes were initiated and received the mark of the devil on their bodies, the sign that they had sold themselves to him.[21] The age of enlightenment and the rise of scientific rationalism in Europe in the Eighteenth century together with far-reaching religious revivals in Europe and America practically abolished witchcraft in the modern civilized world, although it still prevails today among savage and semi-savage races.

C. NECROMANCY AND MODERN SPIRITISM

The distinguishing feature of modern spiritism, frequently misnamed "spiritualism,"[22] is its purported intercourse with the spirits of the dead. In this, it is identical with ancient necromancy. Although much that passes for present-day spiritistic manifestation is pure chicanery, nevertheless, that real communications from the spirit-world are at times received, cannot for one moment be doubted, if both Scriptural and non-Scriptural evidence is to be given credence.

---

[19]Cf. G. L. Kittredge, *Witchcraft in Old and New England*.

[20]See W. N. Gemmil, *Salem Witch Trials*.

[21]Article on "Witchcraft," *Encyclopedia Americana*, 29 (New York, 1951), 430-31.

[22]Gray, *op. cit.*, pp. 16-17; Nevius, *op. cit.*, p. 360; and J. K. Van Baalen, *The Chaos of Cults*, 7th ed., p. 22.

Facts are not lacking to indicate that modern spiritism is nothing more nor less than ancient sorcery revived, with particular emphasis on communication with the supposed spirits of the dead, which are really deceiving, impersonating demons, so that the phenomenon is basically demonism. Its modern claim of being a "new dispensation," ushering in a wholly new advance in communication with the spirit-sphere, is entirely without factual basis. So far from spiritism being anything new, it dates from the most ancient times.

1. Necromancy in the Ancient World

Traffic in the realm of evil spirits goes back in most ancient times to the antediluvian world. Illicit intercourse with spirit beings was the underlying cause of the flood. The earliest history of Egypt, Mesopotamia, and the Graeco-Roman world is replete with examples of the cultivation of the demoniacal arts.[23] These, to which man's religious history bears eloquent witness, fall into three classes. First, there is the divination by signs, omens, and forbidden sciences, evidently under demon manipulation, to indicate the desired course to take. Secondly, there are ceremonies, incantations, and spells to enlist the spirit forces (demons) to give their aid to accomplish the desired course. Thirdly, there is the employment of every method of direct communication and co-operation with the demon forces.

The actual direct intercourse with the demon spirits is, in reality, the domain of so-called necromancy. But since the intercourse is, in reality, not with the spirits of the departed dead, but with lying, seducing spirits (the widely used term "necromancy" being a misnomer and the prevailing idea of communication with the dead being a delusion), *all* the phenomena involving actual traffic with evil spirits, whether purporting to come from the spirits of the deceased or not, is properly included under this category. This being the case, ancient history contains innumerable instances of what is today termed "spiritualism," for demons, pythonesses, sybils, augurs, and soothsaying men and women are constantly encountered in the records of ancient history.

---

[23]See Lewis Bayles Paton, *Spiritism and the Cult of the Dead in Antiquity;* and E. F. Hanson, *Demonology, or Spiritualism, Ancient and Modern.*

Ancient Sumerian, Babylonian, and Assyrian historical records literally swarm with demons; and clay tablets, containing countless incantations, spells, omens, exorcisms, magic rituals, and evidences of spirit traffic, have been dug up by the modern archeologist from the mounds of buried Mesopotamian cities. As Oesterreich notes: "The exorcisms are so numerous that they constitute the major part of cuneiform religious inscriptions; and they must certainly date back beyond the purely Babylonian tradition to the Sumerians."[24]

Likewise, in the records of ancient Egypt, magical texts, charms, and incantations abound. A. V. Harnack says that the priests of Egypt were "celebrated exorcists from very remote times."[25] The religious innovator, Ikhnaton, effected a temporary reformation, however, about 1380 B.C. In his reign the tomb of the deceased "was no longer disfigured with hideous demons and grotesque monsters which should confront the dead in the future life; and the magic paraphernalia necessary to meet and vanquish the dark powers of the nether world, which filled the tombs of the old order at Thebes, were completely banished."[26] Old Testament notices, connecting Egyptian learning with occultism (Exod. 7:11, 22; 8:18; *et al.*), show the prevalence of magic and divination of every conceivable sort in the nations surrounding Israel and stress the ever-present peril to Israel of this traffic in spirits (Deut. 18). As noted in the foregoing, the spiritistic medium of the Canaanites was under rigid ban in Israel (Lev. 19:31; 20:6, 27), and the account of Saul and the medium of Endor is the Bible's once-for-all condemnation of mediumistic traffic.

Greek and Roman antiquity also furnishes abundant evidence of intercourse with the world of evil spirits.[27] In Homer's *Odyssey* there are clear references to necromancy.[28] Pagan antiquity took pride in its renowned oracles—for example, those at Claros, Trophonius, and the most famous of all at Delphi, where trance-mediums received messages from the gods (demons). Healing mediums were

---

[24]*Op. cit.*, pp. 147-48.

[25]*Die Mission und Ausbreitung des Christentums in den ersten drei Jahrhunderten* (Leipzig, 1915) I, 138.

[26]James H. Breasted, *A History of Egypt*, pp. 369-70.

[27]For an able summary of the testimony of Greek classical authors on the existence of phenomena in their day, similar to modern spiritualism, see Leonard Marsh, *The Apocatastasis* or *Progress Backwards*.

[28]Book XI.

also numerous. Such episodes as Vespasian's remarkable experience in the temple of Serapis at Alexandria, Egypt[29]—where he evidently glimpsed a spiritistic materialization—furnish pictures in the Graeco-Roman world of phenomena now known to occur in modern spiritism.

Spiritistic phenomena are recounted in the early Christian centuries. Clement of Rome makes mention of the practice of calling up a soul from Hades "by the art which is termed necromancy" for the purpose of consulting it "upon some ordinary matter."[30]Tertullian makes a remarkable allusion to the same thing that modern mediums profess to do (and do, if abundant evidence is to be given credence): namely, producing apparitions and trafficking in spirits of men who are now dead (really impersonating demons).[31] Augustine again and again ascribes the inspiration of Greek and Roman oracles and soothsayers to evil spirits, and recognizes their powers of prediction. He believed demons had power to produce appearances and visions, as they do through modern mediums.[32]

The Dark Ages of medieval superstition and popery with its magicians, enchanters, astrologers, and mediums produced levitations, apparitions, spirit communications, and miraculous cures quite similar to those of modern Spiritism, Christian Science, and other similar cults. The fearful prevalence of spiritistic phenomena in England, and the survival of heathen superstitions could not be more plainly demonstrated than in the ecclesiastical and the civil laws against all types of sorcery, extending from the seventh to the eleventh centuries.[33] Up to the threshold of the modern era similar conditions prevailed in all medieval Europe.[34]

2. Spiritism in the Modern World

With the far-reaching revival of spiritism in the nineteenth century, old foes of Christianity appeared in new forms. The

---

[29]Pember, pp. 292-93.
[30]Clement of Rome, *Homilies* 1:5.
[31]*Apology XXIII.*
[32]*DeCivitate Dei*, II:24, 26; XVIII:5. See also the practical study of the modern medium by Minot J. Savage, entitled *Psychics.*
[33]Oesterreich, *op. cit.*, pp. 65-73.
[34]*Ibid.*, pp. 352-612.

strange psychic experiences of the Shakers at New Lebanon, New York, in 1843, and especially the famous "spirit-rappings" in the family of John D. Fox in 1848 at Hydeville, New York, excited wide attention; and as a result, mediums through whom these manifestations were said to occur, were multiplied very rapidly all over the country. The seances of the Fox girls, before the Civil War, attracted many prominent people in both Europe and America. Spiritualistic societies were organized (The Society of Psychical Research in England in 1882, and in America in 1888), seances became common, and a prolific literature began rolling off the press. Men of science began subjecting its purported phenomena to severe scientific scrutiny, and some, like Sir William Crookes and Sir Oliver Lodge, the physicists, became its adherents.

A whole complex of phenomena, purportedly tried and proved, was advanced as the result of the widespread activity in psychical research and experimentation with mediums: such as telepathy, spirit-rapping, trances, luminous apparitions, automatic writing, inspiration, clairvoyance, oral and written spirit communications, mediumistic drawings, materializations, levitations, physical healing, and others, and these form the basis of the new belief in spirits. Says Oesterreich, "In various periods and circles, now one and now another phenomenon prevails and is, so to speak, in fashion."[35] Certain states of trance are commonly conceded to be closely related to demon possession.[36]

Spiritism received a new impulse after World War I, especially in England where there was hardly a home from which a son had not been lost. Such prominent men as Sir Oliver Lodge and Sir A. Conan Doyle alleged that they had had communication from their boys and their comrades who had perished on the battlefield. The result was a widespread recourse to mediums, where people were deceived by lying spirits impersonating the departed dead. In no case, it must be concluded, was there what there was purported to be: namely, actual communication of the living with the dead, either with the souls of the righteous or the unrighteous. Spiritism is based on a lie, howbeit a most craftily concealed one,

---

[35]*Op cit.*, p. 366.
[36]*Ibid.* For a classified summary and description of the physical and mental manifestations of modern spiritualism, see Pember, *op. cit.*, pp. 322-327.

and has its source in him whom God's Word says is "a liar and the father of it" (John 8:44).

A remarkable case, that of a Mrs. Piper, [37] was reported in five different volumes of the proceedings of the Society of Psychical Research, and is said to offer the best mass of scientific evidence extant in support of possible spirit communication. It was through this case that Sir Oliver Lodge was finally convinced that the dead may speak to the living. The Bible, however, contradicts his conclusion. James Gray correctly summarizes the evidence thus:

> It reveals the possibility of materializations, but not the actual talking with the dead. By materialization in this case we mean the assumption of a material and bodily form by evil angels or demons, who wickedly personate the dead and deceive the living, but nothing more.[38]

It must be remembered that the calling up of Samuel from the spirit-world (I Sam: 28:7-25) was by God himself, as a test case to pronounce divine condemnation on the whole forbidden traffic with evil spirits. The medium in this case had nothing to do with the procedure.

3. The Doctrines of Modern Spiritism

Inasmuch as present-day spiritism is basically the demonism practiced in hoary antiquity, those who embrace the modern variety do not go forward to something new in Christianity, but backward to that which is as old as fallen man himself—to demon-inspired and demon-impelled paganism. The teachings of this cult would accordingly be expected to be "doctrines of demons" (I Tim. 4:1). And in the light of God's Word, such they are, especially as spiritists have no official creed,[39] and their general tenets are based largely on the pronouncements of mediums under a controlling demon at a seance.

Spiritists have a pantheistic idea of deity and generally abrogate the idea of a personal God.[40] They deny the foundation doctrine of the deity of Christ, making him only a "Master Medium,"[41]

---

[37]M. Sage, *Mme. Piper et la Société Anglo-Americaine pour les Recherches Psychiques.* See also Oesterreich, *op. cit.,* pp. 371-375.

[38]*Op. Cit.,* p. 21.

[39]Van Baalen, *op. cit.,* p. 42.

[40]*Ibid.*

[41]Gray, *op. cit.,* pp. 25-26; and see also Van Baalen, *op. cit.,* p. 42.

and His miraculous conception is to them "merely a fabulous tale."[42] They reject the Bible doctrine of atonement, alleging that "one can see no justice in a vicarious sacrifice, nor in the God who could be placated by such means."[43] They scoff at man's depravity, insisting "never was there any evidence of a fall."[44] In their thinking, "Hell . . . drops out altogether" as an "odious conception, so blasphemous in its view of the Creator" and "as a permanent place does not exist."[45]

Spiritists regard the Christian church as a deadly enemy and as an impediment to true spiritual progress. One of them writes:

Step by step the Christian church advanced, and as it did so, step by step the torch of Spiritualism receded, until hardly a flickering ray from it could be perceived amid the deep darkness . . . For more than 1800 years the so-called Christian church stood between mortals and spirits, barring all chance for progress and growth. It stands today as a complete barrier to human progress, as it did 1800 years ago.[46]

Fully conscious of the irreconcilable antagonism between their cult and Christianity, they say:

If the latter (Christianity) lives, Spiritualism must die; and if Spiritualism is to live, Christianity must die. They are the antithesis of each other . . . Modern Spiritualism has come to give its *coup de grace;* and those who would hold back that flow are the enemies of spiritual truth.[47]

In the following statement Wilbur M. Smith correctly evaluates the followers of this cult: "If they are true spiritualists they are the sworn enemies of the Christian faith."[48]

No cult so blatantly sets aside the Word of God at will or so unashamedly confesses that many of its tenets are in open opposition to the Scriptures. It is obvious, in their *Outlines of Spiritualism,* (Feb. 1, 1952) that spiritists consider the teaching of the divine inspiration and the authority of the Bible as thoroughly untenable and misleading to the public.

Although modern spiritism has performed a beneficial service in calling attention to the supernatural spirit realm (albeit evil)

---

[42]*Spiritual Telegraph,* No. 37.
[43]A. Conan Doyle, *The New Revelation,* p. 55.
[44]*Ibid.*
[45]A. Conan Doyle, *op. cit.,* p. 68.
[46]*Mind and Matter* (May 8, 1880).
[47]*Ibid.* (June, 1880).
[48]*World Crises and the Prophetic Scriptures,* p. 344.

in a grossly materialistic era, extremely skeptical of anything purporting to transcend the purely natural realm, yet that it is a pagan, anti-Christian heresy, characterized by the most direct demonic deception, is thoroughly obvious. Its roots strike deep into demonism, and its fruits bear all the traits of Satan, the deceiver and the destroyer.[49]

---

[49]See R. B. Jones, *Spiritism in Bible Light;* and J. T. Stoddard, *The Case Against Spiritualism.*

CHAPTER X

BIBLICAL DEMONOLOGY AND HERESY

THE WHOLE BODY of revealed truth, as constituting the Bible, inspired and God-given, is the great bulwark and defense against all wicked power and evil supernaturalism. Implicit faith in its teachings, and hearty appropriation of its precepts, moreover, constitute the only, but all-sufficient, guarantee against Satanic subtlety and demonic cunning. As long as Scriptural truth is accepted and followed, Satan and his hosts are stripped of their power to harm or to lead the child of God astray. It is only when revealed truth is neglected or rejected, either in whole or in part, that the powers of darkness have opportunity to inflict damage and work havoc upon the Christian.

It is not surprising, therefore, in the light of these facts, to find Satanic and demonic assault directed particularly and relentlessly against the Word of God, nor is it amazing to discover that attack against the citadel of revealed truth is, perhaps, the most conspicuous and potent role played by demons.

A. DEMONISM AND DOCTRINAL DECEPTION

Warnings against error and doctrinal corruption assume a position of remarkable prominence and importance in Scripture, and particularly on the pages of the New Testament. Whether it is Moses, passionately exhorting the Israelites to serve Jehovah and not to forget His precepts (Deut. 9), or David, in solemn assembly, giving counsel to Israel and to his son Solomon (I Chron. 28), or the prophets advising with stern uncompromising voice, or our Lord himself predicting the rise of "false Christs and false prophets" (Matt. 24:24), or the Apostle Paul cautioning the Ephesian elders against the inroads of "grievous wolves" (Acts 20:29), or Peter forewarning against apostate teachers (II Pet. 2), the Bible usually portrays heresy and false doctrine as simply the result of defection in the human agent. But there is not lacking definite revelation of a deeper cause than the mere manifestation of error and apostasy in human conduct. As usual, Scripture conducts one to ultimate realities and final causes, rather than to mere effects and developments.

1. DEMONISM AS THE SOURCE OF DOCTRINAL DECEPTION

The Apostle Paul, in a pivotal prophetic passage, traces all doctrinal aberration to its deeper cause and its ultimate source in the invisible demon agents behind visible human actors. He presents the perversion of truth and godliness as the direct work of Satan's minions, the demons. "But the Spirit saith expressly, that in later times some shall fall away from the faith, giving heed to seducing spirits and doctrines of demons" (I Tim. 4:1). The "seducing spirits" *are* the deceiving "demons," who are ceaselessly diligent in perverting the truth and in leading God's people astray from sound doctrine.

As the Church is guided "into all truth" by the "Spirit of truth" (John 16:13), the foundation head of all true inspiration, so He is opposed, in His beneficent ministrations, by Satan, "the spirit of error" (I John 4:6), the arch-enemy of truth and the great deceiver, who, with his demon-helpers, is the source of all false inspiration. But since Satan is a mere creature, and, unlike the Holy Spirit, neither infinite nor omnipresent, he requires the aid of an innumerable host of wicked, deluding spirits to carry on effectively his vast program of doctrinal corruption and deception. As the "Spirit of truth" inspires the genuine prophets and teachers of God (I Cor. 12:3), so the "spirit of error," and his spirit-satellites, energize the "many false prophets" who "are gone out into the world" (I John 4:1). Hence the Apostle John, like the Apostle Paul, traces error to its real source in satanic and demonic activity, rather than in the human agent.

The spurious inspiration takes the precise form of "doctrines of demons." The Pauline phrase does not mean "doctrines about demons," or demonology. Still less does it denote heresiarchs, or the human promulgators of strange isms and cults. It emphatically links demonism with false doctrine,[1] and has direct reference to

---

[1] Wilbur M. Smith's words are here pertinent: " . . . I am becoming more and more convinced that many of the awful and blasphemous teachings that

wicked supernatural spirits, and specifically to the "doctrines taught by demons," which the Apostle James vigorously describes as representing "not a wisdom that cometh down from above," but which is "earthly, sensual, devilish," (*daimoniodes*, "demoniacal") (Jas. 3:15). In other words, James views what Paul calls "teachings of demons" as a perverted wisdom, which "belongs to earth, to the unspiritual nature, and to evil spirits" (Jas. 3:15, Weymouth).

The immediate occasion which evoked the revelation of demonism as the source of doctrinal perversion was an erroneous teaching taking the form of a false asceticism, condemning marriage and the eating of certain foods. The Apostle Paul had just ended on a triumphal note, as he reviewed the "mystery of godliness," and, then sweeping majestically over the great events of redemption, from the incarnation to the glorious ascension (I Tim. 3:16), he offered the finished work of Christ as a fitting background for his contrasting somber reference to satanic power in opposition to the faith and truth of God, and set forth the finished work of Christ as a sure and certain guarantee of the future triumph of truth over error, despite the present prevalence and grievous opposition of evil.

The prophetic warning against latter-day demonic activity in corrupting the truth, and in turning many away from the faith, is couched in particularly solemn and impressive language. Paul seems almost to speak as if, under the prophetic influence, he had an activity independent of himself as an apostle. "But the Spirit saith expressly (*hreros legei*, "distinctly declares") that in later times some shall depart from the faith" (I Tim. 4:1). The faith is, of course, the whole body of revealed truth, which, as the bastion of the believer's defense, is the special target of demonic assault, and which, Jude reminds us, "was once for all delivered unto the saints," and is to be earnestly contended for, as a treasure and resource subject to diabolic spoliation. The "later times" are the closing days of the gospel dispensation, as the professing Church lapses more and more into the prophesied lukewarm Laodicean condition (Rev. 3:14-22). Departing from the faith, neglecting and rejecting God's truth, the dupes of Satan will devote

---

are now found in the literature of our day, indeed, in some of the most widely circulated and highly praised books of our generation have been prompted . . . by evil spirits." *Therefore Stand*, pp. 176 ff.

their attention to misleading spirits and pernicious doctrines instigated by demons.

The Apostle is obviously describing a certain class of persons,
who are themselves deceived, but who are not actively and aggres-
sively deceiving others, and who do not maintain the direct and
intimate intercourse with deluding demons that is characteristic
of another class, represented in the succeeding verses. This
second group manifestly consists, not of those falsely taught, but
of the false teachers who instruct them. These are not only themselves deceived, but are actively engaged in deceiving others. They
are the human agents through whom the seducing spirits work, and
so completely are they under demon tutelage and control, that their
disciples, who listen to them, and follow them, are actually represented as giving "heed to seducing spirits and doctrines of demons."

It is the empty insincerity, the base pretense, and the perfidy
of these lying teachers, together with a conscience so hardened and
seared as to be devoid of the sense of right and wrong, which
enable the demons to make use of them as their special tools of
deception. It is thus apparent that those who "fall away from the
faith," and give "heed to seducing spirits and doctrines of demons,"
do so "through the hypocrisy" of their false religious leaders and
teachers, who are exposed as "men that speak lies," and who are
"branded in their own conscience as with a hot iron" (I Tim.
4:1-2).

Although the precise form of error assumed by the "doctrines
of demons," in this particular instance, is seemingly circumscribed
and limited to some local heresy that immediately threatened the
peace and purity of the Church at that time, yet it must not be
supposed that demonic deception is confined to unsound teaching
inculcating a hypocritical asceticism, forbidding marriage, and
frowning upon certain kinds of foods. The multifarious forms
and almost endless variety, which the "doctrines of demons" may
assume, are illustrated by the manifold perversions of pure Christianity, which have been perpetrated in the Church in the course
of the Christian era, and especially, by the bewildering Babel of
cults and sects that afflict modern Christendom.

However, the distinct type of doctrinal vagary emphasized
by the Apostle has been significantly prominent in ecclesiastical

history. Men under demon tuition early began to teach these heresies, even in apostolic times; and they developed into systems like Gnosticism, and later into Roman Catholicism, where priests are forbidden to marry, and people are commanded to abstain from certain meats on certain days. Today, precisely the same principles are advocated in spiritistic and other occult movements.[2]

Such advocates of unscriptural austerities, which are really mere pretensions to superior piety, in forbidding what God has plainly sanctified and established as incompatible with their own assumed higher and holier character, thus exalt themselves against the authority of Him who ordained the institution of marriage, and the eating of all foods, and cast an aspersion upon Him, as though He were an imperfect being. The inveterate satanic spirit of rebellion against God (Isa. 14:12-14), of confirmed falsehood (Gen. 3:4), and of calumination of the divine goodness (Gen. 3:5), is characteristic of all "doctrines of demons," and is discernible, in greater or less degree, in one form or another, in all their multitudinous variations. The same is true if one sees in the phrase "forbidding to marry" the promulgation of doctrines of "free love," and the abrogation of the marriage relation, or whether one construes "commanding to abstain from meats," as following a prescribed diet, which will make one more amenable and susceptible to spirit communication.[3] In any case, the essential satanic character is always apparent in the particular perversion of God's truth.

In view of the ceaseless industry of Satan and his vast cohorts of demon-helpers, zealously bent upon instigating error, and perverting and distorting the truth of God as the chief barrier to the progress and success of their nefarious program for the world, the oft-perplexing problem of the prevalence of so many conflicting sects and isms in professing Christianity, with such contrariety of doctrinal opinion, even among those of the same denominational affiliation, becomes less and less difficult of explanation. The recognition of demonism as the source of doctrinal deception is the only adequate basis upon which to account

---

[2]Cf. Jan K. Van Baalen, *The Chaos of the Cults,* pp. 46-47.
[3]Clarence Larkin, *The Spirit World,* p. 37.

for the modern religious Babel, and the present-day confusion of tongues.[4]

2. DEMONISM AS THE DYNAMIC OF DOCTRINAL DECEPTION

The zeal and energy with which leaders of new and strange cults disseminate their falsehoods and promote their propaganda are matters of common observation.[5] Too often those who possess the truth sit idly and supinely by, while those who advance flagrant error and espouse fantastic heresy, propagate their vagaries with indefatigable enthusiasm and unflagging fervor. The only adequate explanation of this glaring fact is that demonism is not only the source, but also the dynamic, of doctrinal deception. Error, which demons instigate, they take endless pains to propagate. The subtle allurement of idolatry and the fanatical zeal of its devotees can be explained only on the scriptural basis (I Cor. 10:19-22), that "behind the idol there are terrible spiritual presences—demons."[6]

It is the Apostle John who reveals the truth that demonism is the impelling power propagating false doctrine. "Beloved, believe not every spirit, but prove the spirits, whether they are of God; because many false prophets are gone out into the world" (I John 4:1). It is arresting and very significant that the Apostle abruptly introduces the expression "false prophets" into this verse, instead of what might naturally be expected, "false spirits." He has been warning against deceiving, lying "spirits," the invisible demon agents, and, suddenly, without any apparent transition, speaks of their visible human agents, as if the two concepts were in the closest possible relationship—indeed, as if they were actually interchangeable. The explanation is that the wicked, deluding spirits are definitely identified with their human instruments, because the demons are the impelling impulse and power that energize the spurious prophets.

False teachers are tireless and relentless in the extension of their aberrations, because the demons, inspiring and energizing

---

[4]Cf. Charles W. Ferguson, *The Confusion of Tongues—A Review of Modern Isms*, pp. 1-14.

[5]As Van Baalen aptly observes: "Cultists are not people who have to be aroused to an interest in religion" (*op. cit.*, p. 297).

[6]Edward Langton, *Essentials of Demonology*, p. 185. Cf. also pp. 183-186.

them, are diligent and industrious. Besides actual heresy, it would seem that any religious fad, doctrinal hobby, or lopsided presentation of the truth, which does little credit to God's message and which does not redound to the divine glory, enjoys special demonical inspiration and assistance, if the strange enthusiasm and assiduity of those who promote such unbalanced teachings are any indication of the fact.

Because many false teachers have gone out into the world, inspired and impelled by evil spirits, the Apostle warns the people of God against the subtle danger of believing "every spirit." He does not say, "Believe not every teacher or prophet," but, "Believe not *every spirit.*" He goes deeper to the source and dynamic of deception behind the false teacher. Heeding and believing the teacher is tantamount to heeding and believing the spirit motivating and controlling him. Putting the spirits to the infallible test of truth, trying them by the unfailing criteria of the Word of God, is the all-important task, if believers are not to "fall easy victims to the latest fads in spiritualistic humbuggery."[7]

In explicit terms, John gives the test of the Spirit of God: "Hereby know ye the Spirit of God: every spirit that confesseth that Jesus Christ is come in the flesh, is of God" (I John 4:2). It is important to notice, that, whereas, in this whole context, the Apostle most definitely implies the existence of "spirits who are of God," that is, the good and elect angels sent forth and commissioned by God, yet the entire emphasis, in matters doctrinal, and in the realm of the revelation of spiritual truth, as is here the case, is very significantly *not* on these benign beings, but altogether on the Holy Spirit. The lesson is plain. Although angelic spirits have a definite ministry to the people of God here on the earth, and are "sent forth to do service for the sake of them that shall inherit salvation" (Heb. 1:14), yet their beneficent activities are concerned with temporal mercies and ministrations, rather than with the revelation of spiritual truth. For this supreme task there is another Spirit, greater than all created spirits, the Holy Spirit of God, and "believers look not to angels for guidance and understanding," as H. A. Ironside says, "but to . . . the Holy

---

[7]A. T. Robertson, *Word Pictures in the New Testament,* VI, 229.

Spirit, who came into the world to take the things of Christ and open them to us."[8]

It is important to note the force of the injunction (the mode of the verb is, in all likelihood, imperative) which is not "Hereby know ye the spirits who are of God," but, "Hereby know ye the Spirit of God." This is the emphasis, and this is the goal and immediate intent of the doctrinal test—to recognize the Holy Spirit as the sole and all-sufficient Revealer of truth to the Christian. In this knowledge alone is the child of God safe amidst the incessant clamor of alien voices. He will know "the spirits who are of God," but by no means is he to be taught and guided by them into truth. They have no such ministry. This work appertains to the office of the Holy Spirit alone, who is infinite, and needs no helpers.

Knowledge of good spirits is necessary in order to furnish the criterion by which to recognize the evil and misleading spirits, because the latter can so subtly imitate the former that they often appear, like Satan himself, as "an angel of light." The never-failing test to differentiate the false from the true is the basic truth of the incarnation of Jesus the Christ. All good spirits, who serve God, and are commissioned by Him, readily confess this foundational fact of Christianity.

On the other hand, the wicked and seducing spirits of Satan conceal, pervert, and deny this glorious truth, embracing, as it does, the finished redemptive work of Christ.[9] And little wonder, for this is the seal and sure guarantee of their own undoing and doom.

In the Book of The Revelation, the Apostle John gives a striking illustration of the fact that demonism is the dynamic of doctrinal deception. What is seen in his Epistle as teaching, is presented in the Apocalypse as practice. In the last days of this age, the kings of the earth and their armies will be led to such a depth of deception by demonic agency, as to imagine that they can fight against God himself, and be triumphant:

And I saw coming out of the mouth of the dragon, and out of the mouth of

---

[8]H. A. Ironside, *Addresses on the Epistles of John*, p. 124.

[9]Spiritism, Theosophy, Unity, Jehovah's Witnesses, Unitarian-modernism, and others here display their essential demonic character. See Van Baalen, *op cit.*

the beast, and out of the mouth of the false prophet, three unclean spirits, as it were frogs: for they are the spirits of demons, working signs; which go forth to the kings of the whole world, to gather them together unto the war of the great day of God the Almighty . . . and they gathered them together into the place which is called in Hebrew Har-Magedon (Rev. 16:13-16).

These frog-like "unclean spirits" are deceiving demons, who come forth from the pestiferous quagmires of darkness, to perpetrate their deadly work of delusion in the evening shadows at the ending of man's day. They creep, and croak, and defile, and fill the ears of the nations with their lies and noisy demonstrations, until they stir up earth's godless populations to undertake an insane march against Palestine to crush out the divine purpose of establishing the kingdom of Christ on the earth. As the "lying spirits" in the mouth of King Ahab's prophets led the iniquitous monarch to his destruction at Ramoth-Gilead (I Kings 22:20-38), so these "demon-spirits" will perform a similar function in arousing whole nations, and recruiting vast armies from all countries, to march to their predestined doom at Armageddon. Such will be the devastating power of demon deception in the last days.

These are the "seducing spirits," who go forth in the end time proclaiming the "doctrines of demons," of whom Paul warned (I Tim. 4:1). They are dispatched on their miracle-working ministry by the satanic trinity—the dragon, the beast, and the false prophet —and the fanatical zeal and unbridled recklessness they engender in their dupes, bear all the earmarks of their prince leader, Satan.

B. Demonism and Modern Cults

It must be obvious, even to the most casual observer, that there is something wrong in this world of ours, in which there can exist such a state of appalling religious confusion and doctrinal jumble as is found in this present day. Many, realizing only too well that there is something awry and yet being ignorant of the unseen world of evil supernaturalism, are consequently at a complete loss to know what it is, or how to account for it. It is ever a matter of amazement to all such inquiring minds, that professing Christian people, having one Bible, following ostensibly one way, serving one Saviour, and led by one Spirit, can arrive at such diverse and contradictory interpretations and conclusions, even from the same passage of Scripture, and be divided into so many sects and isms.

The lamentable facts of Christian disunity and disharmony must largely remain an unsolved riddle, a source of endless misunderstanding, and a prolific cause of stumbling to those ignorant of the devices of Satan (II Cor. 2:11) and the reality of the spiritual world of evil. Satan has thus gained large advantage over many, because of a widely prevailing incomprehension of even the first principles of Biblical demonology, and because of a manifest unacquaintance with even an elementary knowledge of the power and reality of demonic deception.

Some have laid the blame for this widespread religious confusion at the door of the Bible; and, imagining it countenances the various errors which false teachers allege to draw from its pages, they have abandoned all faith in it as divinely inerrant. Others do not hesitate to fasten the guilt on Christianity itself, and account it an unsatisfactory religion to give shelter to such a motley array of cults as parade under its banner. Others stumble over the inconsistencies and failures of Christian leaders and professors, and repudiate all religious faith as impracticable and unworkable, producing mere hypocrisy. All, failing to understand the powerful and sinister forces of spiritual evil at work behind the scenes, are incapable of accurate evaluations and correct interpretations, and, consequently, suffer great disadvantage and often irreparable injury, at the hands of satanic cunning and deceit.

1. DEMONISM AND DOCTRINAL DIVISIONS

The Holy Spirit of God, the Spirit of truth, is the great Unifier. In answer to the Saviour's fervent intercessory prayer that those whom the Father had given Him "may all be one" (John 17:11, 21, 22), the Holy Spirit came at Pentecost to unite all God's people positionally into "one body," the Church, by the baptism with the Spirit (I Cor. 12:13; Rom. 6:3-4; Eph. 4:5; Col. 2:12; Gal. 3:27). The most impassioned exhortations of the Holy Spirit, through this Apostle, are to the end that God's people may maintain experimentally the unity which they possess positionally, by the Spirit's baptizing work (Eph. 4:1-6; Phil. 2:2-3).

Whereas the "Spirit of truth" is the great Unifier, "the spirit of error" (I John 4:6) is the great divider. Satan and demons have the keenest perception and appreciation of the eminent practicality of the old adage, "in unity there is strength." When unable to keep their victims from contact with truth, light, and salvation, they resort to the next best device to further their detestable plans. With serpentine subtlety and venomous malignity, they strike at the very foundations of Christian unity to disrupt and disorganize the efficiency and testimony of those, who, when standing together, possess such exhaustless energy, and wield such tremendous power against them.

Since truth unites, and error divides, Satanic strategy launches its most ferocious and fearful assaults on the Word of truth, the Holy Scriptures. In proportion as the truth of God is concealed, perverted, or distorted, in that proportion are the people of God divided and despoiled. Surely, in view of these facts, the great prominence given in Scripture to warnings against false teachers, heresies, and divisions, and the appalling spectacle of such a multiplicity of sects and cults in Christendom, lose all aspect of singularity.

That Scripture views the destruction or impairment of Christian unity as one of the chief disasters and calamities of demonic deception and the satanic introduction of false doctrine into the Church, appears clear from the prevailing New Testament use of the term "heresy" (*hairesis*). This word is never employed in its strict modern sense, as meaning "heterodoxy" or "doctrinal aberration," but consistently denotes a "sect" or "faction" produced by the introduction of such error—thus inseparably identifying heresy with factional division.

It is true, however, that the later meaning attached to the word in ecclesiastical language and common parlance is, perhaps, implied in one passage in Peter's second Epistle; yet even here the emphatic idea is the doctrinal divisions themselves, rather than the erroneous "opinions" or "tenets" producing such divisions. "But there arose false prophets also among the people, as among you also shall be false teachers, who shall privily bring in destructive heresies (*haireseis apoleias*, "sects of perdition"), denying even the Master that bought them, bringing upon themselves swift destruction" (II Pet. 2:1). *The Twentieth Century New Testament* accurately renders the expression "ruinous divisions," and Weymouth gives "fatal divisions," both recognizing the descriptive force of the

genitive *apoleias,* as well as taking into account the primary emphasis of the word, as elsewhere in the New Testament, upon the effect
produced by the false teaching, rather than upon the false teaching
itself, as the cause of that effect.

In conformity with the general denotation of an effect, rather
than a cause, the word "heresy" is employed to designate a "sect,"
"party," or body of men who have separated themselves from others,
advocating some particular doctrine or special mode of life, in
accordance with their own peculiar beliefs. Thus the term is used
to refer to "the sect" or "party" of the Sadducees (Acts 5:17) and
the Pharisees (Acts 5:15; 26:5). Likewise, the expression is applied derogatively to Christians (Acts 24:5, 14; 28:22).

In Galatians 5:20 "heresies" are listed under "the works of
the flesh," along with three other terms of similar import: "factions"
(*eritheiai,* "party spirit, feuds"), "divisions" (*dichostasiai,* "splits"),
and "parties" (*haireseis*). This list of three vices is evidently arranged in accordance with the progressively aggravated character
of the sins enumerated. "Party spirit" degenerates into actual
"divisions," which, when developed into distinct and organized
parties, are called "heresies." A similar use of the word occurs
in I Corinthians 11:19: "For there must be also factions (*haireseis*)
among you, that they that are approved may be made manifest
among you." But the force, in this particular verse, is likely simply
"dissensions" arising from diversity of opinions and aims. In Titus
3:10 the adjectival form of the word occurs, signifying "creating
or fostering factions": "A factious (heretical) man after a first and
second admonition refuse."

In the fixed ecclesiastical sense, which it untimately attained,
the term "heresy" indicates not only any doctrinal distortion, but
open espousal of fundamental error with respect to the central
truths of Christianity, in the face of all better instruction, often
combined with aggressive assault upon the common faith of the
Church, and its defenders. However, its strictly New Testament
usage is seen not to contain these elements, except, perhaps, by
implication in II Peter 2:1, but is found significantly to center all
emphasis on the connection of heresy with disunity and division
in the Church of Jesus Christ.

The inference is clear. The Holy Spirit, the Creator of Christian unity, the Revealer of the truth by which that unity is nurtured

and maintained, the infinitely efficient Worker, who operates with unimpeded power in the sphere of true Christian concord and agreement, emphasizes Christian solidarity as a supreme blessing to be realized experientially by God's people, and views heresy not at all as primarily false doctrine, as is done in the extra-Biblical conception, but first and foremost, as sectarian disharmony, and factional division, and lays practically complete emphasis upon the thought of a deadly and damnable satanic device, utterly destructive of Christian oneness.

Hence it is apparent why demonic industry is indefatigably directed against the bastion of God's revealed truth, and why distortion or obscuration of any part of the divine revelation is a real asset to Satan and a victory for his kingdom. There being but one divine standard of truth, and that being the norm of all Christian faith and practice and the basis of all Christian harmony, and there being but one Spirit of truth opening the divine revelation of truth to man, any deviation from that norm, either in doctrine or practice, must inevitably lead to disunity and disharmony, and must be accounted the direct and destructive work of Satan and demons.

2. Demonism and Doctrines of Demons

Throughout the Christian centuries, from the very days of the Apostles themselves, new sects and isms have arisen to trouble the purity and peace of the Church. Taking leave of the Ephesian elders at Miletus, Paul warned that "grievous wolves" would enter in among them, "not sparing the flock," and that even from their own select group would "men arise, speaking perverse things, to draw away disciples after them" (Acts 20:29-30). With prophetic sweep, the Apostle scanned the centuries and saw the rise of innumerable sects in Christendom, and particularly the great apostasy and the multitudinous cults of the latter days, which he brands as "doctrines of demons" (I Tim. 4:1). Peter, in similar prophetic vision, beheld them as "destructive heresies," or "ruinous divisions" (II Pet. 2:1). Jude boldly inveighs against the wickedness of their human promulgators (Jude vv. 12-13). John sketches a historical tableau of their progress and development, and the interminable confusion they cause in the professing Church (Rev. 2:3).

But "doctrines of demons" are not to be thought of as errors and aberrations wholly beyond the Apostles' times and ministries, and confined to succeeding centuries, from whose bane early Christians were immune. So far from this being true, the Apostles themselves were harassed by every imaginable form of unorthodoxy—legalism, antinomianism, Gnosticism, humanism, materialism, false asceticism, and pseudo-rationalism. Demonic deception left no cardinal Christian doctrine unattacked, from the deity of Christ, to the resurrection of the dead. Of course, sufficient time had not elapsed for the formation of elaborate systems of heterodoxy, and the organization of well-defined sects, as proceeded apace in succeeding centuries, but the doctrinal perversions were present none the less, if unformulated and unsystematized.

With the formation of systems of error, and the organization of weakening schisms, the Church of Rome, in alarm, sought to establish a man-made unity instead of a Spirit-inspired one, and, in the place of the infallible Word of God, substituted an infallible so-called "Church."[10] In thus attempting to escape the inevitable ravages of "doctrines of demons" from without, in dethroning the Word of God, it laid the foundation for a whole new brood of "doctrines of demons" from within, and became a well-knit and brilliantly organized system of incredible error, a very citadel for the "doctrines of demons."[11]

Many of the so-called "heretical sects" which arose during the course of the Christian centuries, were true and sincere children of God, often, however, poorly instructed, and ignorantly embracing certain fanatical and erroneous notions. Others were so misled as to have had no essential conception of Christ's saving work at all.

Modern cults offer an interesting study in the various degrees of demonic deception. Spiritism, theosophy, Christian Science, Christadelphianism, Swedenborgianism, humanism, Mormonism, atheism, agnosticism, the New Thought, and Bahaism are systems of almost incredible distortion and fantastic obscuration of truth, displaying everywhere the evidences of extreme demonic deception. Such sects as Russellism (Jehovah's Witnesses, or International Bible Students' Association), Seventh-Day Adventism, Buch-

---

[10]Cf. Jospeh Cullen Ayer, *A Source Book for Ancient Church History*, pp. 356-396.

[11]Cf. *Ibid.*, pp. 401-418.

manism, and British Israelism offer the tragic spectacle of a mass of truth vitiated by error, and demonstrate a more keen and subtle type of demonic distortion. Perhaps, the most deadly and devastating of all, parading with pious sanctimoniousness "as an angel of light," and perniciously and ingeniously working within the great historical denominations, is modernism, Satan's masterpiece of delusion.[12] Others may slay their thousands. It slays its tens of thousands as a cancerous growth within, eating at the vitality of historical Christianity.

Rejecting the truth that "*all* Scripture is inspired by God" (II Tim. 3:16) and consequently doubting and denying the authority of the Word, the supreme tragedy of our day is a far-reaching departure in the large evangelical denominations from the great doctrines of historical New Testament Christianity. The appalling result is a weakened, worldly Church impotent to regenerate, powerless to attract, and unable to answer the distressed cry of sinful humanity for spiritual reality. A prey to seducing spirits, only a sweeping revival of the Spirit of God can keep the professing Church from lapsing more and more into that lukewarm state, in which our Lord threatend he would "spew" Laodicean professors out of his mouth (Rev. 3:16).

Elmer T. Clark, in writing on the smaller church denominations, says that there are approximately four hundred religious denominations of various kinds in the United States.[13]

He further adds:

One who regards the present as an 'age of doubt' has evidently failed to study the convictions of the small sects; for one familiar with the doctrines held by multiplied thousands and even millions of their adherents will rather be impressed with the amazing credulity of a large section of our population. Many strange beliefs are crystallized in the dogmas of these churches. Some of them are undergirded by erratic interpretations of Scripture. Trivial differences of opinion have caused groups to split up into various independent denominations. It is difficult to see how the voices speaking to the American conscience in the name of God could be more completely confused.[14]

In the midst of this appalling confusion of modern cults and the innumerable sects of Christianity, the Bible, God's living Word

---

[12]Cf. Van Baalen, *op. cit.*, pp. 241-286.
[13]Elmer T. Clark, *The Small Sects in America*, rev. ed., p. 13.
[14]*Ibid.*, p. 15.

of Truth, is the Christian's only sure protection against doctrinal deception and demonic despoliation—the Bible, rightly understood, however, and implicity obeyed. Satan and his hosts can by-pass human opinions and men's interpretations, but *they cannot penetrate the impregnable defense of God's Holy Word!*

CHAPTER XI

BIBLICAL DEMONOLOGY
AND WORLD GOVERNMENTS

I N EVERY AGE of human history and in every phase of daily life demons have played a tremendous and very important role. In no realm is their activity more significant than in the sphere of human government. In this area possibly more than in any other field of their operation their activity has frequently not been clearly discerned or even partially understood. Their invisible nature, their close and inseparable identity with their visible human agents, and the supernatural character of their operations have combined to clothe them and their wicked machinations and evil enterprises in ominous mystery. Innumerable multitudes without the light of divine revelation, and other multitudes possessing the Bible, but uninitiated into the truths of the "mystery of lawlessness" (II Thess. 2:7), cannot get beyond "flesh and blood" (Eph. 6:12). They can see only the human actors upon the stage of history. Wicked rulers, ruthless dictators, tyrants, oppressors, kings, governors, and presidents are, to them, the real and only characters in the great drama of life as it affects the political realm. They have no idea at all of the unseen realm of evil personalities, energizing and motivating their human agents. "The principalities . . . the powers . . . the world rulers of this present darkness," and "the spiritual hosts of wickedness in the heavenly places" (Eph. 6:12, R.S.V.) are, so far as they are concerned, mere theological nonentities with which they do not reckon.

However, in the realm of human government the unseen personalities of the evil supernatural sphere are just as real and active as their visible human agents, and any deeper interpretation of human history, tracing in it a divine purpose and goal, must take into account the invisible yet very real realm of spirit. Thus interpreted, human history is seen to be not merely an account of human activities and events independent of spiritual forces, but a continuous interaction of spiritual and human personalities, in which demons play a prominent part.

Although demonic activity is prominent in this and preceding ages, and will be augmented as the age draws to a close, it is not uncurtailed. God is permitting Satan under certain restrictions and through his myriads of demon-helpers to work out his own unholy ambition to be like God and to attempt all the functions of God. But Satan's program is foredoomed to failure and destruction and serves to demonstrate to the entire universe the utter folly of a creature attempting to act in independence of and in opposition to the Creator.

Divine restrictions upon Satan's program are evident from Scripture. There is significantly a present ministry of the Holy Spirit in restraining the full development of evil until the end of the age. "For the mystery of lawlessness doth already work: only there is one that restraineth now, until he be taken out of the way" (II Thess. 2:7, A. R.V.). Moreover, the saved part of humanity, which has been "delivered . . . from the power of darkness" (Col. 1:13) is not under the satanic and demonic direction (unless it yields), but rather through the indwelling Spirit is the salt of the earth, hindering its untimely dissolution. Even more important from the governmental point of view is the clear intimation of Scripture that Satan, though in authority, is not wholly free from his Creator, but that any power he exercises in directing the governments of the world is by divine permission. "Let every person be subject to the governing authorities. For there is no authority except from God, and those that exist have been instituted by God" (Rom. 13:1, R. S.V.).

Though Satan's power is divinely curbed, according to scriptural testimony, he nevertheless exercises authority over unregenerate mankind. The unsaved are unwittingly organized and, under Satanic and demonic leadership, governmentally directed in a great evil system or federation. This satanic order or "kosmos," described in numerous Biblical passages, is frequently ambiguously translated "world." It refers to the world of unredeemed men with their ideals and principles of living and acting in independence of God, which are in salient contrast to the ideals and principles given to the redeemed, and in perfect accord with Satanic ambition and pride. For this reason the world system furnishes an ideal sphere for the operation of Satan and his satellite demons.

A. DEMONISM AND THE SATANIC WORLD SYSTEM

In more than thirty important passages the Greek word "kosmos," signifying in Greek literature from Homer on down "an apt and harmonious arrangement or constitution, order"[1] is employed in the New Testament to portray the whole mass of unregenerate men alienated from God, hostile to Christ, and organized governmentally as a system or federation under Satan (John 7:7; 14:27; I Cor. 1:21; 11:32; I Pet. 5:9; I John 3:1, 13; *et al.*). A study of these various passages discloses the nature of this world order.

1. THE CHARACTER OF THE SATANIC WORLD SYSTEM

Satan is its directing head. Three times Jesus refers to Satan as "the prince (*archon*, ruler or governmental chief) of this world" (John 12:31; 14:30; 16:11). The same word is used of the rulers of the nations (Matt. 20:25; Acts 4:26). The Apostle Paul alludes to Satan as the governmental chief or ruler of the realm of evil supernaturalism, employing the same word *archon* ("prince") that Jesus used to describe Satan's leadership over this evil world system—"the prince of the power of the air" (Eph. 2:2).[2] In II Corinthians 4:4 the Apostle portrays Satan in a religious rather than a political sense as "the god of this age." John, the beloved, mentions Satan as the recognized head of this present world-system. "Because greater is he that is in you than he that is in the world (the Satanic system)" (I John 4:4). "And we know that we are of God, and the whole world (the Satanic system) lieth in the wicked one" (I John 5:19).[3] Jesus' message to the Church in Pergamos reveals that Satan's sway is over the earth and that he

---

[1]Joseph H. Thayer, *A Greek-English Lexicon of the New Testament*, corrected ed., pp. 356-7.

[2]For a thought-provoking discussion of this Pauline designation of Satan in the light of modern man's conquest of the air and his air-mindedness, see Wilbur M. Smith, *This Atomic Age and the Word of God*, pp. 222-248.

[3]On the Satanic *Cosmos* see Lewis Sperry Chafer, *Systematic Theology*, II, 76-90. For an excellent interpretation of I John 5:9 see Robert C. Candlish, *The First Epistle of John Expounded in a Series of Lectures*, pp. 486-500.

attacks God's people.[4] "I know . . . where thou dwellest, even where Satan's seat (throne) is" (Rev. 2:13). Satan's leadership as a governmental chief thus extends to both the celestial and the terrestrial spheres, and these two realms interact in the events that transpire upon the earth.

Satan's puissant sway over the earth is further revealed by the prophet Isaiah in the vision in which he glimpses the entire career of Satan (Isaiah 14:12-17). In this he is depicted as the one "that didst lay low the nations" (v. 12), "that made the earth to tremble, that did shake the kingdoms" (v. 16), "that made the world as a wilderness, and overthrew the cities thereof; that let not loose his prisoners to their home" (v. 17). The panoramic sweep of this passage under the poetic figures employed seems clearly to embrace Satan's conquest of man through the temptation and the fall, his consequent usurpation of authority over man and the earth, and his inveterate resistance toward man's acceptance of God's gracious plan of salvation in Christ.

In Isaiah 14:12-20 the prophetic perspective recedes still farther into the past, to outline under the figure of "the king of Babylon" Satan's primeval fall as "Lucifer, son of the morning." This evidently was his splendid title in the day he was created, when the world was young and "the morning stars (evidently other glorious ruling beings like himself) sang together, and all the sons of God (angels) shouted for joy" (Job 38:7).

The pristine harmony, however, was soon disturbed by Satan's rebellion. Intimations are not lacking that Satan was placed in charge of the earth when this planet was originally created. G. S. Faber calls Satan "the Viceregal Governor of this Planetary Mansion of the Father"[5] and that it was then that he said in his heart, "I will ascend into heaven, I will exalt my throne above the stars of God (other ruling powers); I will sit also upon the mount of the congregation in the sides of the north; I will ascend above the height of the clouds; I will be like the most High" (Isa. 14:13-14). Evidently for this presumptuous act God pronounced judgment upon this pre-Adamite earth and it became chaotic as described in Genesis 1:2.

---

[4]Cf. E. M. Bounds, *Satan: His Personality, Power, and Overthrow*, pp. 81-94.
[5]*The Many Mansions in the House of the Father*, p. 300.

If this is true, it furnishes added evidence to the numerous Scriptures which assert Satan's sway over the earth, and that the offer Satan made to give our Lord all the "power" and the "glory" of the "kingdoms of the world" if He would worship him (Luke 4:5-7) was intensely real. It was no idle word that Satan uttered when he said to Christ: "All this power will I give thee, and the glory of them (the earthly kingdoms): for that it is delivered unto me; and to whomsoever I will I give it. If thou therefore wilt worship me, all shall be thine." Satan said, "All these are delivered to me." That was true, but be careful. These were not delivered unto the devil by God. They had been delivered unto him by man. Man had yielded to him, and consequently these kingdoms had all passed under the mastery of the devil.[6]

In the light of these facts Satan's persistent efforts to keep man under his dominion—which he won when he caused man's fall in Eden—and to keep men away from the saving grace of Christ, become more understandable, as does the ceaseless war Satan is waging against the Most High to retain possession of the earth.

Not only is Satan the directing head of the Satanic world system, but according to Scripture, *the system itself is wholly evil.* In the light of the moral, educational, religious, scientific and cultural aspects of man's civilization many believers hesitate to admit that the Satanic system is totally corrupt. Unbelievers deny it altogether. But men forget that this appraisal of fallen humanity, federated under Satan, is made according to the standard of divine holiness and not according to the faulty estimate of human morality. Unregenerate men, lacking spiritual discernment and subject to demonic deception, are incapable of comprehending God's standards; for His thoughts and ways are above their thoughts and ways as the heavens are higher than the earth (Isa. 55:8-9). Neither can they understand that in consequence of their Christ-rejecting attitude before God they stand condemned (John 3:18); and their morality, refinement, culture, and religiousness are only external-ities unable to cover the unrighteousness of their hearts in the sight of God, who declares concerning fallen humanity, "there is none righteous, no, not one" (Rom. 3:10) and "all have sinned and come short of the glory of God" (Rom. 3:23).

---

[6]G. Campbell Morgan, *The Voice of the Devil*, p. 41.

The lurid picture of unregenerate humanity presented in Romans 3:10-18, with all its sordid details of human depravity, seems almost incompatible with the culture and accomplishments of civilized man, until it is realized that this description of the fallen race is as it appears before God's holiness, stripped of all externals, and as it will be manifest in reality in the end of the age when at last the hand of God, now restraining evil, will be removed.

The Satanic world system is thus invariably presented in Scripture as inveterately evil in character, according to God's appraisal, not only in those conditions which the world confesses to be morally wrong, but also in those which it considers to be ideal. The Apostle John connects the "spirit of antichrist" with "the world" or the Satanic system (I John 4:3). He also declares that "whatsoever is born of God overcometh the world" or the Satanic system (I John 5:4). James asserts that "friendship with the world (the Satanic system) is enmity with God" (James 4:4). He, moreover, lists keeping one's self unspotted from the world (the Satanic system)" as one of the necessary elements of "pure religion" (James 1:27). Peter speaks of "the corruption that is in the world" (the Satanic system) (II Pet. 1:4) as well as "the pollutions of the world (the Satanic system)" (II Pet. 2:20). The Apostle Paul emphasizes the truth that the believer has been "delivered from the present evil age" (Gal. 1:4) and "from the power of darkness" (Col. 1:13) and is not to be conformed to the present world (Rom. 12:2).

The Satanic world system is not only wholly evil, but as a world order *it is limited and temporary*. It is limited in its leadership. Satan, although powerful, is not, like Christ, omnipotent. "Greater is he that is in you, than he that is in the world (the Satanic system) (I John 4:4). It is limited in its knowledge and understanding. "There is none that understandeth, there is none that seeketh after God" (Rom. 3:11). "And even if our gospel is veiled, it is veiled only to those who are perishing. In their case the god of this world has blinded the minds of the unbelievers, to keep them from seeing the light of the gospel of the glory of Christ, who is the likeness of God" (II Cor. 4:4-5, R. S.V.). "Now the natural man receiveth not the things of the Spirit of God: for they are foolishness unto him; and he cannot know them, because they are spiritually judged. But he that is spiritual judgeth all things, and he himself is judged of no man" (I Cor. 2:14-15). This system is temporary and transient. "And the world (the Satanic system) passeth away and the lust thereof: but he that doeth the will of God abideth forever" (I John 2:17).

The Satanic world system is characterized by pride, lust, and war. Its temptations, which are directed to selfish cravings of the fallen nature without thought of God, are those to which Eve succumbed in the garden (Gen. 3:6), and which Satan perennially employs to hold those who are slaves of his system or to win back those who have, through faith in Christ, broken with his program. "For all that is in the world (the Satanic system), the lust of the flesh, and the lust of the eyes, and the pride of life, is not of the Father, but is of the world (the Satanic system)" (I John 2:16).

James traces the source of wars and dissensions to yielding to these temptations of the Satanic system. "What causes wars and what causes fightings among you? Is it not your passions that are at war in your members? You desire and do not have; so you kill. And you covet and cannot obtain; so you fight and wage war" (James 4:1-2, R. S. V.). The same spirit of pride and rebellion against God that motivated Satan in his proposed revolt against God takes possession of one who forms ties of amity with the Satanic system in following its ways and yielding to its temptations. "Unfaithful creatures! Do you not know that friendship with the world is enmity with God? Therefore, whoever wishes to be a friend of the world makes himself an enemy of God" (James 4:4, R. S. V.). The spirit of Satan, which thus dominates this evil world system, is basically antagonistic toward God—whatever cloak civilization, human culture, or man's religiousness may cast over it.

Jesus distinctly disavowed that the royal power he exercised as King of the Jews, had any connection with the Satanic world system. "My kingship is not of this world (the Satanic system); if my kingship were of this world (this Satanic system), my servants would fight that I might not be handed over to the Jews, but my kingship is not from the world (the Satanic system)" (John 18:36, R. S. V.).

In emphasizing that His kingly prerogative had no alliance whatever with the Satanic world system, our Lord incidentally enunciated a truth all too apparent to a war-weary generation which has already witnessed the agony and devastation of two world wars, with the paralyzing fear of a third hanging like a Damoclean sword over a distraught globe; namely, that the world governments of the Satanic system depend upon war and armed might to maintain or extend their power. This is even more disconcerting, that although wars usually have an end, "the ends of wars on the earth appear to be getting more and more unsatisfactory."[7] Wars are also coming more frequently; and since the Satanic system is based upon and perpetuated by war, peace will not ensue until Satan's world rule is destroyed at the second coming of Christ. As Daniel foresaw: "And even unto the end shall be war: desolations are determined" (Dan. 9:26, R.V.); and as our Lord himself forewarned: "And ye shall hear of wars and rumors of wars; see that ye be not troubled; for all these things must come to pass, but the end is not yet. For nation shall rise against nation, and kingdom against kingdom: and there shall be famines and pestilences, and earthquakes in divers places" (Matt. 24:6-7).

Summarizing the evidence of some of the best commentators on our Lord's amazing prediction concerning war, in Matthew 24, Wilbur M. Smith correctly concludes: "This then, fundamentally, we will all agree upon, that our Lord in the last week of his life here on earth clearly predicted that wars, national conflicts, would definitely mark the entire age following between His first and second advents."[8] In other words, Jesus was simply warning that despite the blind optimists and the multiplicity of vain prognosticators of peace—like Ahab's lying prophets of old (I Kings 22:6-28) —there can be no peace until the "Prince of Peace" comes to destroy the Satanic system and bind its prince-leader in the abyss (Rev. 20:1-3).

The Satanic world system presents a perpetual peril to the child of God. Not only is the believer continually faced with its subtle temptation addressed to the carnal nature in the threefold appeal to the "lust of the flesh, the lust of the eyes, and the pride of life" (I John 2:16), but Satan and his demon-helpers can in other ways gain access to the saints of God. He can exercise a cruel and harsh control over them. Jesus was anointed "with the

---

[7]Theodore Schwarze, *The Program of Satan*, p. 192.
[8]*This Atomic Age and the Word of God*, p. 254.

Holy Spirit and with power" to heal "all that were oppressed by the devil" (Acts 10:38). He can fetter one. "And ought not this woman, being a daughter of Abraham, whom Satan hath bound, lo, these eighteen years, be loosed from this bond on the Sabbath day (Luke 13:16)?" By divine permission and for a divine purpose he can touch a believer's possessions, his health, and his family (Job 1:9-12), and even his physical life (I Cor. 5:5).

Moreover, Satan can sift a Christian as wheat (Luke 22:31-32). Through his satellites he can work in human government and hinder prayer (Daniel 10:12-13), and through kings and magistrates stir up trouble and persecution against the people of God (Acts 4:25-27). He can buffet a Christian, as he did Paul: "And lest I should be exalted above measure through the abundance of the revelations, there was given to me a thorn in the flesh, the messenger of Satan to buffet me, lest I should be exalted above measure" (II Cor. 12:7). He has the power of physical death (Heb. 2:14) and can in other ways gain access and cause damage to a believer as well as to an unbeliever.

Scripture is emphatic in setting forth the power and the authority of Satan in this age. And though his activity is circumscribed within certain divinely set limits, the precise extent of these boundaries is not revealed. However, that he is the god of this age, the head of a powerful world system, and through human governments is the director of the affairs of unregenerate men, albeit unknown to them, is certain.

2. The Destruction of the Satanic World System

It is plain from the testimony of Scripture that God is permitting Satan's career and program of pride and rebellion to run its course, both as it affects man and the earth and the angelic beings, in order to bring glory to Himself in His redemptive grace in Christ (Eph. 2:7) and to furnish a stern lesson for eternity, to all created intelligences, of the wicked folly of revolt against their Creator (Matt. 25:41; Rev. 19:20). But the concluding acts of this great drama of evil, ending in tragedy for Satan and his followers and in the destruction of Satan's world system, will be enacted in the closing years of this age, in the day of the Lord, after the Church has been translated to heaven (I Thess. 4:13-18; II Thess. 2:1-4).

Satan, who still has his abode in the heavenlies with the privilege of access to God during the period his world system exists
on the earth, will with his angels be cast out of the upper air upon
the earth in the middle of the last amazing seven years which
wind up this era (Rev. 12:7-17). Jesus referred to this yet future
event graphically when he declared: "I beheld Satan as lightning
fall from heaven" (Luke 10:18). Cast out of heaven upon the
earth, Satan will operate through the Antichrist, that mysterious
and ominous personage predicted both in the Old and the New
Testament to arise in the last times. In the Old Testament this
fearful antagonist is prefigured under the titles of "the king of
Babylon" (Isa. 14:4), "Lucifer" (Isa. 14:12), "the little horn"
(Dan. 7:8; 8:9), "a king of fierce countenance" (Dan. 8:23), "the
prince that shall come" (9:26), and "the king" that "shall do
according to his will" (Dan. 11:36). In the New Testament he
appears as "the man of sin," "the son of perdition" (II Thess. 2:3),
"the wicked (lawless) one" (II Thess. 2:8), "antichrist" (I John
2:18), and "the beast" (Rev. 13:1-10).

Considerable confusion has been precipitated in prophetic
teaching by identifying the second beast of Revelation 13:11-18
with the Antichrist[9] rather than with the first beast of Revelation
13:1-10.[10] That the first beast, and not the second, is the Antichrist of Scripture, is amply demonstrated by W. R. Newell.[11]
Through this sinister person, whom Satan will indwell (which
he may do since he is "a spirit, and therefore unseen by mortal
eyes,")[12] he will strike his final furious blows at the God-fearing
remnant of Jews, who will then preach the "gospel of the kingdom"
(Matt. 24:14), and the God-fearing Gentiles, who will believe
the good news that Christ will shortly come to establish His
millennial kingdom upon the earth. Satan's evil design will be
to take full possession of the earth himself, banish the name of

---

[9]Walter Scott, *Exposition of the Revelation of Jesus Christ*, p. 280; W. Kelly,
The Revelation Expounded, pp. 159-164; A. C. Gaebelein, *The Annotated
Bible*, IV (James–Revelation), 242-3; C. I. Scofield, *Reference Bible*, p. 1342,
note on Rev. 13:16; F. W. Grant, *The Numerical Bible, The Gospels*, p. 228.
[10]J. A. Seiss, *The Apocalypse, II*, 388-412; Clarence Larkin, *The Book of
Revelation*, pp. 103-125; and Larkin, *Dispensational Truth*, 115-123.
[11]*The Book of the Revelation*, pp. 195-201.
[12]Walter Scott, *op cit.*, p. 268.

God from the globe, and defeat the divine plan to set up the Messianic kingdom.

To this end this devil-indwelt "man of lawlessness . . . the son of perdition . . . opposes and exalts himself against every so-called god or object of worship, so that he takes his seat in the temple of God (at Jerusalem), proclaiming himself to be God" (II Thess. 2:3-4, R. S. V.). Power will be "given him over all kindreds, and tongues, and nations" (Rev. 13:8). He will inaugurate a world-wide reign of terror, blasphemy, and murder. "He shall speak words against the Most High, and shall wear out the saints of the Most High, and think to change times and laws" Dan. 7:25). It will be his supreme and most desperate attempt to be "like the Most High" (Isa. 14:14). "He shall stand up against the prince (Christ)" (Dan. 8:25). His brief but horrible reign and mad career of God-defying pride and selfish ambition will bring into full fruition all the latent evil elements of the Satanic world system and reveal it to be, what it has always been and what God's Word appraises it to be, wholly evil. When its iniquity is full, as in the case of the ancient Amorites (Gen. 15:16), it shall be irremediably destroyed.

The destroyer of Satan's evil world system will be the all-glorious returning Christ, He who at the cross "spoiled principalities and powers," and "made a show of them openly, triumphing over them in it" (Col. 2:15), and who thereby not only purchased man's redemption, but at the same time redeemed the earth from Satan's ultimate usurpation. He who alone was found worthy to unloose the seven-sealed book, the title deed to the earth, by virtue of His sacrifice (Rev. 5:1-7), will then have finished opening the seals and loosing the judgments upon the earth that will result in the utter annihilation of the Satanic system and the dispossession of Satan.

At the end of the Great Tribulation the confederated armies under the Antichrist, Satan's tool, will be assembled in the plain of Megiddo, in preparation for moving against Jerusalem (Zech. 14:2) to annihilate the Jew. Pouring the "spirit of grace and supplications" upon "the house of David" (Israel) and the inhabitants of Jerusalem (Zech. 12:10), the glorious Christ, leading the "armies of heaven," will come to their rescue (Rev. 19:11-16), clashing with the Antichrist and the wicked kings and their demonized armies of earth, assembled by unparalleled demon activity (Rev. 16:13-16) to make war against the Lord. The Beast (Antichrist) and the False Prophet, his helper, will be taken and "cast alive into the lake of fire," and their armies "slain with the sword of him that sat upon the horse" (Rev. 19:20-21). In the terrific carnage "all the fowls will be filled with their flesh" (Rev. 19:21).

The last event marking the collapse of the Satanic world system will be the descent of an angel from heaven, who seizes "the dragon, that old serpent, which is the Devil, and Satan, and bound (will bind) him a thousand years," and "cast him into the bottomless pit and shut him up, and set a seal upon him, that he should deceive the nations no more, till the thousand years should be fulfilled" (Rev. 20:1-3). Although only Satan, as the great head of the kingdom of darkness, is mentioned as incarcerated in the bottomless pit, it would be inconceivable in view of the nature of the Messianic Kingdom to suppose that the demon powers were left free to act. In this case the whole body of spiritual evil is to be thought of as included in the head, especially as the bottomless pit is also the prison house of the demons (cf. Rev. 9:1-11).

With the Satanic system destroyed and Satan and demons locked up, the time will have at last come for the restoration of the kingdom to Israel (Acts 1:6), that glorious era of peace and blessing so magnificently predicted by the seers of the Old Testament.

B. DEMONISM AND THE GOVERNMENT OF THE SATANIC WORLD SYSTEM

Satan as "prince (ruler) of this world" (John 12:31; 14:30; 16:11) and "prince (ruler) of the power (forces) of the air" (Eph. 2:2) is chief of the realm of evil supernaturalism, but he is not alone in the exercise of spiritual authority. As an eminent spirit-creature, whose position is so exalted that even Michael the Archangel in a dispute with Satan about the body of Moses did not dare to "bring against him a railing accusation (Jude v. 9), he has a vast host of spirit beings under him who fight to hold and extend their dominion over men's lives and who assist in the government of the world system.

Under their king (Matt. 12:26) and supreme military commander, Satan's subjects and soldiers consist of "the principalities" (chief, not inferior spirits, five-star generals over various divisions of the host); "the powers" (subordinate generals and lesser officers); the world-rulers of this darkness" (martial spirits, considered in their political rather than their military capacity, who rule, as spirit beings may, in and through human governmental agents in a sphere of darkness, descriptive of "the ethical character of their realm as away from God: Light");[13] and "the spiritual hosts of wickedness in the heavenly places" (the mass of common soldiers comprising the demon hordes) (Eph. 6:12, R.V.). The Apostle Paul refers to these same evil spirits in Romans 8:38 as "angels . . . principalities . . . powers," in connection with their inability to separate the believer from Christ. They are "emissaries of the destroyer," as Joseph F. Berg points out, "because holy angels would never either desire or endeavor to separate God's people from Jesus Christ."[14]

1. HUMAN AND SUPERHUMAN AGENCIES IN
WORLD GOVERNMENTS

That the Holy Spirit guides and ministers through godly kings, presidents, and governors, of course, no one can reasonably deny. In addition, there is a wide and varied ministry of good angelic spirits to rulers in their temporal administrations, as well as believers in general. "Are they (the angels) not all ministering spirits, sent forth to minister for them who shall be heirs of salvation?" (Heb. 1:14). There are numerous instances of the ministry of good angels in both the Old and the New Testaments—to ancient Israel, our Lord, and the early Church.[15]

Scriptural intimation on the other hand is also clear, that as the holy angels are active in behalf of the heirs of salvation, demons are engaged in the interests of the Satanic world system, especially governmentally. "Satan enters into rulers, governors, and kings and uses them to oppose the people of God and the Word

---

13F. C. Jennings, *Satan: His Person, Place, Work, and Destiny,* p. 144. Cf. Lewis
  Sperry Chafer, *Systematic Theology,* II, 16-17; and VI, 194-95.
14*Daemons and Guardian Angels,* p. 182.
15Cf. Clarence Larkin, *The Spirit World,* pp. 79-81.

of God."[16] This fact appears in clear light in the tenth chapter of the prophecy of Daniel. The revelation there given concerning demonism in world governments is understandable in the light of the very significant circumstances that evoked it.

Daniel had been fasting and praying "three whole weeks" in deep humiliation of soul, to know the future of the remnant of his nation which had returned to Judah and Jerusalem. The answer when it came was undoubtedly far broader in scope than Daniel had asked, commencing with his own day and culminating in the ushering in of the millennial kingdom (Dan. 10-12). Since the vision extended to the overthrow of the Satanic world system at the Second Advent, it aroused intense demonic opposition through one of Satan's powerful spirit agents—a principality, perhaps, or a power, or age-ruler of darkness—here called "the prince (evil spirit-ruler) of the kingdom of Persia" (Dan. 10:13).

This prince, as Edward J. Young correctly says, "is not the king of Persia (Calvin, Haevernick), for the thought here is that of spiritual warfare. (Cf. Rev. 12:7.) Furthermore, the earthly kings of Persia are designated by the words *kings of Persia;* Israel has an angelic 'prince,' Michael: hence it is expected that the prince of Persia should also be an angel."[17] To be sure, an evil angel (demon); and so powerful was he that he was able to hinder Daniel's prayer for three weeks, the answer to which was given "from the first day" that Daniel set his heart "to understand" and to chasten himself before God (Dan. 10:12); but the angel dispatched with the revelation was intercepted by the hostile spirit of the kingdom of Persia and was not able to convey the vision to Daniel until the archangel Michael, special guardian of the interests of Israel (Dan. 12:1), came to the assistance of the messenger.

Carl F. Keil aptly defines "the prince of the kingdom of Persia" as "a spirit-being; yet not the heathen national god of the Persians, but, according to the view of Scripture (I Cor. 10:20-21), the *daimonion* (demon) of the Persian kingdom, i.e., the supernatural spiritual power standing behind the national gods. . . ."[18] H. A. Ironside makes the significant observation that

---

[16]A. D. Muse, *The Spirit World: Demonology,* p. 61.
[17]*The Prophecy of Daniel: A Commentary,* pp. 226-27.
[18]*Biblical Commentary on the Book of Daniel,* reprint, p. 416.

the prince is "not Cyrus himself, but an evil angel evidently, delegated by Satan to seek to influence the hearts of the Persian kings
against the people of God."[19] And Edward J. Young notes, "this
spirit influenced the kings of Persia to support the Samaritans
against Israel."[20]

At this very time, it will be recalled, efforts were being made
by appeal to the Persian kings to frustrate God's purposes concerning the Jews. Sanballat and his henchmen sought maliciously
in every possible way to stop the work of the Lord at Jerusalem.
What is of the utmost importance is that what was transpiring upon
the earthly scene (commonly considered to be simply the activity
of human governmental leaders) was most intimately connected
with, in fact was the result of, what was going on in the upper
air. The episode, as W. C. Stevens points out, "suggests to our
minds that governmental organizations in Satan's interest exist
in the skies corresponding to and interlocking with the governmental organizations of the earth."[21]

Human and superhuman agencies in the government of the
earth were interacting. Satan as the prince of the power of the
air and his evil spirit subordinates were clashing with God's holy
angels. The attempt was being made to thwart the purpose of
God for His earthly people; they knew full well that the divine
plan invoked challenge to their sway in the world system. In
this instance this was true in a pre-eminent sense; for Daniel was
about to be given a momentous vision, looking forward to the
Second Advent and the establishment of the Messianic earthly
kingdom over Israel, which would ultimately spell the doom of
Satan's rule through human governments.

The great passage on the spiritual conflict of the believer
with the evil spirits operating in the Satanic world system in
Ephesians 6:10-18 ties up inseparably with this passage in Daniel
10, especially in the matter of demon forces in human government. "The principalities . . . the powers . . . the age rulers of
darkness of this world . . . the wicked spirits in the heavenly
places (v. 12, literal translation) are the Christian's foes as they

---

[19]*Lectures on Daniel the Prophet*, p. 176. Similarly, A. C. Gaebelein, *Gabriel
and Michael the Archangel*, p. 97.
[20]*Op. cit.*, p. 127.
[21]*The Book of Daniel*, rev. ed., p. 179.

were the inveterate enemies of God's ancient people Israel. These wicked spirits, like the prince of the kingdom of Persia, are ruling the hearts of unregenerate men, especially men in places of power and authority, in these days of darkness. It is against the subtle stratagems of these evil spiritual forces that the Word of God especially warns. So cunningly deceptive are these hosts of evil that nothing short of the whole armor of God for the protection of the whole body of the believer will avail. The girdle of truth and the breastplate of righteousness for the body proper (v. 14); shoes—the gospel of peace for the feet (v. 15); the shield of faith for the hand (v. 16); the helmet of salvation for the head (v. 17); the sword of the spirit for the mouth (v. 17).[22]

The world of unregenerate humanity and human leaders, unprotected by God's armor, are, except by the restraining grace of God's Spirit (II Thess. 2:7), utterly at the mercy of the deceptions of these crafty perverters of the truth. As Joshua and the people of Israel were deceived by the trickery of the wily Gibeonites (Josh. 9), many of God's people, not availing themselves of the full armor of God, are becoming a prey to the cults; and multitudes of the unregenerate throughout the world are falling helpless victims to the utopian lies of communism.

The most interesting designation of the evil spirit forces behind the scenes in world governments mentioned in Ephesians 6:12 is "the world rulers of this darkness." Who are these world rulers? They are not the dictator of the Soviet Socialist Republic, nor the queen of England, nor the dictator of Spain, nor of Yugoslavia, nor the president of our own great Republic, nor the men associated with them in human government. Human rulers are frequently great and good men, "the powers that be" who are ordained of God (Rom. 13:1); yet even these good and great men, except as God's restraining Spirit and the prevailing prayers of believers intervene, are like pawns on the international chessboard, moved to and fro by the *real* rulers of this darkness. Wicked rulers and dictators, on the other hand, renouncing Christianity and abandoning themselves to pride, ambition, conquest, and rebellion against God, offer the ideal medium for the untrammelled operation of these evil ruling spirits.

---

[22]Norman B. Harrison, *His Very Own*, p. 161.

History, since the fall of man, has been an unbroken attestation of the ominous fact of evil powers working in human rulers, whether it be a Pharaoh of Egypt, oppressing the people of God, or a Nebuchadnezzar, leading them into captivity, or a Nero, brutally torturing and massacring them. However, perhaps the most solemn demonstration of the utter barbarity and horrible cruelty and wickedness of men energized by demon power has, it seems, been reserved for the boasted civilization and enlightenment of the twentieth century.

Hitler, the demon-energized and demon-directed scourge of Europe, has come and gone, leaving behind him only a trail of agonized suffering and a state of chaos upon which atheistic communism is determined to perpetrate even greater evils. This system proclaims more blatant doctrines of demons, enslaves more persons, and murders even greater numbers of innocent victims, people whose only crime is opposing communist lies with truth and the communist program of slavery with ideas for human freedom.

Under Hitler, Europe underwent an intensive process of demonization, resulting in the horrors of the second World War. From the fourth in a series of leaflets entitled "Leaves of the White Rose," issued by an underground movement of German Youth under Hitler's regime, come the following significant thoughts, which might also be aptly applied to present-day communism and its leaders:

Every word out of Hitler's mouth is a lie. If he says peace, he means war, and if he calls frivolously on the name of the Almighty, he means the power of Evil, the Fallen Angel, the Devil. His mouth is the stinking throat of hell, and his power is fundamentally rotten. Certainly one has to fight against the Nazi terror state with rational weapons, but whoever still doubts the real existence of demonical powers has not understood the metaphysical background of this war. Behind the concrete and perceptible things, behind all real and logical considerations, there is the irrational, there is the fight against the Demon, against the messenger of Anti-Christ. Everywhere and at all times the demons have lurked in the dark for the hour when man becomes weak, when he arbitrarily abandons his human situation in the world order founded by God for him on freedom . . . After the first voluntary downward step he is compelled to the second and third with rapidly increasing speed; but everywhere, and at all times of the greatest human distress, men and women who have retained their freedom have risen as prophets and saints, and called on men to turn back to God. Certainly man is free, but he is unprotected against Evil without the living God; he is like a boat without oars, exposed to the tempest, or like a baby without a mother, or like a cloud which dissolves.[23]

Under communism, satellites in Europe and Asia are undergoing a more fearful process of demonization than under Hitler; this, unless averted by divine grace, must inevitably lead to a third world war, more frightful and terrible than its predecessors. Never before have demon forces, as though let loose from the abyss (compare Revelation 9), so blatantly published their lies as truth, paraded their slavery as freedom, pronounced wrong as right, been so ambitious of world conquest, so cunning in their deception, or so malevolent in their lawlessness and rebellion against God, as they are today in the program and propaganda of Russian communism. The only effectual weapon, as in the case of Daniel in his struggle against the wicked spirit of Persia, who hindered the answer to his petition for three whole weeks (Dan. 10:12), is the earnest, prevailing prayer of the believer, accoutered with the full armor of God (Eph. 6:10-20). For if our real foes are spiritual—"we wrestle not against flesh and blood" (Eph. 6:12)—our effective weapons are also spiritual; "for the weapons of our warfare are not carnal, but mighty to the pulling down of strongholds" (II Cor. 10:4).

2. DEMONISM AND WORLD GOVERNMENT IN THE LAST DAYS

The fearful demon forces in human government, manifested so recently in Hitler and the leaders of German Naziism and now in the leaders of International communism, are but precursors to fearfully augmented demon activity in the period of apocalyptic judgments preceding the Second Advent. In Revelation 9:1-12 innumerable hordes of wicked spirits under the general form of locusts are let loose out of "the pit of the abyss" (Rev. 9:1-2, R. V.)—which is evidently the lowest part of the prison region of the demons (Luke 8:31)—to delude and torment wicked earth-dwellers.

The period will be one of abounding demon worship (Rev. 9:20) and what is so intimately connected with it (I Cor. 10:19-29): idolatry (Rev. 9:20). Corresponding to the pagan character of the prevailing religion there will exist a heathen state of morality also— with murder, sorceries, fornication, and theft abounding.

---

[23]Quoted by Leslie Paul in *The Age of Terror*, p. 221.

The general lifting of the divine restraint against iniquity in the end of the age, after the translation of the Church, will not only eventuate in the loosing of myriads of demons out of the abyss, the rise of the personal Antichrist (Rev. 13:1-10), the False Prophet (Rev. 13:11-18), and the casting out of Satan upon the earth with his evil angels (Rev. 12:9), but it will involve an unparalleled outburst of demon activity, thus furnishing the government and the cause of the Dragon, the Beast, and the False Prophet (the Satanic Trinity) with a universal ministry. "And I saw three unclean spirits like frogs come out of the mouth of the dragon, and out of the mouth of the beast and out of the mouth of the false prophet. For they are the spirits of devils (demons), working miracles, which go forth unto the kings of the whole world (inhabited earth), to gather them to the battle of that great day of God Almighty" (Rev. 16:13-14).

Thus Scripture shows with exceeding clearness the intimate connection of demon-spirits with world potentates and earthly governments; in this case, it is crystallized into their final evil form, ripe for destruction. These unclean emissaries are sent forth by this infernal Trinity. They issue from it. They do its bidding and act for it and its interests. They display startling powers of evil supernaturalism to offset the divinely miraculous. They deceive by their acts. They delude by their words. Blatant, noisy propogandists like the vile spirits that energize the lies of present-day communism, they arouse the governmental powers of the whole inhabited earth to assemble in one gigantic foolhardy move to crush the Lamb and to banish His incoming kingdom from the earth.

Their superlative success in congregating the kings and potentates of the earth and their armies is not to be wondered at. Rejecting God's truth and God's Christ inevitably means accepting the devil's lie and Satan's Anti-christ. When men's iniquity is full, divine Holiness makes speedy retribution, as it did for Ahab into the mouth of whose prophets the Lord put a lying spirit to conduct the wicked monarch to his doom at Ramoth-Gilead (I Kings 22:19-38). "Therefore God sends upon them a strong delusion, to make them believe what is false, so that all may be condemned who did not believe the truth but had pleasure in unrighteousness" (II Thess. 2:10-11).

How great was the stir, and how intense the enthusiasm, awakened through Europe by the crusader craze set on foot by Peter the Hermit! How were the nations aroused and set on fire to recover the holy places from the dominion of the Moslem! What myriads rushed to arms, took the mark of the cross upon their shoulders, and went forth as one man, never once calculating by what means they should live, much less reach the expected victory! And what thus happened throughout Europe in a campaign professedly *for* Christ, may readily happen throughout the whole habitable world when the question of the sovereignty of the earth hangs upon the success or failure of one last, grand, and universal engagement of battle.[24]

"And they (the evil spirits) assembled them at the place which is called in Hebrew Armageddon" (Rev. 16:16), the hill of Megiddo, in the plain of Esdraelon, a battle field made famous by the centuries. Here by divine appointment, albeit by Satanic agency and deception, "the rulers of this age, who are coming to nought" (I Cor. 2:6), are gathered with their armies and brought to nought. At the acme of its rebellion and insolence the Satanic system with its recalcitrant and God-defying leaders, the Dragon-Satan operating through the Antichrist and his False Prophet and the kings of the earth and their deceived and demonized followers, is destroyed. As the Amorites were destroyed when their iniquity was full (Gen. 15:16), so this wicked world system with its demon-directed leaders and followers is destroyed at the zenith of its wickedness. Then the heavens will open and the returning all-glorious Lamb, the Lion of the Tribe of Judah, the Redeemer of man and the earth, "the King of kings and Lord of lords" (Rev. 19) will slay the lawless one (Antichrist) "with the breath of his mouth and destroy him by his appearing and coming" (II Thess. 2:8, R. S. V.).

The most heinous and foolhardy war that fallen man under Satan's dominion has ever yet rushed into is never joined. The Lamb has but to come forth and the Beast is taken and the False Prophet and hurled into the lake of fire (Rev. 19:20), the Devil is imprisoned in the abyss (Rev. 20:1-3), and the demonized kings and their followers are slain (Rev. 19:21). Such is the future of this evil world system of Satan. Such is the future of Satan. How then can he proceed with his program when God has foreordained it to complete destruction? The only answer is that it is fitting that he who deceives his myriads of followers should himself be abjectly deceived.

---

[24]J. A. Seiss, *The Apocalypse*, III, 89-90.

CHAPTER XII

BIBLICAL DEMONOLOGY AND ESCHATOLOGY

A LTHOUGH DEMONIC activity in human history has always been undeniably great since the sin of our first parents exposed mankind to its baneful attacks, yet the full realization and augmentation of its destructive power are reserved for the consummation of the age. Demonism bears a striking relation to the doctrine of last things; and all classes of mankind, Jew, Gentile, and the Church of God (I Cor. 10:32) will be intimately and vitally affected by the last-day upsurge of evil supernaturalism.

Despite the fact that the Holy Scriptures are not only clear but quite emphatic in their repeated warnings against augmented latter-day demonic activity, the professing church of the twentieth century to an alarming extent refuses to recognize the existence of evil supernatural forces. This condition of unbelief can be attributed only to the low level of spiritual life and power in the church. "The existence of evil spirits is recognized by the heathen, but it is generally looked upon by the missionary as 'superstition' and ignorance; whereas, the ignorance is often on the part of the missionary, who is blinded by the prince of the power of the air to the revelation given in the Scriptures concerning the Satanic powers."[1]

In the light of the prophesied onslaught of deceiving spirits against the Church in the last days (I Tim. 4:1-3), so apparent in its incipient fulfilment now, the unbelief of Christian people is all the more tragic as many believers suffer demonic deception and despoliation because of sheer ignorance of Satan and his devices. Even many spiritual believers are unable to wage a successful war against this army of wicked spirits, through lack of knowledge of what is involved. Many shrink from the subject altogether, insisting that so long as Christ is preached, occupation with Satan and

---

[1]Mrs. Penn-Lewis and Evan Roberts, *War on the Saints*, p. 30.

demons is unnecessary and spiritually unhealthy. All the while, however, Satan is continuously gaining advantage because of the believer's ignorance. Many untaught in the prophetic Scriptures, knowing little or nothing of God's ultimate purposes for the Jew, the Gentile, and the Church of God, and the momentous role of evil supernaturalism in future events as they pertain to these three distinct groups of humanity, suffer great disadvantage in their Christian life and testimony.

A. The Demonology of the Last Days and the Church

From its very birth in the riven side of a crucified and risen Lord, the Church of the living God, as the body of Christ (Eph. 1:23), and "the pillar and ground of the truth" (I Tim. 3:15), has ever been the object of Satan's most venomous attacks and the special target of demonic malignity. Scarcely had the infant Church been born when Satan loosed a storm of persecution against it to stamp out its very life (Acts 4:3; 5:18; 8:1). Failing in this, he stirred up false teachers to harass the Apostles in their work of spreading Christianity. What Satan failed to do by schismatics and heretics, he tried to accomplish by fire, sword, and death in the first three centuries, but with as little success. He won a triumph, however, when, under imperial favor, the Church became wedded to the world in the Pergamos and Thyatira periods (Rev. 2:12-29).

The Sardis period of the Reformation promised a great blessing and revival, but soon the Church of that age lived only in name; it was dead (Rev. 3:1). The blessings it missed were realized in the great world-wide missionary movements and the modern revivals of the glorious Philadelphian era (Rev. 3:7-13). The secret of the Philadelphian power and growth is revealed in the commendatory words of Christ to this, His favored Church: "Thou . . . didst keep my Word, and didst not deny my name" (Rev. 3:8). They kept the impregnable fortress intact against demon incursion. They retained their fidelity to the Word of God, and the doctrine of the deity of Christ. This is precisely what the Church of the latter days is failing to do, with the inevitable result of the terrific inroads of demonic power and delusion.

1. DEMONISM AND LAODICEAN MODERNISM

In Christ's very significant prophecy concerning the founding of His Church, He not only clearly implied that perpetual and implacable Satanic assault would be relentlessly directed against it, but also distinctly promised that "the gates of Hades" should not prevail against it; for it was built upon the rock of His deity and lordship (Matt. 16:18). But in the last days, under the powerful impact of augmented demonic activity, the very foundations of truth will be blatantly denied; and already in Laodicea even the doctrine of the deity of our Lord is found to be discarded. In a church which is no longer the true Church, against which the gates of hell are promised never to prevail and in which Christ walks in the midst of the golden candlesticks (Rev. 1:13; 2:1), Satan is seen to triumph, and Christ is found to be excluded. "Behold, I stand at the door and knock" (Rev. 3:20).[2] What a tragic scene! Christ outside what was once His own Church, knocking for entrance! And why is He shut out? The answer is plain. In contrast to Philadelphia, Laodicea does not keep His Word and wickedly denies the power of His name.

A perfect genius at compromise, a mixer of unmixables, of righteousness with iniquity, of light with darkness, of Christ with Belial, of the portion of a believer with that of an unbeliever, and of the temple of God with idols, this offshoot of the church of the latter days stands as a stern prophetic warning to modernistic Christendom of the nauseating effects of spiritual lukewarmness. Outwardly religious, inwardly apostate; having a form of godliness, but having denied the power thereof; temporally rich, but spiritually destitute; self-satisfied and contented, but wretched and miserable; boastedly wise and scientific, but utterly blind to God's truth; clothed in self-righteousness and the garments of man-made salvation without vicarious sacrifice, but shamefully naked and sinful before God; proudly democratic and free, but enslaved by license, and victimized by anarchy. Such is Laodicean modernism, the master delusion, the chief doctrine of demons of the predicted latter-day apostasy.

This treacherous and deadly error stands revealed, in all its demonic craftiness and cunning, by the application of the simple

---

[2]F. W. Grant, *The Revelation of Christ*, pp. 219-20.

yet searching test which the Apostle John gives to determine teachings instigated and promulgated by "spirits not of God," which Paul calls "doctrines of demons" (I Tim. 4:1). It is this: "Every spirit that confesseth that Jesus Christ is come in the flesh is of God; and every spirit that confesseth not that Jesus Christ is come in the flesh is not of God; and this is the spirit of the antichrist" (I John 4:2-3). Modernism denies this foundational truth of Christianity, the doctrine of the incarnation, that Jesus Christ, the Eternal Word (John 1:1), became flesh (John 1:14) to take upon Himself man's iniquity and sin, and to make reconciliation for them (II Cor. 5:19, 21). Instead of an incarnation, it substitutes an apotheosis:[3] Jesus was, like other children, begotten by natural generation. In no sense was He virgin-born, nor the eternal Christ made flesh. He was merely a remarkable youth, in many respects superior to any other child, a great religious genius, who, from His earliest years, was so pre-eminently God-conscious, and God-occupied, so perpetually and insatiably eager for greater knowledge and appropriation of deity, that eventually He became so absorbed in Him, that He became like Him. Therefore, in Him we see God manifested.

But all such theological bombast that professes to honor Jesus as the mightiest of the mighty, and the greatest of the great men of the world, the most superlative of all its ethical teachers, goes down in disgrace and defeat, branded as a doctrine of demons, denounced as an ignominious degradation of Him who alone "is over all, God blessed forever" (Rom. 9:5). The very name given Him at his nativity, "Immanuel" (Matt. 1:23), calls for a Godman, not a superman, and demands, not One who began to be when He was born into the world, but One who *was* from all eternity and who *came* from heaven. All such inane objections as "biological miracle," or "biological impossibility," which would mean only a superman, are too foolish to discuss. W. H. Griffith Thomas says: "In the Incarnation there was, and still continues, a union between God and man."[4]

It is a mistake to think of so-called "modernism" as a recent fad, or something progressive, and entirely new. While Laodicean or 'modern" modernism takes its descent from the academic toys and theological inanities of so-called "higher criticism," the real source

---

[3]H. A. Ironside, *The Epistle of John*, pp. 126-134.
[4]*The Apostle John*, p. 296.

of this troubler of the Church, as a particular mode of thinking, can be clearly traced to the Satanic method employed in the Edenic temptation. As the first protagonist of the cult, Satan reveals its essence. "Yea," representing a diplomatic affirmative, "hath God said . . . ?"—a subtly expressed doubt, immediately negativing the affirmation, presented as a question. "Ye shall not eat of any tree of the garden?"—a perversion of God's utterance, "Ye shall not eat of *it*" (Gen. 3:1). "Ye shall not surely die" (Gen. 3:4)—a complete denial of God's Word.

Although the most characteristic marks of modernism can be clearly discerned in some heresy in practically every century of the Christian era, the modern revival of this unbelieving sect can be traced from the latter part of the seventeenth century to the present day, through such representative names as Spinoza, Jean Astruc, Eichhorn, De Wette, Julius Wellhausen, and Harry Emerson Fosdick.

2. Demonism and Laodicean Moral Degeneracy

Vitiated and corrupted doctrine cannot help producing distorted and degenerate morals. The rampant spirit of compromise and easy-world conformity, so saliently characteristic of the Church of the latter days, will result in all manner of complicity with evil among professing Christians, with worldliness sweeping in, paralyzing all spiritual life, and counteracting all efficiency and testimony. The salt losing its savor (Matt. 5:13), moral putrefaction inevitably sets in.

If the popular preachers and teachers in Laodicea, who promise their followers "liberty," are "themselves the bondservants of corruption" (II Pet. 2:19), little can be expected from their disciples. "Like priest, like people" is a saying that expresses a perennial truth. Sin countenanced among the professing people of God, there will be little spiritual power to act as a deterrent upon the sweeping cataclysm of immorality among the people of the world. Satan and demons will be free to augment their mischief in human hearts both within, and without, the Church.

The Apostle Paul warns thus of this perilous sag in morality:

But know this, that in the last days grievous times shall come. For men shall be lovers of self, lovers of money, boastful, haughty, railers, disobedient to parents, unthankful, unholy, without natural affection, implacable, slanderers, without control, fierce, no lovers of good, traitors, headstrong, puffed up, lovers of pleasure rather than lovers of God; holding a form of godliness, but having denied the power thereof (II Tim. 3:1-5).

B. The Demonology of the Last Days
and the Gentile

If Satan and demons work such appalling havoc among the professing people of God in the latter days of the Church, what dire evil and destruction may they not be expected to perpetrate among those who make no religious profession at all, the Christless masses of the world's populations, unsheltered from demonic despoliation and delusion, as they necessarily are? And what must be the pathetic plight of wicked earth dwellers left upon this scene after the out-taking of the true Church, left to face increased demonic pressure and fearful demonic eruptions from the underworld of evil and the terrible prospect of the expulsion of Satan and his angels from the heavenlies upon the earth (Rev. 12:7-9)?

1. Demonism and the Mystery of Lawlessness

The translation of the Church of Jesus Christ to heaven (I Thess. 4:13-18; II Thess. 2:1) will precipitate vast and far-reaching changes upon this earthly scene, and will occasion the simultaneous removal of the Holy Spirit, who, having come at Pentecost to form the body of Christ, will leave with it when that body is completed. With the people of God gone, and the Holy Spirit, the great Restrainer of sin and ungodliness, "taken out of the way" (II Thess. 2:7), at last there will be nothing to hold back the full manifestation of diabolic power, which will then burst upon a Christ-rejecting world with shocking violence and unbridled fury. The dammed-up tides of iniquity and evil supernaturalism, so long held in check by God's restraining Spirit, will deluge the earth, as the floods held back by some gigantic dike are let loose to inundate a whole countryside, when the dam is suddenly demolished.

Apostasy, which has been in progress throughout the Church age, and which reaches especially formidable proportions in the defection of Laodicea (I Tim. 4:1-3; II Tim. 3:1-5; II Pet. 2; Jude) now gives way to *"the* apostasy"(*he apostasia*) (II Thess. 2:3).[5] Partial falling away gives way to complete falling away. Appalling defection brings in thorough-going abandonment of all faith by Christendom (Luke 18:8). Darkness merges into gross darkness. "The mystery of lawlessness" yields to "the lawless one" (II Thess. 2:3-4, 8). Curbed demonic might is now fully unleashed, and produces "power, and signs, and lying wonders." Formerly restricted and resistible, demonic delusion now becomes unrestricted, irresistible, and overwhelming "deceit of unrighteousness for them that perish."

Those who in the Church period rejected the overtures of grace, who heeded not the call of the gospel and "received not the love of the truth, that they might be saved" (II Thess. 2:11), and doubtless also the multitudes of Christless professors in Laodicea, left behind when all true believers were translated to heaven—these are now abandoned by divine justice to judicial blindness and Satanic error, that "they should believe a lie, that they all might be judged who believed not the truth, but had pleasure in unrighteousness" (II Thess. 2:11-12). It will be pre-eminently the period of Satan's sway and the hour of the power of darkness, the heyday of demonic deception, the moment for the revelation of the "mystery of lawlessness."

The revelation of the vast ramifications and the complex outworkings of the introduction of sin into the moral universe, by the intrusion of the Satanic will against the divine law and order, is "the mystery of lawlessness." As the principle of evil operating in the world—the special sense in which it is employed by the Apostle in this context—it is no new thing springing into existence in the last evil days of this age; for it existed and was already at work in Paul's day (II Thess. 2:7)—yes, and long before that, in Eden with our first parents (Gen. 3:1-7). In fact, it began even before the creation of man, in the pristine sinless sphere, and received its essential and invariable character in the heart of Satan, when he said, "I will exalt my throne above the stars of God . . . I will make myself like the Most High" (Isa. 14:13-14). God's purpose in permitting the incursion of lawlessness into His sinless universe, and Satan's object and failure in pursuing such an iniquitous course, are constituent elements revealed in the "mystery."

---

[5]A. C. Gaebelein, *The Annotated Bible, The New Testament,* III, pp. 133-4.

With the manifestation of the lawless one, the man of sin (II Thess. 2:3, 8, 12), the mystery of lawlessness will cease to be a mystery. Every unrevealed element in it will be fully made known. Satanic treachery and demonic perfidy will then be disclosed in all their stark and hideous reality. Satan will demonstrate that he has not, for one moment, given up his original inveterately lawless determination to exalt his throne above the stars of God and to make himself like the Most High. Through his tools, he will oppose and exalt himself "against all that is called God or that is worshipped, so that he sitteth in the temple of God, setting himself forth as God" (II Thess. 2:4). He will support his deceptive claims to deity with full and startling display of diabolic miracle (v.9). Efficiently assisted by his hosts of demon-helpers, with their ranks augmented by myriads of seducing spirits let loose from the abyss (Rev. 9:1-11), the delusion of earth's Christless masses will be complete. They will accept "the man of sin" as God, and Satan will at last have apparently achieved his goal—to be like the Most High, and be accorded divine worship.

Full Satanic triumph cannot be attained, nor complete enjoyment of divine honors realized, until that which is a necessary concomitant is achieved. There must be the thorough-going extirpation from the earth of "all that is called God or that is worshipped" and Satanic power must gain the total possession and domination of this terrestrial sphere, thus assuring the frustration of the divine plan to establish the Millennial Kingdom of Christ upon the earth. To this end multitudes of demons go forth to consummate the apostasy and complete man's abysmal deception, in gathering earth's deluded armies to the most disastrous and foolhardy enterprise of the ages—the battle of Armageddon (Rev. 16:13-16).

The mad cry will arise: "On to Jerusalem! Annihilate the Jew! Banish the names of God and Christ from the earth!" It will be the most desperate and devastating outburst of anti-Semitism the world has ever seen, the heinous culmination of demonic malignity and hatred against God and His plans for the earth. It will end in colossal defeat and wholesale destruction of the impious armies by the glorious revelation of the all-conquering Christ from heaven, defending His earthly people Israel, slaying His enemies, consigning the beast and the false prophet to Gehenna and Satan to the abyss, and setting up His own righteous and peaceful kingdom upon the earth (Rev. 19:11-20:3).

2. DEMONISM AND LAST-DAY GENTILE DEPRAVITY

No one can imagine the depths of wickedness and woe to which the rejectors of the truth will be exposed under augmented demonic tyranny after the Church leaves the world, and the restraining power of the Holy Spirit has gone. All the malicious treachery and vicious uncleanness of depraved demonic nature will be reproduced and manifested in human beings victimized by vile spirits. Wicked earthdwellers, subjected to the God-hating influence of these vile spirits, will be hardened under apocalyptic judgments and will cry for the rocks and the mountains to fall on them, to hide them from "the wrath of the Lamb" (Rev. 6:16); but they will utter not one word of repentance.

Like a doleful dirge, the terrible words, "they repented not," re-echo through the apocalyptic passages depicting these redoubtable end-time scenes (Rev. 9:20-21; 16:9, 11). Under the devastating bowl judgments, men gnaw their tongues for pain, yet curse and blaspheme God, being enmeshed in such amazing demon-control, that, like their tyrannous oppressors, they are confirmed in rebellion and wickedness (Rev. 16:9, 11).

Under the fifth trumpet, and the first woe, the loosing of myriads of tormenting demon-locusts from the abyss will occasion such agonizing torture that "men shall seek death, and shall in no wise find it; and they shall desire to die, but death shall flee from them" (Rev. 9:6). After the demon-like infernal cavalry under the sixth trumpet, two hundred million strong, has decimated one-third of earth's godless populations in terrific judgments upon rampant sin and unbridled vice, the unrepentant and abandoned state of those who survive constitutes a shocking disclosure of the profligate and utterly reprobate condition of society under end-time demonic domination, revealing a startling reversion to the crudest and most sordid levels of demon-inspired and demon-energized paganism:

And the rest of mankind, who were not killed with these plagues, repented not of the works of their hands, that they should not worship demons, and the idols of gold, and of silver, and of brass, and of stone, and of wood, which can neither see, nor hear, nor walk: and they repented not of their

murders, nor of their sorceries, nor of their fornication, nor of their thefts
(Rev. 9: 20-21).

Idolatry, as in the most ancient times, produces its same foul
brood: violence and bloodshed; illicit traffic in the spirit-realm and
in every kind of occult art; fornication and every form of uncleanness; dishonesty and every type of deception. Utterly deceived
and despoiled by demon power, men will be so blinded and
beguiled as to believe "the lie" (II Thess. 2:11), Satan's lie, and
will accept his false Christ, the usurper of the earth, instead of
the true Christ, the rightful Possessor (Rev. 5:1-10). The acme
of human folly and iniquity will be laid bare by the apocalypse
of the true Christ, the King of kings and Lord of lords, to destroy
the false Christ, and to oust him as the usurper of the earth.

C.   The Demonology of the Last Days
and the Jew

Direct and potent demonic activity and deception can be
discerned in every phase of the Jewish rejection of the Lord
Jesus Christ, their Messiah, at His first advent. The venomous
hatred of the scribes and the Pharisees, their secret and under-
hand plottings, the fraud and the crooked methods resorted to in
His trial, His unjust condemnation, and shameful death—all bear
the unmistakable stigma of demonic treachery. The insensate cry
of the populace, "His blood be on us, and on our children" (Matt.
27:25), and the blindness which has rested on Jewish hearts
down through the Christian centuries (Rom. 11:25), prove the
grip that demon power has over this people. But, however great
Jewish deception and demon domination have been in the past,
the full force and manifestation of demonic tyranny, as in the
case of unbelieving Gentiles, will not be reached until the last
awful days of this dispensation, just preceding the second advent
of the Messiah.

1. Demonism and Last-Day Jewish Unbelief

It was very significant prophecy which Jesus uttered concerning the abysmal delusion which would be the penalty for
Jewish skepticism in the last days. "I am come in my Father's
name, and ye receive me not: if another shall come in his own

name, him ye will receive" (John 5:43). Refusing the light, they will accept gross darkness. Rejecting the true Christ, they will welcome the false one, even him "whose coming is according to the working of Satan with all power, and signs, and lying wonders" (II Thess. 2:9), who "opposeth and exalteth himself against all that is called God or that is worshipped; so that he sitteth in the temple of God, setting himself forth as God" (II Thess. 2:4).

Regathered to their homeland, established there as a nation in unbelief, with a rebuilt temple, and a reinstated Judaism, under demon tutelage and imposture, they will make a league with the Antichrist at the beginning of the amazing final seven years of this age (Dan. 9:27). The ungodly alliance will prove a covenant with "death and hell" (Isa. 28:18), for in the middle of the period the false, flattering Messiah will break his agreement, sit in the temple, demanding worship for the image he will set up, and for himself. The cruel and terrible "abomination of desolation, (Matt. 24:15) will mark the commencement of the most intense and diabolical persecution of the Jew the world has yet seen, the horrible "time of Jacob's trouble" (Jer. 30:7). Through the fiery ordeal of death and desolation, the nation will be made to see its supreme folly and crime in rejecting its true Messiah, and choosing the false one. Through the refining crucible they will learn the deadly power of demonic delusion, and in their dire extremity, will turn their eyes heavenward, and cry for their true deliverer, as the godless demon-led armies close in to destroy them completely from the face of the earth. When their Messiah breaks through the heavens in unspeakable glory, the scales will at last fall from their blinded eyes, and when they look upon Him whom they have pierced, they will recognize Him not only as the Messiah, the King of kings and Lord of lords, but as the meek and lowly Jesus of Nazareth, whom they slew on Golgotha's brow. Unbelief will give way to radiant faith, and hardness of heart to great mourning and "the spirit of grace and supplications" (Zech. 12:10).

2. DEMONISM AND LAST-DAY JEWISH DEMONIC POSSESSION

The twelfth chapter of Matthew is a scathing exposure of the wickedness and gross unbelief of the Jews in rejecting and slandering their King and Messiah. Their dreadful guilt in repudiating divinely attested truth, in refusing inward light, and thus sinning against the Holy Spirit, made them more culpable than the ancient heathen (Matt. 12:38-42), and furnishes the background and occasion for Jesus' vivid prophetic parable incisively emphasizing the appalling fact, that, although the nation was then wicked, in the future it would become even more so.

Using the graphic and significant figure of a demoniac, Jesus sketches in that chapter the history of the Jewish people (Matt. 12:43-45). The illustration begins at the point of dispossession. "But the unclean spirit, when he is gone out of the man, passeth through waterless places, seeking rest, and findeth it not" (v. 43). The demon-possessed man represents, according to the scope of the passage indicated by our Lord himself, "this evil generation" (v. 45). The reference to "race" (*genea*) is clearly to the Jewish nation, which had so signally exhibited its crime, and so deservedly merited the epithet "evil" in its abysmal unbelief and deliberate rejection of its rightful Messiah. The man in the original demonized state speaks of the nation "from the time of the Exodus to the period of the Captivity," when the worship of other gods exercised a strange and horrible fascination over the people," and "deprived them . . . of light, reason, and the true freedom of will," so that they were enslaved and possessed by the "unclean spirit" of idolatry.[6] The expulsion of the demon from the man suggests the departure of the unclean spirit of idolatry from the nation after the exile, when, not so much by the teaching of the prophets as by that of the scribes and the Pharisees, idolatory seemed banished forever. The house, "empty, swept, and garnished" (v. 44), describes the condition of the Jews under their freedom from idolatry and with their moral and social improvements.

However, the arresting word is "empty." The nation was (and is) undeniably improved in certain ways, "swept clean, and in good order." But the calamitous thing is that it was (and is) "empty," unoccupied by God's Spirit, unpossessed by a living faith, and uncontrolled by any genuine spiritual life. The resulting improvements are of no avail, and are to be swept away.

---

[6]E. H. Plumptre in *A New Testament Commentary for English Readers,* ed. by C. J. Ellicott, I, 75.

The seven other more evil idolatrous spirits,[7] joined with the first, enter into the man and forewarn of the last and worst state of the nation in the great tribulation. Then, destitute of faith, and bereft of God's Spirit, the nation will be the pitiable prey of more numerous, more depraved and destructive demons than at any previous period in its history, and will be held in the grip of a more intense, complete, and tyrannous state of demon possession than ever before. It will be this condition of complete demonic domination and subjugation that will account for the nation's supreme act of idolatry and wickedness, the colossal blunder of making a covenant with the Antichrist, incurring unparalleled disaster and ruin.

The "seven other spirits,"[8] whom Jesus characterized as "more evil" (Matt. 12:45), are doubtless to be connected with the demons now imprisoned in the abyss, who, seemingly more depraved and vicious than the free demons—perhaps accounting for their confinement—are let loose in vast numbers (Rev. 9:1-11) to plague and delude all mankind, but constitute "a special judgment upon apostate Israel," as A. C. Gaebelein correctly concludes.[9] That these sinister occupants of the abyss direct the ferocity of their horrifying attacks principally against Israel, appears from the command issued to them to hurt "only such men as have not the seal of God on their foreheads" (Rev. 9:4). Since the elect of Israel, the one hundred and forty-four thousand, are the only people who are thus sealed (Rev. 7:3-8), and thus escape their fury, it is clearly suggested that their assault is aimed primarily against those of whom they form a number. The fact is also apparent in the descriptive name of the angel-custodian, the king of the abyss, given first in Hebrew (Abaddon), and afterwards in Greek (Apollyon), indicating that the gigantic demon outburst has to do with the Jew and also affects the Gentile (Rev. 9:11).[10]

---

[7]F. W. Grant, *The Numerical Bible*, p. 133.

[8]For parallels to the idea of "seven spirits" in general Semitic demonology, see R. Campbell Thompson, *Semitic Magic: Its Origin and Development* in Luzac's *Oriental Religion Series*, III, 47-56; see also Edward Langton, *Essentials of Demonology*, p. 150.

[9]*The Revelation*, p. 63.

[10]J. A. Seiss, *The Apocalypse*, II, 82.

Chapter XIII

BIBLICAL DEMONOLOGY AND DELIVERANCE

THE STUDY OF Biblical demonology reveals the important fact, that, although Scripture is remarkably reserved on some aspects of demonological thought, yet it is found to be strikingly full and detailed on some other phases of the topic. For example, in the examination of the question of the origin and the identity of demons, Scriptural reserve shows that the consideration of practical moment is not whence they came, nor precisely who they are, but that they actually do exist and that they are wicked and deleterious; they are pernicious enemies, to be ceaselessly resisted, and no "believer dare say he is exempt from peril."[1]

In like manner, the Bible displays a noteworthy reticence in regard to such questions, involving deity and demonism, as the following: How can demonism be consistent with the goodness and wisdom of God? Why did God create beings He foreknew would sin, and be eternally doomed? If, at the outset, the universe was without sin, why did not God keep it so for all time? And, if Satan and demons are the chief cause of misery and sin, why does not God immediately remove them to some place where they can no longer perpetrate their mischief?[2]

But again, Scriptural reticence reveals that, while these questions involve admittedly great difficulties for finite creatures, at the best of immature spirituality and circumscribed vision and exposed to the ravages of human sin and ignorance, they are by no means questions of primary import for faith and life, and practical godliness, and, hence, are developed only in the barest outline.

---

[1] Mrs. Penn-Lewis and Evan Roberts, *War on the Saints*, pp. 16-17. See also Charles Hodge, *Systematic Theology*, I, pp. 644-5.

[2] For objections to the doctrine of evil angels answered, see Augustus H. Strong, *Systematic Theology*, pp. 460-464; and Lewis Sperry Chafer, *Systematic Theology* II, 28-32; 37-8.

In contrast, however, the subject of deliverance from Satan and demons and of immunity from their incessant and baleful attacks—so vitally and indispensably practical to man's temporal and eternal welfare—fittingly receives full and detailed treatment, not only being accorded large space and prominence on the sacred page, but also calling forth God's vast, gracious, and all-efficacious redemptive plans and purposes in Christ.

A. DEMONOLOGY AND THE NEED FOR DELIVERANCE

From whatever angle Biblical demonology is approached, whether it be the existence, the identity, the origin, the numbers, or the organization of the demons, Scripture lays pre-eminent and continual stress upon one central fact: man requires deliverance and protection from these malignant and destructive creatures. No phase of the subject accentuates this urgent and inescapable need more than that dealing with the essential wicked and unclean nature of demons, and especially the irretrievable and abandoned character of their corruption.

1. DEMONISM AND THE DOCTRINE OF CONFIRMED DEPRAVITY

If, perchance, there were some faint prospect held out that Satan and the demons might some day repent of their wickedness, or some feeble hope entertained that eventually they might realize their folly and turn from their lawlessness, then need for protection and release from their disastrous machinations might not appear to be so urgent or imperative and the finished work of Christ might not seem to be so completely indispensable. But the Bible offers no such vain prospect or empty hope. Not only are Satan and his demon-helpers portrayed as utterly incorrigible, confirmed in depravity, and destined for the eternal flames of Gehenna (Matt. 25:41), but those from the human family, who follow in their lawless train and refuse God's provided way of deliverance through Christ, must suffer the same inevitable fate.

The doctrine of confirmed depravity loses any aspect of singularity or unusualness when contemplated in the light of common every-day events noticed in the natural history of transgression. It is a matter of frequent observation that a sinful tendency, long indulged, becomes a fixed habit, and a fixed habit, in the course of time, becomes an unalterable destiny. When

Satan and the demons yielded to temptation in their primeval
defection, and became sinners, a tendency to sin, which had not
previously existed, resulted. This corrupt disposition would remain
forever, unless provision were made to overcome it. But it is
apparent that such provisions could not be made, nor remedial
agencies prove availing, so long as rebellion and a state of unre-
pentance continued in the hearts of the sinners.

Moreover, in the case of angelic offenders, repentance and
reformation were all the more unlikely, even in the initial stages
of their lawlessness, because of their deliberate, willful, and intelligent transgression in the face of the full glow of light, and the
unobscured recognition of the divine goodness and perfection. This
greater privilege, as wise and powerful direct creations of God,
and the consequent greater responsibility involved in their fall,
are doubtless prime factors in their incorrigibility and irretrievable
moral and spiritual obliquity. The added fact that Satan and
demons are sinners of long standing contributes further reason for
the overwhelming probabilities that there will be no reformation.
The advanced stages in the career of the drunkard, the gambler,
and the libertine, for example, offer a similar parallel; long continuance in evil-doing seems to seal the sinner's doom. But the
comparison is imperfect, for the rich grace of God (Rom. 5:20)
abounds in Christ, who died to repair the damage done by Satan
and his demons in the human family; and often, by virtue of the
finished work of Christ, even such abandoned characters are
rescued and saved as special tokens of divine love. On the other
hand, the case seems quite otherwise among angelic offenders,
wherein the sin and the doom of Satan and demons fall under a
code of universal laws, upon the maintenance and execution of
which depend the safety and permanency of the moral universe.

Then, too, the special heinous and destructive character of
Satan and the demons is evident, not only in the facts of their
wicked and lawless nature, but also in their aggressive activity
in deceiving and harming others and in winning over as many
deluded adherents as possible to their God-hating and God-opposing
program. In this is evidenced their deadly nature. They are not
passively wicked, as if they were in a state of sullen and peevish
inaction, morosely sulking under the restraints of detested divine
omnipotence. But, on the contrary, they are militantly malevolent,

seemingly, completely obsessed with insane optimism and the blind delusion that eventually their cause must triumph and God's program be overturned.

2. Demons and the Fact of Human Peril

It is startling enough to realize that there are such wicked and destructive beings as Satan and demons abroad in the world, who are not only irretrievably confirmed in wickedness themselves, but assiduously bent on confirming others in the same condition. But when it is apprehended that these emissaries of evil, these malicious agents of darkness, are concentrating their energies and directing their attacks upon the human family as their target, the fact is truly appalling. Man's peril is grave. He must go down in disgraceful defeat, and be completely despoiled and ruined forever, unless he takes advantage of the salvation so graciously provided in Christ.

The precise reason why Satanic and demonic hatred is directed so relentlessly against man is wrapped in mystery. It may be that Satan and certain angels were given the suzerainty over the earth when it was primevally created, and that it was in that high position of responsibility and trust that Satan first obtruded his will against the will of God (Isa. 14:12-14), bringing divine judgment and chaos upon this sphere (Gen. 1:2). If this explanation is true, it would account for Satan's jealousy and temptation of Edenic man (Gen. 3:1-6), who was given dominion over the renewed globe (Gen. 1:28), as well as justify Satan's claim that this world belongs to him (Matt. 4:8-9), and would furnish, in addition, a valuable commentary on why he is waging such a persistent war against God to retain his usurped possession of the earth.

Whatever may be the ultimate reason for Satan's implacable hostility toward the human family, it is certain that man, through his fall, lost his sovereignty over the earth to the usurper, and was thus alienated from his Creator. To repair the damage instigated and wrought by Satan, the Logos, the image of the invisible God, left the bosom of the Father (John 1:1, 14), took upon Himself humanity (Phil. 2:5-7), and wrought redemption, not only for man's salvation (Col. 1:14; II Cor. 5:21), but for the earth's deliverance as well (Matt. 13:44; Eph. 1:14; Rev. 5:1-10). Therefore, Satan and the demons tried, in every possible way, to tempt or to kill Christ, in order that there might not be the shedding of blood, according to the Scriptures (Matt. 2:16; 4:1-11; Luke 4:29; 22:3, 44). The same intense opposition, shown against Christ, is manifested against all believers united to Him, and who are one "in Him" (Eph. 6:10, 12).

Israel, moreover, as God's elect nation, in whom He is to consummate His plan on the earth, is marked as a special target for diabolic fury (Rev. 12:13-17). Those whom Satan alienated and turned from God when he seduced the human race, he holds with a fierce and tenacious grip, and relentlessly fights to keep them from cleansing salvation provided in Christ (Col. 1:13-14; II Tim. 2:26). No one in the human family, whether saint or sinner, is exempt from Satan's incessant attacks, and salvation and safety are to be found only in the blood of Christ (Rev. 12:11). Temporal and eternal ruin must inevitably be the portion of all who do not avail themselves of the divinely provided way of escape (Rev. 20:15).

B. Demonism and the Way of Deliverance

It must be obvious, to all who have even a cursory knowledge of Biblical demonology, that, since such beings as Satan and demons actually exist, since they have caused so much havoc and mischief in the world in the past, since they are still relentlessly pursuing their wicked depredations, and since they are to be allowed an augmented sphere of influence and activity in the future, the possibility of release and exemption from their destructive doings is a matter of personal and paramount concern to everyone.

It would indeed be strange if the good and all-wise Creator of the universe would not have made a fully efficacious provision for human safety and salvation where it is most desperately needed, especially, when it is clearly the divine method to provide for every possible emergency in the course of events. If all things on earth are made for man's comfort, help, and happiness—which is no less the testimony of science than of the Holy Scriptures (I Cor. 3:21-22)—certainly the all-gracious God would not fail man in this most momentous need of all: deliverance and safety from Satan and demons.

1. Demonism and the Cure For Spiritual Disease

Cure comes before prevention, because man is already spiritually sick. "All have sinned" (Rom. 3:23). "Death has passed unto all men, for that all sinned" (Rom. 5:12). Rescue comes before preservation, because man has already been despoiled, and lies under the heel of the Devil, and the power of demons (Eph. 2:2; Col. 1:13). Realization of even the most elementary principles of Biblical demonology must at once strip man of all vain hopes of salvation by merely his own puny efforts, by his own merits, works, character, or self-improvement (Eph. 2:8-10). All men, both Jews and Gentiles, are "under sin" (Rom. 3:9), a prey to Satan and demons, totally unable to save themselves, and without God's grace, appropriated by faith (Rom. 3:25), must perish forever (Rom. 5:6, 18). Christ died, "the righteous for the unrighteous, that He might bring us to God" (I Pet. 3:18), and we must ever remain away from God, under the thraldom and tyranny of Satan and demons, unless He, who is the only way to the Father (John 14:6), delivers us from the power of evil supernaturalism and brings us hither by His grace. The blood of Him "who His own self bare our sins in His body upon the tree" (I Pet. 2:24) is the only antidote against the poison of sin, the only cure for the deadly disease, which, unless healed, must result in eternal death in the lake of fire with Satan and his demons (Rev. 20:10, 15).

By the law of correspondence between what is seen in the natural world, and what exists in the spiritual world (Rom. 1:20), the cure and prevention of spiritual disease may be vividly illustrated by the cure and prevention of natural sickness. As medical science, by the use of pathological antiseptics, can cure and provide comparative immunity from malignant bacteria, so by the use of spiritual antiseptics, religious science can provide deliverance and immunity from Satan and demons. The all-sufficient remedy for the venom of sin is "the blood of Jesus" which "cleanses us" (I John 1:7). Without the shedding of blood, there could be no remission of sin, no recovery from spiritual malady (Heb. 9:22). Moreover, as there are agencies provided in nature, which, under certain conditions, affect the renewing or regeneration of the human body when suffering from physical sickness, so there is an agency in the spiritual realm, the Holy Spirit of God, who, under the simple condition of faith in Christ, can give the human

soul a new birth and eternal life. "That which is born of the
flesh is flesh; and that which is born of the Spirit is spirit. Marvel
not that I said unto you, Ye must be born anew" (John 3:7). "For
God so loved the world, that He gave His only begotten Son,
that whosoever believeth in Him should not perish, but have
eternal life" (John 3:16).

2. Demonism and the Prevention of Spiritual Disease

Cure for spiritual disease is offered to the unsaved. Prevention of spiritual disease is provided for the saved. Cure from sin,
providing deliverance from its penalty and assuring the believer's
safety and security for eternity, is important and indispensable,
but it is not enough. Prevention of further sin, providing emancipation from its power, and guaranteeing the believer's victory
and usefulness in time, is also necessary. Both are fully provided
for in the finished work of Christ; so, although the cure of sin
(regeneration) exposes the newborn believer to the special buffet-
ings, temptations, and assaults of Satan and demons, yet the prevention of further sin enables him to triumph over all the power
of these enemies, and to live a life of holiness, happiness, and
usefulness.

However, victory over all the power of the evil one is not by
human works or self-effort but on the basis of the believer's faith
in his position in Christ. It is the Christian's being baptized into
vital union with the Lord Jesus Christ (I Cor. 12:13; Rom. 6:3-4;
Gal. 3:27; Col. 1:12), Satan's Vanquisher, that is the ground of
all his positions and possessions as well as his victories over the
evil one. The victory that "overcomes the world", Satan's evil
world system (I John 5:4) as well as the "prince of the world,"
is "our faith." It is our believing that we are what we are "in
Christ" that alone routs the devil. Moreover, the reason for this
is not difficult to see; for all of our resources against the enemy
spring not from ourselves or our unregenerate position "in Adam"
(Rom. 5:12-21), but from our regenerate position "in Christ"
(Rom. 6:3-4). Victory is possible because we are united to the
Victor. Victory is appropriable as we realize and reckon upon our
position.

But what *is* our position in Christ, which is the basis of our
victory over sin and Satan? In briefest statement it is that of

"death" (Rom. 6:2). "How can we who died to sin live in it?" (R.S.V.). The believer died to sin and, since life and death are two mutually exclusive principles, it is impossible that he should live any longer in it. In more detailed statement (Rom. 6:3-10) the Apostle explains his summary statement that the believer's position is that of "death" by showing that the Christian has been baptized by the Holy Spirit into vital union with Jesus Christ, (Rom. 6:3-5), hence into His death (v. 3), His burial, (v. 4) and His resurrection (v. 5). Accordingly he has been judicially set free from sin (Rom. 6:6-7) and is now the recipient of resurrection life (Rom. 6:8-10). All this is the believer's position "in Christ" and is to be converted into experiential victory over Satan and sin by faith. "Even so reckon ye also yourselves to be dead unto sin, but alive unto God in Christ Jesus" (Rom. 6:11, R.V.). The believer *is* "dead unto sin" and "alive unto God" (Rom. 6:2-10) whether he reckons (counts it true) or not. The difference is that when he does believe it is true, the indwelling Holy Spirit is set free to make it *experientially real.* Then, and only then, is he conqueror in the conflict with Satan and sin, and then solely because Christ conquered Satan and the powers of evil at the Cross (Col. 1:14-15), and the believer united with Christ shares the victory. "Now thanks be unto God who always causeth us to triumph *in Christ*" (II Cor. 2:14).

The phenomena observed in the natural world concerning the prevention of physical disease offer instructive and suggestive parallels to the prevention of ills in the spiritual realm. As those who are robust in body may be infested with millions of bacilli, and yet enjoy immunity from their mischief, so those whose spiritual health is guarded and kept hale and vigorous will escape any spiritual liability that the Devil and all the demons may attempt. This does not signify, however, that spiritual robustness exempts its possessor from Satanic and demonic assault and temptation. Rather the opposite is true. Genuine spirituality is ever the target of incessant demonic attack in this world, and it is maintained only through continuous contact with Christ.

In a magnificent passage which fittingly closes the Ephesian letter, containing lofty truth addressed to the spiritual man, the Apostle Paul describes the warfare of the spirit-filled believer against the powers of darkness (Eph. 6:10-20). He mentions first what is of primary importance—the believer's strength for the conflict. "Be strong in the Lord" (v. 10). He does not say "from the Lord," but "in vital union with the Lord." "Strong in the position which is ours in Him, just as the hand or the foot has its strength in the body to which it belongs."[3] As S. D. F. Salmond says, the strengthening is such "as can take effect only in union with Christ."[4]

Realizing we are what we are "in Christ" (Rom. 6:1-10) and reckoning upon our wondrous position of union (Rom. 6:11) is the ground and the source of our power over the devil and his hosts. Just as the reckoning in Romans 6:11 is a present tense and must be continuous, so the strengthening in Ephesians 6:10 is a present tense and is to be continuous. H. C. G. Moule thus renders the passage: "Strengthen yourselves always in the Lord"; and he adds "your one possible Sphere and Magazine of inexhaustible resource, to be drawn upon by obedient trust."[5]

It is important to note the term "Lord" is employed—His family deity name. He is now our Master (John 13:13) and is coming as Lord over all (Rev. 19:16). Here, then, we are bidden to be strong in our victorious Lord, in him who gained the victory for us and is coming to complete it in ultimate triumph. In the interim we are to triumph in Him.[6]

The Apostle, after describing the believer's strength for the conflict, indicates his equipment against the foe—full armor provided by God (6:11-17). The necessity for the armor is emphasized by a description of the spiritual nature of the warfare and the power and subtlety of the foe (6:12). "Wherefore, take unto you the whole armor of God" (6:13). "Take" not "make" is the divine direction. Pitiable indeed is man's perennial attempt to make his own armor. For the nature of the enemy proves how foolhardy this is. God has made the panoply, a perfect product of His redemptive grace. We have only to put it on to "be able to stand successfully against our foe and having done all to stand."

"Stand, therefore!" That is what God asks of the believer. Stand as the victors we are—*stand in the victory of Calvary.* It

---

[3]Norman B. Harrison, *His Very Own*, p. 156.
[4]"The Epistle to the Ephesians" in *The Expositor's Greek Testament*, III, 382.
[5]*Ephesian Studies*, 2nd ed., p. 323.
[6]Norman B. Harrison, *op. cit.*, pp. 156-57.

is the grand note sounded throughout the Ephesian letter. We are "in Christ." We stand victors in Him. Our armor is significantly defensive rather than offensive. God has provided the panoply primarily to protect what is nearest His heart on earth, as His Son is nearest His heart in heaven—the Church, "which is his (Christ's) body, the fullness of him that filleth all in all" (Eph. 1:23).

The Apostle, having set forth the Christian warrior's strength and equipment against the enemy, lastly describes the full use of these resources—constant prayer in the Spirit (6:18-20). "Praying always with all prayer and supplication in the Spirit, and watching thereunto with all perseverance and supplication for all saints" (6:18). The provision of prayer is not to be regarded as a part of the warrior's resources, equipment, or another weapon.[7] It is the actual use of his resources of strength "in Christ" and his equipment in the "full armor of God." Only through prayer which is "all sorts," "at all seasons," "for all saints," "with all perseverance and supplication" and "in the Spirit" can the believer utilize the strength which is his "in the Lord." Only through prayer can he put on and use the whole armor, and "therefore, stand." Prayer in Ephesians 6 is the actual conflict in which the foe is vanquished and the victory won, not only for ourselves, but also by intercession for others (6:19-20).

It is quite obvious from such a conflict resulting in such a victory that benefiit will accrue to the believer. But the question is frequently asked, What possible good purpose may evil powers have?

The facts of pathological medicine may be used to illustrate the frequent use that powers of darkness may serve. As serums and inoculations, that would be harmful and perhaps fatal to sick men, may be of incalculable value when introduced into the systems of those in hearty health, so Satan and demons may not only not harm, but be a positive blessing in disguise and an inestimable service to those having spiritual stamina. They assault and tempt the Spirit-filled, but the resistance evoked calls forth the noblest faith and effort and issues in the development of the highest types of sterling character. Except for the rough and

---

[7] Cf. John Bunyan in *Pilgrim's Progress*, ed. by Cassell, Petter, Galpin and Co. p. 63, *n.d.*: "So Christian was forced to put up his sword, and betake himself to another weapon, called All-Prayer . . ."

unpleasant things in life, the fierce battles, and the resulting call
to achievement, the human race would never have advanced
beyond its spiritual infancy and immaturity. In this fact there
doubtless lies, at least a partial answer, to the mysterious problem
of the divine permission of evil in the universe.

Again, as fresh air, pure water, sunlight, nourishing food,
proper exercise, and general cleanliness are prime and basic factors
in preserving the normal functions of the human body, in main-
taining physical fitness, and rendering one exempt from the depredations of millions of malicious disease-causing germs, so an invig-
orating atmosphere of prayer (Eph. 6:18), living in the heights,
where Scripture urges people to dwell (Col. 3:1-3), appropriating
the Word of God, which is substantial food (John 6:32-58), being
continually filled with the Holy Spirit (Eph. 5:18), who satisfies
the spiritually thirsty (John 7:37-39), walking in Christ, the light
of the world (John 8:12; I John 1:7), engaging in true spiritual
service (Rom. 12:11), and diligently remaining in separation from
the world and complicity with evil (II Cor. 6:17)—these are the
simple, never-failing rules of good spiritual health, and automatically work immunity for the human soul against demonic
danger. As violation of the laws of health exposes the transgressor,
sooner or later, to the fatal attacks of disease-producing bacteria,
so every sinful act or neglect is a direct invitation to Satan and
demons to gain a foothold, and work harm to the human soul.

3. Demonism and the Banishment of Spiritual Disease

The dark cloud of evil which hangs today like a pall over
the moral universe is not without a silver lining; for Christ has
conquered the unseen realms of evil, and Christians conquer in
Him. Already foregleams of the coming glory may be discerned
through the present darkness. And so secure are Christians in
our all-conquering Redeemer, that we look forward with assurance
to walking the streets of gold and treading the spotless corridors
of the heavenly mansions. Every shadow will then pass away,
and the cloud of evil, now so ominous, will dwindle and pale
into insignificance in the clear blue of God's cloudless and sinless
tomorrow, when "he shall wipe away every tear . . . and death
shall be no more; neither shall there be mourning, nor crying,
nor pain, any more; the first things are passed away" (Rev. 21:4).

But where in that sinless and tranquil universe will Satan and the demons be? Will they ever again have permission to roam at large? No; when evil has accomplished its divine purpose, it will be rigidly isolated and eternally imprisoned. Satan, demons, and incorrigibly wicked men are to move onward and downward into a place all to themselves, there to remain forever (Matt. 25:41; Rev. 20:10; 21:8). Nor will that dread habitation mar the harmony and tranquility of God's illimitable empire.

Just as the public health and the welfare of society demand that certain persons afflicted with contagious diseases be quarantined, and that criminals afflicted with moral and spiritual distempers be imprisoned, so the safety and general good of the universe require the final segregation and imprisonment of those whose case is hopeless, and whose freedom would jeopardize the peace and security of the moral universe.

This prison-abode of the wicked will be the one dismal region of disobedient and miserable inhabitants, and the only one, in the infinite spheres. No sun will rise upon its endless night. No peace will give relaxation to its endless confusion. These evil creatures will never be permitted to cross over the divinely set confines nor to burst out of the divinely sealed prison-house. Nor will the wretched inhabitants ever be permitted to perpetrate further mischief, nor to mar the perfections of a blissful and sinless eternity.

Yet, like everything else in the divine economy, this doleful region of the depraved exists to accomplish its purpose, a two-fold purpose—one from the standpoint of the creature, the other from the standpoint of the Creator.

From the standpoint of the creature, this "lake of fire" will serve as a witness to the destructiveness and folly of sin. It will be like a danger signal, advertising to the universe of created beings, both angels and men, the utter futility of resisting God's will; and it will act as a sufficiently potent deterrent, even for all the eons of eternity, to keep created intelligences from the folly of Satan, demons, and incorrigibly wicked men. The picture of Satan, the once-glorious "anointed Cherub," "full of wisdom," "perfect in beauty," whose covering was "every precious stone," who "was upon the holy mountain of God," who once majestically "walked up and down in the midst of the stones of fire," who was "perfect" in his way from the day he was created "till iniquity was found" in him (Ezek. 28:12-15), then reduced so abysmally to the depths of shame—this picture will be a stern warning against apostasy that even eternity will not erase. Satan will not have a throne there; he will no longer reign. But having "the unenviable title of chief of all sinners . . . the original sinner," the one who "has wrought the most injury," who "has practiced sin longer than any other," who "sinned against the greatest light,"[8] it is fitting that he should "sink to a lower depth of shame and suffering than any other creature,"[9] and thus, at least in so far as the creature is concerned, justify his creation and apostate existence, in being a grim reminder of the irretrievable ruin of sin.

From the standpoint of the Creator, this doleful region serves another purpose. It will glorify the Creator. It will be a continual witness to the infinite perfection of God's character. All else in a sinless universe of holy angels and redeemed men will speak of the majesty, the holiness, and the love of God. This will show his *just*ness, his *right*eousness. *This,, too,* is a part of the divine glory. Had sin never risen to defy God's authority, an important question would have ever remained unanswered: How would God react if His will were opposed and evil introduced? Would He be overcome by it, or would He use His power alone and annihilate it, or would His essential nature of love offer a way of rescue from it?

Sin came. And time and eternity will proclaim, to the glory of the all-glorious Creator, His manner of dealing with it—in infinite love and holiness: "For God so loved the world, that he gave his only begotten Son, that whosoever believeth in Him should not perish, but have everlasting life." In unapproachable wisdom, yet not compromising His infinite holiness, but rather magnifying His grace, He furnished a way to maintain His creation, though sin-defiled, drawing His beloved race of men back to Himself with more tender ties, giving them a "new song" of redemption (Rev. 5:9)—even more exquisite music than was heard in the primeval creation, "that in the ages to come he might show the exceeding riches of his grace in his kindness toward us through Christ Jesus"

[8]Lewis Sperry Chafer, *op. cit.,* II, 73.
[9]F. C. Jennings, *Satan: His Person, Work, Place, and Destiny,* p. 226.

(Eph. 2:7). These re-born, happy creatures are free moral agents, drawn but not driven.

But what if some of His creation should reject the way of salvation and pass into eternity as moral lepers still? What can be done to justify *their* existence, that in the ages to come they may show the infinite holiness of God, as the redeemed show forth "the exceeding riches of his grace"? Their incarceration in that dreadful abode will be, as stated by F. C. Jennings, an eternal witness to the power, the holiness, and the severity (the justice) of God—with even *Satan's* knee bowing, "even *his* tongue joining in the universal confession that Jesus Christ is Lord, to the glory of God the Father."[10]

Meanwhile, as the child of God journeys on his pilgrimage through this world, still exposed to the attacks of these demon creatures, he can well marvel at the complete provision the rich grace of God has made for his protection and immunity. Although the Bible contains clear revelation concerning the reality and wickedness of these agents of evil, it also gives explicit directions on how to secure and maintain immunity from their crafty assaults. The Christian, possessing all the benefits of a finished redemption in Christ, having the Holy Spirit within to guide and to preserve and the Word of God without to point the way to victory and blessing, finds himself so supplied with resources of every kind, so panoplied with the full armor of God, that with these divine aids he can hold aloft the highest standards of Christian living, as he appropriates the full power of God for effective serving and witnessing.

Reckoning faithfully upon his position in Christ (Rom. 6:11), the believer's joyful testimony becomes: " . . . thanks be unto God, who always causeth us to triumph in Christ" (II Cor. 2:14). Facing the foe, "strong in the Lord and in the power of His might" (Eph. 6:10), the Christian warrior finds that soon every foe is vanquished from the field of battle, as his glad shout ascends: " . . . thanks be to God, who giveth us the victory through our Lord Jesus Christ" (I Cor. 15:57).

---

[10]*Opus cit.*, pp. 228-29.

BIBLIOGRAPHY

Abbot, Ezra. "Demon, Demoniac," *Smith's Dictionary of the Bible*, I, rev. ed. by H. B. Hackett, 1885.

Agrippa, Heinrich C. *Three Books of Occult Philosophy*. Chicago: Hahn and Whitehead, 1898.

Albright, William Foxwell. *From the Stone Age to Christianity*. Baltimore: Johns Hopkins Press, 1940.

——————————. "The Oracles of Balaam," *Journal of Biblical Literature*, 63, September, 1944, pp. 207-33.

Alexander, William Menzies. *Demonic Possessions in the New Testament: Its Relations Historical, Medical, and Theological*. Edinburgh: T. and T. Clark, 1902.

Almquist, David. "Demon Possession in Our Day," *Missions Vannen* (a Swedish weekly). Trans. by Oscar W. Hallin, *Sunday School Times*, February 28, 1942.

Augustine. *The City of God*. Trans. by Marcus Dods. (Nicene and Post-Nicene Fathers of the Christian Church, edited by Philip Schaff), II. Buffalo: The Christian Literature Co., 1887.

Ayer, Joseph Cullen. *A Source Book for Ancient Church History*. New York: Charles Scribner's Sons, 1948.

Babylonian Talmud (new ed.). New York: New Amsterdam Book Co., 1906.

Barry, Alfred. "Demon, Demoniac," *Smith's Dictionary of the Bible*, I.

Baudissin, Wolf W. G. *Studien zur Semitischen Religionsgeschichte*, Heft I. Leipzig: verlag von F. W. Grunow, 1876.

Beacham, C. Gordon. *New Frontiers in the Central Sudan*. Toronto: Evangelical Publishers, 1928.

Berg, Joseph F. *Daemons and Guardian Angels*. Philadelphia: Higgins and Perkinpine, 1856.

Bevan, E. R. *Sibyls and Seers*. Cambridge: Harvard University Press, 1929.

Binns, L. E. In *Westminster Commentaries*. 1927.

Blau, Ludwig. *Das Altjuedischen Zauberwesen*. Berlin: Verlag von Louis Lamm, 1914.

Bouché-Leclercq, Auguste. *Histoire de la Divination dans l'Antiquité*, 4 vols. Paris: E. Leroux, 1879-1882.

Bounds, Edward M. *Satan: His Personality, Power, and Overthrow*. New York: Fleming H. Revell Company, 1922.

Breasted, James H. *A History of Egypt*. New York: Charles Scribner's Sons, 1912.

Broydé, I. "Demonology," *The Jewish Encyclopedia*. New York: Funk & Wagnalls, 1903, pp. 514-21.

Bunyan, John. *The Pilgrim's Progress.* New York: Cassell, Petter, Galpin Co., n.d.

Burr, George Lincoln. "The Literature of Witchcraft," *American Historical Association Papers,* IV, iii, pp. 235-266. New York: American Historical Association, 1890.

Canaan, Taufik. *Daemonenglaube in Lande der Bibel.* Leipzig: J. C. Hinrische Buchhandlung, 1929.

Candlish, Robert C. *The First Epistle of John Expounded in a Series of Lectures.* Edinburgh, 1866.

Chafer, Lewis Sperry. *Major Bible Themes.* Chicago: Moody Press, 1942
————————————. *Satan.* Chicago: Moody Press, 1942.
————————————. *Systematic Theology,* II. Dallas, Texas: Dallas Seminary Press, 1947.

Charles, R. H. *The Apocrypha and Pseudepigrapha of the Old Testament,* 2 vols. Oxford: Clarendon Press, 1913.

Cheyne, T. K. "Demons," *Encyclopedia Biblica,* I, pp. 1070-74. New York: Macmillan Co.

Chisholm, William H. "Casting Out a Deaf and Dumb Spirit in Korea," *Sunday School Times,* January 1, 1938.

Cicero, Marcus Tullius. *De Divitatione,* VI, No. 3, ed. by A. S. Pease. Urbana: University of Illinois, publisher, 1920.

Clark, Elmer T. *The Small Sects in America,* rev. ed. New York: Abingdon-Cokesberry Press, 1949.

Clemens, Romanus. *Apostolic Fathers.* Amstelasdami: apud R. and G. Wetstenios, 1724.

Clement of Rome. *Homilies.* In Ante-Nicene Library, XVII (1870), 1-331; and VIII (1886), 215-346.

Clementine Recognitions. In Ante-Nicene Library, XII (1867), 143-471; and VIII (1886), 77-211.

Colville, William J. *Universal Spiritualism: Spirit Communion in All Ages among All Nations.* New York: R. F. Fenno and Co., 1906.

Conway, Moncure Daniel. *Demonology and Devil Lore,* I and II. New York: Henry Holt and Company, 1879.

Conybeare, F. C. "Christian Demonology," *The Jewish Quarterly Review,* 9 (October, 1896), 59-114; 9 (April, 1897), 444-470; and 9 (July 1897), 581-603.

————————————. "The Demonology of the New Testament," *The Jewish Quarterly Review,* 8 (July, 1896), 576-608.

Cruikshank, William. "Astral Theory," *Hastings' Encyclopedia of Religion and Ethics,* VIII, p. 63. Edinburgh: T. and T. Clark, 1912.

Daney, H. E. and J. R. Mantey. *A Manual of the Greek New Testament.* New York: Macmillan Co., 1946.

Davies, Thomas Witton. "Divination," *International Standard Bible Encyclopedia,* Vol. I, 860-863; "Magic, Magician," Vol. III, 1963-64; and "Witch, Witchcraft," Vol. V, 3097-98. Grand Rapids, Mich.: Eerdmans Publishing Co., 1939.

——————————. *Magic Divination, and Demonology among the He-brews and Their Neighbors.* London: James Clarke and Co., 1898.

Delaporte, Father. *The Devil: Does He Exist? And What Does He Do?* New York: D. and J. Sadlier and Company, 1871.

Doyle, A. Conan. *The History of Spiritualism,* 2 vols. New York: Doubleday, Doran & Co., 1926.

——————————. *The New Revelation.* New York: Doubleday, Doran & Co., 1918.

Driver, S. R. Deuteronomy, *International Critical Commentary.* New York: Charles Scribner's Sons, 1906.

Easton, Burton S. "Python," *International Standard Bible Encyclopedia,* IV, 2511. Grand Rapids, Mich.: Eerdmans Publishing Co., 1939.

Edersheim, Alfred. *The Life and Times of Jesus the Messiah,* I and II. New York: Longmans, Green and Co., 1940.

Edman, V. Raymond. *The Light in Dark Ages.* Wheaton, Illinois: Van Kampen Press, Inc., 1949.

Edman, V. Raymond. *Storms and Starlight,* Chapters XI, XIII, XIV, and XXVII. Wheaton, Illinois: Van Kampen Press, Inc., 1951.

Eliezer, Pirqé de Rabbi, trans. by Gerald Friedlander. New York: Bloch Publishing Co., 1916.

Ellicott, Charles John. (ed.) *A Bible Commentary for English Readers* (Old and New Testament). New York, n.d.

Ellinwood, F. F. Introduction to J. L. Nevius's *Demon Possession and Allied Themes,* 5th ed. New York: Fleming H. Revell Co., *ca.* 1900.

Encyclopedia Americana, XXII. 1951.

Ewen, C. L'Estrange. *Witchcraft and Demonianism.* London: Heath, Cranton, Ltd., 1933.

Faber, G. S. *The Many Mansions in the House of the Father.* London: Royston, 1851.

Farmer, Hugh. *An Essay on the Demoniacs of the New Testament.* London. 1775.

——————————. *The General Prevalence of the Worship of Human Spirits in the Ancient Heathen Nations, Asserted and Proved.* London: Galabin and Baker, 1783.

Farmer, John S. *Spiritualism as a New Basis of Belief.* London: E. W. Allen, 1880.

Farrar, F. W. *The Book of Daniel.* New York: George H. Doran Company, n.d.

Fell, John. *Demoniacs.* London: for Charles Dilly, 1779.

Ferguson, Charles W. *The Confusion of Tongues—A Review of Modern Isms.* Grand Rapids, Mich.: Zondervan Publishing House, 1940.

——————————. *The New Books of Revelations.* New York: Doubleday, Doran and Co., 1930.

Ferré, Nels F. *Evil and the Christian Faith.* New York: Harper and Sons, 1947.

Fox, John. "Spiritist Theologians," *Princeton Theological Review,* 1920.

Frazer, James George. *Folklore in the Old Testament,* 3 vols. New York: Macmillan Co., 1918.

——————————. *The Golden Bough: A Study in Magic and Religion,* 12 vols. New York: Macmillan Co., 1935.

Gaebelein, A. C. *Gabriel and Michael the Archangel.* New York: *Our Hope* Publication Office, 1945.

——————————. *The Angels of God.* New York: *Our Hope* Publication Office, 1924.

——————————. *The Annotated Bible,* 9 vols. The Pentateuch, and Vols. III and IV, and The Revelation. New York: *Our Hope* Publication Office, 1913-1921.

——————————. *The Gospel of Matthew.* New York: *Our Hope* Publication Office, 1910.

Garcon, Maurice and Jean Vichon. *The Devil,* trans. from 6th French ed. New York: E. P. Dutton and Company, Inc., 1930.

Gemmil, William Nelson. *Salem Witch Trials.* Chicago: A. C. McClurg Co., 1924.

Gesenius, William. *A Hebrew and English Lexicon of the Old Testament,* trans. by Robinson, rev. ed. Boston: Houghton Mifflin Co., 1882.

Gilgamesh Epic and Old Testament Parallels. Chicago: University of Chicago Press, 1946.

Gilmore, George W. "Demon, Demonism," *New Schaff-Herzog Encyclopedia of Religious Knowledge,* III, 399-401. New York: Funk & Wagnalls, 1909.

Gilpin, Richard. *Daemonologia Sacra.* Edinburgh: Nichol, 1867.

Graf, Arturo. *The Story of the Devil,* trans. from the Italian by Edward N. Stone. London: Macmillan and Co., 1931.

Grant, F. W. The Gospels in *The Numerical Bible.* New York: Loizeaux Bros., 1899.

——————————. *The Numerical Bible.* New York: Loizeaux Bros., 1913.

——————————. *The Revelation of Christ.* New York: Loizeaux Bros., n.d.

Gray, G. Buchanan. "Demons and Angels," *Encyclopedia Biblica,* I, 1069-70. New York: Macmillan Co.

Gray, James M. *Satan and the Saint.* New York: Fleming H. Revell Co., 1909.

——————————. *Spiritism and the Fallen Angels.* New York: Fleming H. Revell Co., 1920.

Greenstone, J. H. *Numbers with Commentary* (The Holy Scriptures). Philadelphia: The Jewish Publication Society of America, 1939.

Gruenthaner, Michael J. "The Demonology of the New Testament," *The Catholic Biblical Quarterly,* 6 (January, 1944), 6-27.

Hafner, G. *Die Daemonischen des Neuen Testaments.* Leipzig, 1894.

Hanson, E. F. *Demonology or Spiritualism, Ancient and Modern.* Belfast, Maine: published by the author, 1884.

Harnack, A. V. *Die Mission und Ausbreitung des Christentums in den ersten drei Jahrhunderten,* I. English translation by James Moffatt. New York: G. P. Putnam's Sons, 1908.

Harrison, Norman B. *His Very Own.* Chicago: The Bible Institute Colportage Association, 1930.

Hastings, James, ed. *Encyclopedia of Religion and Ethics,* IV. 565-635. New York: Charles Scribner's Sons, 1935.

Heidel, Alexander. *The Babylonian Genesis,* 2nd ed. Chicago: University of Chicago Press, 1951.

Heinze, Richard. *Xenokrates.* Leipzig: B. G. Tuebner, 1892.

Herodotus, edition by A. D. Godley. London: W. Heinemann; New York: G. B. Putnam's Sons, 1921-24.

Hesiodus, *The Works of Hesiod,* the Anderson Robert edition, translated by Thomas Cooke.

Hodge, A. A. *Outlines of Theology.* New York: A. C. Armstrong and Son, 1891.

Hodge, Charles. *Systematic Theology,* I, reprint. Grand Rapids, Mich.: 1940.

Homer. *The Iliad,* trans. by Alexander Pope. New York: A. L. Burt Co., n.d.

————. *The Odyssey,* trans, by Alexander Pope. New York: A. L. Burt Co., n.d.

Ironside, Henry A. *Addresses on the Epistle of John.* New York: Loizeaux Bros., 1930.

————————. *Lectures on Daniel the Prophet.* New York: Loizeaux Bros., 1911.

Irvine, William C. *Heresies Exposed,* 11th ed. New York: Loizeaux Bros., 1940.

Jamieson, R., and others. *A Commentary on the Old and New Testaments.* New York: S. S. Scranton and Company, 1873.

Jastrow, Morris, *Hebrew and Babylonian Traditions.* New York: Charles Scribner's Sons, 1911.

————————. *The Religion of Babylonia and Assyria.* Cambridge: Harvard University Press, n.d.

Jennings, F. C. *Satan: His Person, Work, Place, and Destiny.* New York: A C. Gaebelein, n.d.

Jewett, E. H. *Diabolology: The Person and Kingdom of Satan.* New York: Thomas Whittaker, 1890.

Jones, E. H. *The Road to En-Dor.* New York: Dodd Mead & Co., 1920.

Jones, R. B. *Spiritism in Bible Light.* London, 1921.

Josephus, Flavius. *The Life and Works of Josephus,* trans. by W. Whiston. Philadelphia: John C. Winston Company, n.d.

Jung, Leo. *Fallen Angels in Jewish, Christian, and Mohammedan Literature.* Philadelphia: The Dropsie College for Hebrew and Cognate Learning, 1926.

Kaufmann, Kohler. "Divination," *The Jewish Encyclopedia,* IV, 622-624.

Kautzsch, E. *Gesenius Hebrew Grammar,* ed. by A. E. Cowley. Oxford: at the Clarendon Press, 1910.

Keil, Carl F. *Commentary on the Pentateuch,* 3 vols., reprint. Grand Rapids, Mich.: Eerdmans Publishing Co., 1949.

Keil, Carl F., and Franz Delitzsch. *Biblical Commentary on the Book of Daniel.* Grand Rapids, Mich.: Eerdmans Publishing Co., 1949.

Kelly, William. *The Revelation,* 6th ed. New York: Loizeaux Bros., n.d.

————————. *Notes on the Book of Daniel,* 7th ed. New York: Loizeaux Bros., 1943.

Kittel, Rudolf. *Biblia Hebraica.* Lipsiae, J. C. Hinrichs, 1905.

Kittredge, George Lyman. *Witchcraft in Old and New England.* Cambridge: Harvard University Press, 1928.

Koenig, Eduard. *Theologie des Alten Testaments*, 3rd and 4th eds. Stuttgart: Belser, 1923.

Lange, Johann Peter. *A Commentary on the Holy Scriptures*. New York: Charles Scribner's Sons, 1865——.

Langton, Edward. *Essentials of Demonology*. London: The Epworth Press, 1949.

——————————.*Good and Evil Spirits*. London: Society for the Propagation of Christian Knowledge, 1942; New York: Macmillan Co.

——————————. "The Reality of Demonic Powers Further Considered," *Hibbert Journal*, July, 1935, pp. 605-615.

——————————. *Supernatural: The Doctrine of Spirits, Angels, and Demons from the Middle Ages to the Present Time*. London: Rider and Company, 1934.

Larkin, Clarence. *Dispensational Truth*, 7th ed. Philadelphia: Clarence Larkin Estate, 1920.

——————————. *Rightly Dividing the Word of Truth*. Philadelphia: C. Larkin, publisher, 1920.

——————————. *The Book of Revelation*. New Rochelle, New York: Clarence Larkin, publisher, 1919.

——————————. *The Spirit World*. Philadelphia: Clarence Larkin Estate, 1921.

Latourette, Kenneth Scott. *A History of Christian Missions in China*. New York: Macmillan Co., 1929.

Liddell and Scott. *Greek-English Lexicon*, rev. ed., I. Oxford, 1939.

Lightfoot, John. *Horae Hebraicae et Talmudicae*, rev. ed., I-IV. Oxford University Press, 1859.

Lincoln, W. *Lectures on the Book of Revelation*. New York: Fleming H. Revell Co., n.d.

Marsh, Leonard. *The Apocatastasis, or Progress Backwards*. Burlington Vermont: C. Goodrich, 1854.

Maunder, E. W. "Astrology," *International Standard Bible Encyclopedia*, I, 295-300. Grand Rapids, Mich.: Eerdmans Publishing Co., 1939.

Mayor, J. B. "The General Epistle of Jude," *The Expositor's Greek New Testament*, reprint. Grand Rapids, Mich.: Eerdmans Publishing Co., n.d.

McCasland, S. Vernon. *By the Finger of God*. New York: Macmillan Co., 1951.

M'Donald, W. *Spiritualism Identical with Ancient Sorcery, New Testament Demonology, and Modern Witchcraft*. New York: Carlton and Porter, 1866.

Meissner, Bruno. *Babylonien und Assyrien*. Heidelberg: Zweiter Band, Carl Winters, Universitaets Buchhandlung, 1927.

Meyer, Heinrich A. W. *Critical and Exegetical Handbook to the Acts of the Apostles*. New York: Funk & Wagnalls, 1883.

Michelet, Jules. *Satanism and Witchcraft*. New York: Citadel Press, 1946.

Miller, M. S., and J. L. *Encyclopedia of Bible Life*. New York: Harper & Brothers, 1944.

Mind and Matter, May 8, 1880, and June, 1880.

Moffatt, James, contributor. *The Expositor's Greek New Testament* (Revelation), reprint. Grand Rapids, Mich.: Eerdmans Publishing Co., n.d.

Mohamet. *Le Koran,* traduction par M. Kasimirski. Paris: Charpentier et Cie, 1873.

Montgomery, James A. *The Book of Daniel: International Critical Commentary.* New York: Charles Scribner's Sons, 1927.

Morgan, G. Campbell. *The Gospel According to Mark.* New York: Fleming H. Revell Company, 1927.

——————————. *The Gospel According to Matthew.* New York: Fleming H. Revell Company, 1929.

——————————. *The Voice of the Devil.* New York: Fleming H. Revell Company, n.d.

Moule, H. C. G. *Ephesian Studies.* London: Pickering and Inglis, n.d.

Murray, M. A. *The Witch Cult in Western Europe.* New York: Oxford University Press, 1921.

Muse, A. D. *The Spirit World:Demonology.* Cynthiana, Ky.: Hobson Book Press, 1944.

Naudé, Gabriel. *The History of Magic by Way of Apology for all the Wise Men Who Have Unjustly Been Reputed Magicians,* trans. from the French by J. Davies. London: printed for J. Streater, 1657.

Nevius, John L. *Demon Possession and Allied Themes,* 5th ed. New York: Fleming H. Revell Company, n.d.

Newell, Philip R. *Daniel, The Man Greatly Beloved and His Prophecies.* Chicago: Moody Press, 1951.

Newell, William R. *The Book of the Revelation.* Chicago: Scripture Press, 1935.

Oesterley, William O. E., and Theodore H. Robinson. *Hebrew Religion,* rev. ed. New York: Macmillan Co., 1937.

Oesterreich, T. K. *Possession, Demoniacal and Other among Primitive Races in Antiquity, the Middle Ages, and Modern Times.* New York: R. Long and R. Smith, Inc., 1930.

Olshausen, Hermann. Matthew, *Biblical Commentary on the New Testament,* rev. ed. by A. C. Kendrick. New York: Shelden & Co., 1861-63.

Origen. *Contra Celsum. Writings of Origen,* II, trans. by Crombie. In Ante-Nicene Christian Library.

Orr, James. "Nephilim," *International Standard Bible Encyclopedia,* IV, 2133. Grand Rapids, Mich.: Eerdmans Pub. Co., 1939.

Owen, John J. "The Demonology of the New Testament," *Bibliotheca Sacra and Biblical Repository,* 16 (January, 1859), 119-139.

Paton, Lewis Bayles. *Spiritism and the Cult of the Dead in Antiquity.* New York: Macmillan Co., 1921.

Paul, Leslie. *The Age of Terror.* London: Faber and Faber, Ltd. (The Scientific Press), 1950.

Pember, G. H. *Earth's Earliest Ages and Their Connection with Modern Spiritualism and Theosophy,* revised and enlarged edition of *Earth's Earliest Ages and Their Lessons for Us,* 1876. New York: Fleming H. Revell Company, *ca.* 1900.

Penn-Lewis, Mrs., and Evan Roberts. *War on the Saints*. London: Marshall Brothers, 1912.

Perkins, William. *A Discourse on the Damned Art of Witchcraft*. Cambridge: C. Legge, Printer to the University of Cambridge, 1608.

Pictorius, George. *A Discourse on the Nature of Spirits*, trans. by R. Turner. London, 1655.

Plato. *Platonis Opera*. Lipsiae: Caroli Tauchnitti, 1829.

——————————. *Symposium*. Cambridge: W. Heffer and Sons, 1909.

Plummer, A. *New Testament Commentary*, III, ed. by C. J. Ellicott. New York: Cassell, Petter, Galpin & Co., 1883.

Plumptre, E. H. *A New Testament Commentary for English Readers*, ed. by C. J. Ellicott. New York: Cassell, Petter, Galpin & Co., 1888.

Plutarch. "De Defectione Oraculorum," XIII, in *Plutarch's Lives and Writings*, edited by A. H. Clough and W. W. Goodwin, Vol. IV. New York: Colonial Company, 1905.

Pratt, Dwight M. "Enchantment," *International Standard Bible Encyclopedia*, II, 942. Grand Rapids, Mich.: Eerdmans Pub. Co., 1939.

Preller, Ludwig. *Griechische Mythologie*, 2 vols., 4th Auflage, bearb. von Carl Robert. Berlin: Weidmann, 1894-1926.

Price, Ira Maurice. *The Monuments and the Old Testaments*. Philadelphia: The Judson Press, 1925.

Pusey, E. B. *Daniel the Prophet*. New York: Funk & Wagnalls, 1885.

Rahlfs, Alfred. *Septuaginta*, I and II. New York: Societate Biblica Americana, 1949.

Ramsay, Sir W. M. *Hastings' Dictionary of the Bible*, I and V. New York: Charles Scribner's Sons, 1902.

——————————. *The Bearing of Recent Discovery on the Trustworthiness of the New Testament*, 4th ed. London: Hodder and Stoughton, 1920.

Renouf, P. LePage. *The Origin and Growth of Religion as Illustrated by the Religion of Ancient Egypt*. New York: Charles Scribner's Sons, 1880.

Robertson, A. T. *Word Pictures in the New Testament*, VI. New York: Harper and Brothers, 1933.

Rogers, Robert W. *The Religion of Babylonia and Assyria*. New York: Eaton and Mains, 1908.

Rohde, E. *Psyche, the Cult of Souls and Belief in Immortality among the Greeks*, 2nd ed. Freiburg, 1898.

Roseberry, R. S. *Black Magic*. Chicago: World-Wide Prayer and Missionary Union, 1935.

——————————. *The Niger Vision*. Harrisburg: Christian Publications, 1934.

Rudwin, Maximilian. *The Devil in Legend and Literature*. Chicago: The Open Court Publishing Company, 1931.

Sage, Michel. *Le Spiritisme, Probléme Scientifique*. Paris: Bibliothéque de Philosophie Spiritualiste Moderne et des Sciences Psychiques, 1931.

——————————. *Mme. Piper et la Société Anglo-Americaine pour les Rescherches Psychiques*. Paris: P. G. Leymarie, 1922.

Salmond, S. D. F. "The Epistle to the Ephesians," *The Expositor's Greek Testament*, III, reprint. Grand Rapids, Mich.: Eerdmans Publishing Co., n.d.

Savage, Minot J. *Psychics*. Boston: Arena Publishing Co., 1893.

Sayce, A. H. *Babylonians and Assyrians*. New York: Charles Scribner and Sons, 1899.

Schneweiss, Emil. *Angels and Demons According to Lactantius*. Washington: Catholic University of America Press, 1944.

Schofield, A. T. *Modern Spiritism: Its Science and Religion*. Philadelphia: P. Blackiston's Son & Co., 1920.

Schwarze, C. Theodore. *The Program of Satan*. Chicago: Good News Publishers, 1947.

Scofield, C. I. *Scofield Reference Bible*, New York: Oxford University Press, 1917.

Scott, Reginald. "A Discourse of Devils and Spirits," appended to Nicholson's edition of *The Discoverie of Witchcraft*.

———————————. *The Discoverie of Witchcraft*, re-edited by E. B. Nicholson. London: E. Stock, 1886.

Scott, Sir Walter. *Letters on Demonology and Witchcraft*, 2nd ed. London: G. Routledge and Sons, 1885.

Scott, Walter. *The Existence of Evil Spirits Proved*. London: Jackson and Walford, 1853.

———————————. *Exposition of the Revelation of Jesus Christ*, 4th ed. London: Pickering and Inglis, n.d.

Seiss, Joesph A. *The Apocalypse*. Philadelphia: Approved Book Store, 1865.

Serafim, Bishop of Ostrog. *The Soothsayer, Balaam*. England, 1900.

Siculus, Diodorus. *Bibliotheca Historica*, translated by C. H. Oldfather. London: W. Heineman Ltd.: New York: G. P. Putnam's Sons, 1933.

Siebeck, Hermann. *Lehrbuch der Religionsphilosophie*. Freiburg and Leipzig: Mohr, 1893.

Smith, Wilbur M. *Therefore Stand*. Boston: W. A. Wilde Co., 1945.

———————————. *The Supernaturalness of Christ*. Boston: W. A. Wilde Co., 1943.

———————————. *This Atomic Age and the Word of God*. Boston: W. A. Wilde Co., 1948.

———————————. *World Crises and the Prophetic Scriptures*. Chicago: Moody Press, 1951.

Sophocles. *The Oedipus Tyrannus*. Cambridge: at the University Press, 1897.

Spencer, Frederick A. M. "Demonic Powers: the Case for Their Reality," *Hibbert Journal*, April, 1935, 443-456.

Spenser, Edmund. *The Faerie Queene*, 3 vols., Vol. I, Book II, edited by J. C. Smith. Oxford: at the Clarendon Press, 1909.

Stevens, W. C. *The Book of Daniel*, rev. ed. Los Angeles: Bible House of Los Angeles, 1943.

Stoddard, J. T. *The Case Against Spiritualism*. New York, 1909.

Strabo. *The Geography of Strabo*, 8 vols. New York: G. P. Putnam's Sons, 1917-1932.

Strauss, David F. *Das Leben Jesu,* zweiter Band. Tuebingen: Verlag von C. F. Osiander, 1836.

Strong, Augustus H. *Systematic Theology.* Philadelphia: The Judson Press, 1907.

Summers, Montague. *A History of Witchcraft and Demonology.* London: Alfred A. Knopf, 1926.

——————————. *The Geography of Witchcraft.* New York: Alfred A. Knopf, 1927.

Sweet, Louis M. "Demon, Demoniac, Demonology," *International Standard Bible Encyclopedia, II,* 827-29. Grand Rapids, Mich.: Eerdmans Pub. Co., 1939.

——————————. "New Testament Demonology," *International Standard Bible Encyclopedia.* Grand Rapids, Mich.: Eerdmans Pub. Co., 1939.

Taylor, A. E. *Socrates.* London: Peter Davies, Ltd., 1932.

Tertullian. *Apology, XXIII,* in *The Ante-Nicene Fathers, II,* 37-38. New York: The Christian Literature Publishing Co., 1896.

Thayer, J. H. *Greek-English Lexicon of the New Testament.*

Thomas, W. H. Griffith. *The Apostle John.* Philadelphia: Harper and Brothers, 1923.

Thompson, R. Campbell. *Reports of the Magicians and Astrologers of Nineveh and Babylon.* 1900.

——————————. *Semitic Magic.* London: Luzac and Company, 1908.

——————————. *The Devils and Evil Spirits of Babylonia.* London: Luzac and Company, 1903-1904.

Thorndike, Lynn. *A History of Magic and Experimental Science, I-VI.* New York: Macmillan Company and Columbia University Press, 1923-1941.

——————————. *The Place of Magic in the Intellectual History of Europe.* New York: Columbia University Press, 1905.

Tisdall, W. St. Clair. "The Magi," *International Standard Bible Encyclopedia, III,* pp. 1962-63. Grand Rapids, Mich.: Eerdmans Publishing Company, 1939.

Townsend, L. T. *Satan and Demons.* Cincinnati: Jennings and Pye, 1902.

Trench, R. C. *Notes on the Miracles of Our Lord.* New York: Fleming H. Revell Company, 1895.

Tsanoff, R. A. *The Nature of Evil.* New York: Macmillan Co., 1931.

Twesten, A. C. D. "The Doctrine Respecting Angels," *Bibliotheca Sacra and Theological Review, I* (November 1844), 769-82; and II (February 1945), 108-40.

Tylor, E. B. *Primitive Culture, I* and II. New York: G. P. Putnam's Sons, Knickerbocker Press, 1924.

Usher, Charles H. *How to Deliver Souls from Deception and Possession.* Brighton: W. T. Moulton and Co., n.d.

Van Baalen, Jan K. *The Chaos of Cults,* 7th ed. Grand Rapids, Mich.: Eerdmans Publishing Co., 1948.

Waite, Arthur Edward. *Occult Sciences.* New York: E. P. Dutton and Co., 1923.

——————————. *The Book of Black Magic and of Pacts, Including the Rites and Mysteries of Goetic Theurgy, Sorcery, and Infernal Necromancy.* Chicago: DeLaurence, Scott and Co., 1910.

Weiss, Johann. "Demoniac," *The New Schaff-Herzog Encyclopedia of Religious Knowledge,* 401-403. New York, 1909.

West, Robert H. *The Invisible World.* Athens, Georgia: University of Georgia Press, 1939.

Westminster Dictionary of the Bible, rev. by Henry S. Gehman. Philadelphia: Westminster Press, 1944.

White, Andrew D. *A History of the Warfare of Science with Theology in Christendom,* 2 vols. New York: D. Appleton and Co., 1896.

White, Hugh. *Demonism Verified and Analyzed.* Richmond, Va.: Presbyterian Committee of Publication, 1922.

Whitehouse, Owen C. "Demon, Devil," *Hastings' Dictionary of the Bible,* I, 590-94.

Wimberly, C. F. *Is the Devil a Myth?* New York: Fleming H. Revell Company, 1913.

"Witchcraft," *Encyclopedia Americana,* XXII. New York: Americana Corporation, 1951.

Young, Edward J. *The Prophecy of Daniel: A Commentary.* Grand Rapids, Mich.: Eerdmans Publishing Co., 1949.

Zilboorg, Gregory. *The Medical Man and the Witch during the Renaissance.* Baltimore: Johns Hopkins Press, 1935.

Zimmern, H., and H. Winckler. *Keilinschriften und das Alte Testament,* 3rd ed. by E. Schrader, 1905.

GENERAL INDEX

SCRIPTURE INDEX